D0022894

THE NAZIS' MARCH
TO CHAOS

THE NAZIS' MARCH TO CHAOS

❖ ❖ ❖

The Hitler Era Through the Lenses of Chaos-Complexity Theory

❖ ❖ ❖

Roger Beaumont

Westport, Connecticut
London

DD253.25
.B43
2000

Library of Congress Cataloging-in-Publication Data

Beaumont, Roger A.
    The Nazis' march to chaos : the Hitler era through the lenses
of chaos-complexity theory / Roger Beaumont.
        p. cm.
    Includes bibliographical references and index.
    ISBN 0-275-96708-5 (alk. paper)
    1. Nationalsozialistische Deutsche Arbeiter-Partei. 2. National
socialism. 3. Power (Social sciences) 4. Germany—Politics and
government—1933–1945. 5. Social systems. 6. Chaotic behavior in
systems. 7. Complex organizations. 8. Bureaucracy. I. Title.
    DD253.25 .B43 2000
    943.086′01—dc21   99-32027

British Library Cataloguing in Publication Data is available.

Copyright © 2000 by Roger Beaumont

All rights reserved. No portion of this book may be
reproduced, by any process or technique, without
the express written consent of the publisher.

Library of Congress Catalog Card Number: 99-32027
ISBN: 0-275-96708-5

First published in 2000

Praeger Publishers, 88 Post Road West, Westport, CT 06881
An imprint of Greenwood Publishing Group, Inc.
www.praeger.com

Printed in the United States of America

∞™

The paper used in this book complies with the
Permanent Paper Standard issued by the National
Information Standards Organization (Z39.48-1984).

10 9 8 7 6 5 4 3 2 1

In memory of and in tribute to my mentors:

Philip Curtin
Chester Easum
John Erickson
Robin Higham
Bernard James
Lee Lawrence
J. Rhodes Zell

FEB 0 8 2002

Contents

Preface

A caveat at the outset: This study is not a technical treatise on non-linearity, but an examination of the *Hitlerzeit* (Hitler era) from the perspective of chaos-complexity. While that may seem appropriate enough, since many have visualized those times as a kind of historical tempest or whirlpool and drawn analogies to chaos in the sense that the Third Reich was a kind of random disorder, that is also true of many other past events, from the fall of Babylon, Carthage, and Rome through the Black Death and the Mongol invasions to the French Revolution. There are no equations, charts, or diagrams in this study, beyond those included for illustrative purposes, nor are there Feigenbaum numbers, Hamiltonian systems, and Julia, Mandelbrot, and Cantor sets and other items, which can be found in many of the cited works on chaos-complexity theory. As Alan Beyerchen has pointed out, insights cannot usually be referenced to a particular source; but I have done my best to mark my trail, although it is hard to draw sharp distinctions between modern theorists' view of chaos as a level order within apparent random turbulence and the sense of chaos being totally random disorder. Many have seen that as the essence of history and as something that cannot be reduced to exact quantities and patterns, since the crafting of history is unavoidably impressionistic and subjective.

What led me to approach this vortex? In the late 1980s, I became interested in chaos-complexity during a visiting year at the Naval Academy, where I was aided and encouraged by several colleagues as well as by relatives and friends. After returning to Texas A&M, I began work on *War, Chaos and History,* which appeared in 1994. Although immersion in the dense conceptual thicket of non-linearity led me to vow that I would proceed no further, as I turned to other projects, I became aware that I had become accustomed to seeing things through the lenses and filters of chaos-complexity. But why Hitler and the Third Reich? I became interested in the *Hitlerzeit* while reading through my father's collection of *Time* magazines in the early 1950s, and my focus was sharpened in stages by Chester Wilmot's *The Struggle for Europe* and by Chester Easum's seminar at Wisconsin in 1959–1960. My major doctoral field in graduate school was Central Europe, and over the last two-and-a-half decades, I have frequently discussed its facets and implications with colleagues, especially Dr. Arnold Krammer of the History Department and Dr. John Robertson of the Political Science Department at Texas A&M, as well as my daughter Anne, and my son, Eric, who helped nudge me onto this track in the late 1980s.

I am especially grateful for the Texas A&M History Department staff's help, especially that of Mary Johnson, a paragon of administrative efficiency; the always cheerful and helpful Judy Mattson; and the very able and enthusiastic Robyn Miller. My department head, Dr. Julia Blackwelder, has been most encouraging, as has Heather Ruland Staines at Greenwood/Praeger. And last, but not least, I thank my wife Penny for her aid in the final stages of this effort.

Chaos-Complexity and History: Perspectives and Paradoxes

Chaos lies all about us, most of it natural and normal, in the form of clouds, waves, smoke, and the wind rippling on grain fields and in a host of images framed by students of non-linearity,[1] including:

the trickle of sand in an hourglass, which creates peaks that suddenly collapse and cascade (see Figure 1)

the dynamics of sand dunes in the deep desert

avalanches

the cutting of a single strand of a spider web, which creates a whole new pattern

the transition from a smooth millpond to a millrace (Figure 2)

the peaks and valleys of stock market price charts and cardiograms

rising smoke

spilled peas, or beans, or marbles

weather and climate patterns

the folding of cloth and pastry dough

the patterns formed in the mixing of different compounds

Some chaos is seen as benign, like our heartbeat, which, if it suddenly becomes regular instead of choppy and uneven, can be fatal. Thunderstorms bring a mix of good and bad things that seem wildly random—rain to parched earth, wind, and hail and lightning—but which are not

Figure 1 A simple phase change in the flow of sand in an hour glass, similar to avalanche dynamics. The slow and steady flow of sand builds steep cones, which suddenly and unpredictably collapse, and then rise again, and collapse again.

wholly formless or limitless. The laws of physics are at work in anvil-head clouds, in the ponderous grinding of glaciers, and in a howling tornado. Even such wild chaos occurs within certain ranges, not as precisely as the swing of a pendulum or the flow of alternating current in a wire, but inside specific dimensions nevertheless. Chaotic systems may appear placid or regular in behavior just before they undergo a dramatic transition, or phase-change, resulting in "patterns which arise when a system is driven away some equilibrium state and undergoes sudden transitions which, with increasing external stress, break the symmetry of the simple, least stressed state, in more and more complicated ways."[2]

The difficulty of measuring the exact limits of the range in which chaos occurs led a mathematician to warn against "anyone who tries to explain the causes behind what happens," or "who claim[s] to predict the future."[3] Not bad advice on the surface, but in the last quarter-century, the ever-increasing power of computers has allowed researchers to probe more deeply into the nature of non-linearity. That has sharpened their view of chaos as a degree of order embedded within apparent turbulence, and not outside the reach of effective analysis and control. In examining such processes as electronic circuits and sequences of the replication of forms like tree branches and rivers (Figure 3), analysts of non-linearity have been able to pinpoint and predict in some cases. However, like nuclear physicists, they have also found that their ability to look more closely at some phenomena did not always give them a clearer picture of what was going on. Despite that, as we will see, researchers in many fields have been able to draw close enough approximations to allow the mapping of certain patterns and processes and

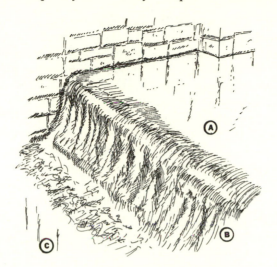

Figure 2 A common example of phase-change: water flowing over a spillway, transitioning from a calm steady-state (A) to chaos (B) and returning to steady-state (C).

the designing of equations and systems that allow them to cope with apparent chaos and uncertainty.[4]

It is not yet clear how much the application of chaos-complexity theory to things like the weather, politics, social processes, and war will produce tools that will allow effective prediction and intervention. The

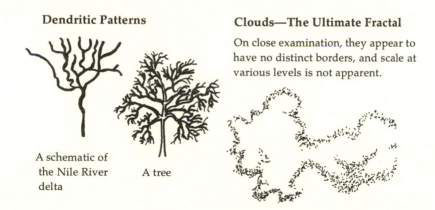

Dendritic Patterns

A schematic of the Nile River delta

A tree

Clouds—The Ultimate Fractal

On close examination, they appear to have no distinct borders, and scale at various levels is not apparent.

Figure 3 Real world fractals include smoke, fog, dendritic patterns like circulatory systems, leaf veins, river valleys.

reflex to simplify and seek out the practical tends to get in the way of seeing the essence of the paradox that Gerry Gingrich pointed out: "The science of complexity ... does not yield answers, at least not in the sense of those we have typically sought to describe our world and predict its events since the beginning of the Scientific Revolution. What it does yield is a new way of thinking about the world."[5]

The basic question underlying this study is: How much does looking at history through the lens of chaos-complexity theory offer new and useful perspectives on how history is crafted by historians and on how it actually works? At the risk of puncturing suspense, the answer is: Only time will tell. At first glance, it may seem useful to increase our ability to foresee and control in any of those, but there may be a dark side to that as well. Understandably, those possessing in-depth knowledge of the mathematics and concepts may rush to point out the dangers of generalizing on certain points and of making assertions and drawing implications. That seems fair enough, but it also loses sight of the fact that Dostoevski's metaphor of a two-edged sword, rather like a fractal pattern, extends far beyond the narrow limits of his metaphor drawn in respect to psychology. Simplified complexities have proven deadly again and again in the working of history. The lack of a detailed knowledge of the underlying scientific apparatus did not prevent millions cursorily familiar with the intricacies of Newton, Darwin, Freud, Marx, and Hitler from acting on their limited grasp, which stirred them to fervor.

At a more abstract level, historians have long wrestled with the mysteries of what caused things to happen. In graduate school, a generation ago, we were warned against getting bogged down in "what-iffing," in trying to puzzle out all the things that might have happened, since that was illogical and a waste of time; but underlying attitudes and assumptions have changed. Deconstructionists and postmodernists, for example, have raised questions about the reliability of evidence and the possibility of drawing conclusions, but although chaos-complexity touches on some of the same questions, the theories touch but do not overlap. The latter lies closer to and builds upon probability, General Systems theory, fuzzy sets, and catastrophe theory, as well as quantum physics, creating a realm in which uncertainty and subjectivity are seen as unavoidable and where theories and devices have been built with those limits in view. Some may see it as contradictory, then, that this study of the *Hitlerzeit* (the Hitler era, 1919–1945) raises the question of finding patterns and drawing implications by searching the evidence of the chaos of those times, just as some historians of the Third Reich and Holocaust may take exception to considering the tangle of the *NS Staat* (National Socialist state) as a historical problem at all. The implied polarity between the unique and the generic here is not merely an academic matter if processes—linear or non-linear, or both—at work in the *Hitlerzeit* raise, even to the slightest degree, the possibility of some kind of reiteration. With that dilemma in view, both assuming uniqueness and waving it aside lie closer to faith than reason. Yet even if the *Endloesung* (the Final Solution) was sui generis, which is true in a narrow sense of all historical events, accepting that without a challenge gives way to true chaos and risks giving evil more than its due, including awarding the Nazis a victory over history as well over their victims. In chaos-complexity terms, the Third Reich extended the distance that a civilized and technically advanced nation might lurch toward brutality. The greatest puzzle here, in chaos-complexity terms, is whether the Third Reich's rise and fall was a single tracing around a "strange attractor" or one of many in a class that includes other brutal regimes—or if it lies outside any category or construct.

PERSPECTIVES ON CHAOS

Chaos is often seen as wild disorder and tumult, bringing to mind such images as crashing waves, billowing smoke, white-water rapids in a mountain stream, storms, battles, riots, and the shrill disorder of a playground. It is not surprising that since chaos has often been linked to massive destruction, it has often been seen as embodying evil. In spite of that, many philosophers and scientists have looked at it from a more or less clinical point of view. Half a millennium ago, for example, Leonardo da Vinci studied cascading and flowing liquids as he tried to identify patterns within the apparent random turbulence of waterfalls. A century later, the mathematician and philosopher Gabriel Pascal searched for forms within what looked like randomness when he used roulette wheels to generate numbers, laying the foundations of the science of probability. Later, students of such intricate processes recognized that some problems could not be successfully attacked with the tools of analysis, like statistical mechanics, that helped them solve other kinds of problems. When marine and hydraulic engineers grappled with the behavior of liquids and aerodynamicists studied air flows, both dealt with chaotic processes that could not be measured exactly, but which did take place within approximate limits. As they assigned numbers and terms to those ranges that allowed them to solve practical problems, they moved closer to modern chaos-complexity theorists, who define chaos as a degree of order that lies buried within what at first glance looks like random turbulence. Others glimpsed bits and pieces of that along the way. Workers in fields like metallurgy and baking had long recognized that mixing different substances by mechanical devices, even over a long time, would not yield a uniform blend. Differential patterns continued to appear, instead of an even mix, and order persisted in spite of attempts to generate total chaos. In the 1930s, Ralph Bagnold, an expert on the movement of desert sand, noted that the distribution and forms in sand dune migration and particle spills were never exactly identical, but always fell within specific mathematical ranges.[6]

In the early twentieth century, physicists and chemists confronted the dilemma of sensing patterns of order within disorder when they tried to explore the inner structure and dynamics of molecules and atoms. Concepts like Planck's Constant and Heisenberg's "uncertainty principle" reflected the inability to determine the precise location and dimensions of the smallest forms of matter despite the increasing resolving power of scientific instruments. On a parallel track, the French mathematician Henri Poincaré "first observed that there is a densely distributed set of periodic orbits" that "would provide the means for understanding the chaotic behavior."[7] He defined some aspects of non-linearity more clearly in equations, but was frustrated by what was later labeled "sensitive dependence"[8]—major, unpredictable outcomes of complex processes produced by very slight differences in the original conditions. Those questions puzzled others as well, like a philosopher of history who, on the eve of the chaos-complexity "explosion," observed that modern "aesthetic forms have been rife with expressions of the chaotic unconscious within us and of the mindless chaos around us."[9] The puzzling effect of seemingly trivial shifts and accidents on the shaping of events reflected in the old poem "For Want of a Nail" had long challenged historians as they tried to trace causality and explain how things happened. It also served as the basis for a host of science-fiction and fantasy "alternative futures," which describe worlds—or "nonfactual histories"—created by very small changes in history.[10] In the early 1970s, as increased computer power allowed researchers to examine such problems, Poincaré's concepts and bit and pieces of other fields of inquiry, including cybernetics, General Systems theory, and catastrophe theory were woven into what became known as chaos theory. Within a decade, chaos-complexity buzzwords had entered popular culture, often oversimplified and sensationalized, even in the popular scientific press. Michael Crichton's *Jurassic Park* dramatized the challenge of chaos theory to "the reductionist viewpoint, ingrained in western science, that a complex can best be understood by breaking it down into component parts."[11]

Although this is not a technical study, some definitions are needed to offer some sense of how chaos-complexity researchers see the phenomena that they have been studying for the last quarter-century, aided by increasingly powerful computers that have allowed them to see chaos as a level of order within apparent turbulence. The technical intricacy of the terms and equations has made it difficult for historians and social scientists who have turned to chaos-complexity for images and metaphors, not only because of their weak grounding in mathematics and the sciences but also because students of non-linearity themselves are not in absolute agreement about definitions or implications, despite many points of concurrence. Unfortunately, the word *chaos* is often used to describe both randomness and technical chaos—a degree of order within apparent disorder—just as the terms *complexity* and *chaos* are often used interchangeably.[12] Frequently used chaos-complexity terms include the following:

Attractors: dual points around which processes orbit on similar but never identical tracks, or "stable limit cycles."[13] As Stephen Kellert pointed out, "Strange attractors" are called strange because "they reconcile two seemingly contradictory effects" as "nearby trajectories converge onto them" and then "suddenly diverge rapidly" through a "combination of stretching and folding," sometimes leaping "to opposite sides of the attractor" but remaining in "a region of phase space with a particular shape."[14] While the orbits of "ordinary attractors" eventually become regular and predictable, in the case of "strange attractors . . . a minute difference in the starting positions of two initially adjacent points leads to totally uncorrelated positions later."[15]

Chaos:[16] levels of approximate order lying within apparent turbulence. Although not totally random and although some phases in their process may seem regular and predictable, chaotic or non-linear systems cannot be precisely monitored, depicted, or predicted. Even if such a process does not unfold within exact limits, it may not be random; even spills and explosions conform to certain patterns and take place within finite ranges.[17]

Complexity: Not all complex systems are chaotic, and not all chaotic systems are complex. An extremely intricate system may look highly regular in its behavior, but become chaotic very suddenly—like a single flat tire jamming freeway traffic, or a chance remark triggering a prison riot. In such instances, a highly charged and delicately balanced system that appears calm at one instant becomes wildly turbulent the next, like the description of the "political upheaval in eastern Europe in 1989" flowing out of "long maintained stable states"[18] and the sudden outbreak of some wars.[19]

Fractals: increasingly ornate sequences of branchings, created by using a generative equation to expand a simple initial pattern into fans of ever-varying and complex configurations. The elaborate and elegant "Persian rug" sequences produced by computerized iterations of Mandelbrot, Cantor, or Julia sets appear similar to such natural phenomena as tree branches and river valleys in nature (Figure 4). Despite their wildly diverse and intricate forms, their unfolding replication conforms to a common ratio known as the *Feigenbaum number,* 4.66.[20]

Fuzziness: the characteristic of equations based on approximate ranges rather than exact numbers. "Fuzzy sets" have been applied in designing control systems that function under uncertain conditions in which a system monitor-controller cannot "distinguish between groups of possible outcomes."[21]

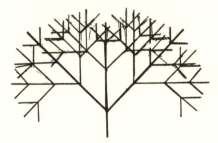

A fractal—a pattern formed by repeating a simple pattern, following an equation or rules, often very simple ones; the crude one at left shows intricacy appearing at the fourth level of repetition of a simple triple branching, with declining scale at each level. Computer generated fractals reveal vast universes of filigrees at millions of replications.

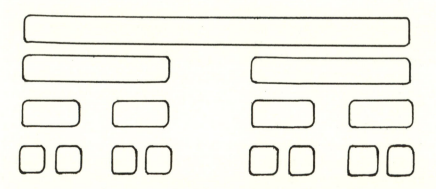

A Roman legion in battle array? Not really. This simple "Cantor Dust" model shows a basic fractal dynamic. Each descending level has the middle quarter removed. In time, the pattern becomes "dust"—a vast number of particles with no actual mass. Computer programs based on Cantor, Julia, and Mandelbrot sets are used to generate fractal patterns.

Figure 4 Fractal patterns—in the realm of theory

Nonlinearity: a characteristic of systems and processes described as "asymmetrically disproportionate,"[22] that is, inputs may vary widely and unpredictably from output. In linear processes, output is proportional to input, and they are often depicted as lines, trajectories, curves, or other coherent forms, while non-linearity is portrayed in such forms as multiple, nonidentical tracks around a common point or points, folded planes, or the myriad branchings of fractals.

Phase changes: alterations in chaotic systems from tranquility to turbulence that can be seen in many everyday occurrences, like the sudden eddying of smoothly rising cigarette smoke, the fluttering of a candle flame in a slight breeze, or the dramatic transition when a smooth millpond flows into a millrace or water begins to boil.

Sensitivity to initial conditions: a key property of non-linear systems, since their ultimate behavior may vary widely from the scale of forces that shaped them at the outset. Konrad Lorenz, while studying weather systems, coined the image of the flap of a butterfly's wing at the very outset of a storm affecting its ultimate course and form. That was not literally true nor measurable, but he wanted to suggest how a wide range of outcomes might result from subtle differences as a complex system evolved, that is, how "small differences in the present will lead in due time to the largest differences that can occur."[23] In the world of practical affairs, "links in . . . accident chains are extremely hard to identify and eliminate."[24]

As we explore some of those diverse aspects of chaos and history, we should keep several guideposts and warning signs in view, including:

Chaos may not be complex, that is, intricate.

Complexity may not be chaotic.

Chaos may resemble order, but change suddenly and without warning.

Chaos is not wholly random.

Evolution may not lead to progress.

Complex processes sometimes conform closely with precedents, and sometimes vary widely from them.

Complex systems consisting of common elements may produce fragments of apparent similarity.

At each point that we examine, in keeping with the dynamics of fractals, we will discover further degrees of complexity, in keeping with William Poundstone's dictum that "In principle, any set of physical laws that permits complex systems allows an unlimited explosion of complexity."[25]

The course of history may be more tachycardic than smooth and harmonic.

The ability to see more details may either enhance predictability or add to confusion.

Rational assumptions and simple stratagems align with reality only by coincidence.

Arraying a great deal of complexity to approximate absolute reality may fall much shorter of actuality than what appears to be the case.

What seems to be wild turbulence may actually be behaving in conformity with a fairly simple sets of parameters, like sudden changes in direction by schools of fish and flocks of birds.

While much in nature and life is chaotic, the greatest challenge for scientists, engineers, and other analysts is determining what is truly random and whether or not "symmetry, or pattern, exists within chaos, or disorder."[26] That could be useful in analyzing forms of social turbulence like migrations, settlement patterns, riots, revolutions, and wars or in resolving long-debated questions such as whether historical events are the waves that appear on a massive flow like a great river whose banks and course are shaped by general laws, or unique bubbles generated by the intricate collisions of myriad forces, great and small. From the perspective of chaos-complexity theory, history looks like a vast spiderweb, an intricate, delicate, and stressed network that springs into wildly different forms when a single strand is cut. If mapping those strands—like the patterns embedded in the stock market—could be detected, measured, and used for prediction, that would have tremendous practical value. That might also be true of politics, ideology, and social systems, but especially of warfare, where there is a special value in knowing if what looks like a messy tangle is not as random as it appears, which led Martha Gellhorn to suggest that "the mind that adapts to the chaos of war risks becoming chaotic too."[27]

Some researchers have seen chaos-complexity theory as a full-blown conceptual revolution, like Nicolis and Prigogine, who asserted that it signifies "the breakdown of the ideal of complete knowledge that has haunted western science for three centuries."[28] Others are less enthusiastic, seeing it as merely old wine in new bottles or an overdramatized fad, like catastrophe theory—or too vague or cult-like.[29] In looking through the lenses of chaos-complexity theory, however, viewers should be aware that some critics see it a fad, doomed to the same ultimate frustration as earlier concepts.[30] Some are put off by the equations and jargon, such as the proposition that scientific "laws are not timeless truths" but "context dependent regularities."[31] Still, it is not clear how really robust the complex causal webs are that converge and produce what actually happens. That suggests that great batches of might-have-beens are crumbling every instant as one of the many possibilities actually happens. Can such questions ever be answered, at least to the satisfaction of scientists? Will we ever know enough about "initial conditions" to make confident statements about how they shaped outcomes, let alone to make effective predictions?

In chaos-complexity terms, "the overall behavior of a dynamical system is for the most part fixed by the number of and character of the attractors,"[32] but building valid models of history is not the same as a laboratory experiment in which models can be kept simple and variables shifted. As we know reality cannot be duplicated, how meaningful can any model short of reality really be? Even trying to draw a "fuzzy logic map" of historical events exceeds the capacity of blackboards and computer spreadsheets. That throws us back on the impressionistic selection and arraying of "facts" that historians have relied on in their craft for roughly the last two centuries. As they make assumptions and impressions in trying to recapture and analyze the past, there is no sure test of their validity. Paradoxically, historians who try to point out the disorder and ambiguity of the "real world" often seem too cautious, while those who resort to exaggeration and self-confident posturing appear more convincing. Although that may seem to be less of a problem when history is read for entertainment, it is a different story when it creates false perspectives while shaping the attitudes and expectations of both elites and the public-at-large.

So what is the value of looking at the Nazi era through the lenses of non-linearity? Clearly it offers a fresh perspective and, hopefully, new insights and implications, a different view of something long seen as chaotic—when that is defined as "dynamics freed from the shackles of order and probability."[33] The *Hitlerzeit* was certainly a "historical surprise" in terms of its being a prime example of what "happens when common sense fails."[34] Anticipating sudden shifts in the flow of history is not something we have become better at doing with the advance of technology. That led a biologist trying to cope with fire ants to lament "our inability to predict how harmful something is going to be" and conclude that "the only thing we can try to do is get better at predictions about what will be the big nasties."[35] The NS Staat was certainly a big nasty. Many of the scars that it inflicted on the world are still plainly visible, and some have not yet healed. Holocaust denials, recurrent genocide, and neo-Fascism provide solid evidence of that. Nor can we be sure it was the biggest or nastiest.

Whatever lenses we use to scrutinize the Third Reich, it presents basically the same challenges to analysts as other events do. There are debates over Fascism's and Nazism's roots,[36] whether the Holocaust stands outside history as a unique event, whether Germany might or could have won World War II, and so on. Ideally, chaos-complexity would help us identify patterns embedded in Nazism or determine if the Third Reich was the symptom of some kind of chronic historical malaise, and whether there is a chance of a recurrence.[37] Of course, the odds may be stacked against us as we look back into history, since we do not know whether our view of the past is only limited by inadequate methods of sensing and analyzing it or whether the nature of things presents absolute limits on our ability to probe it. If, for example, we could be absolutely sure that Nazism sprang from the pent-up rage and emotion seething beneath the surface in civilized societies that Freud anguished over, what difference would that make? That uncertainty does not justify faintheartedness; the argument that, since Nazism arose from a bewildering tangle of forces, analysis can be of little practical value, could have been made about theoretical physics in the mid-1930s.

In looking at the *NS Staat*, we will see all kinds of chaos, including the broad array of theories about how it came to be and how it worked. Was, for example, Nazism the fifth in a series of uprisings against Western civilization in German history, in "what they believe is their national destiny: the periodic rejuvenation of mankind through barbarism?"[38] Or was it merely a facade that masked a gang of greedy manipulators?[39] Although speculations have been aimed at making sense out of that frightfulness, they have not led to a consensus about what National Socialism really was and why it attracted many Germans. Close scrutiny of it at the time and since has shown that what many saw as a ruthless and efficient monolith was actually riddled with cracks and flaws, leading to some overcorrection in that direction. The fragmented afterimages of the *Hitlerzeit* in popular culture have added to the sense of chaos by presenting glimpses of mass hysteria and the howling frenzy of Hitler's speeches, leaving out of focus the fact that the National Socialists—the Nazis—offered themselves as an antidote to the chaos of the Weimar Republic era of 1919–1933. How, then, do that fragmentation and complexity align with chaos-complexity theory? By the mid-1990s, scientists and analysts had applied chaos-complexity theory to a wide array of problems with some practical effect, from cryptanalysis to control systems.[40] Studies of the dynamics of circular wave fronts that led researchers to hope they might be able to predict the "onset of collapse"[41] generated enthusiasm for its potential in military circles.[42] At the very least, considering the history of the *Hitlerzeit* from that vantage point offers fresh perspectives, whether or not it helps us identify impending pathologies analogous to those stirred up by Hitler and the Nazis. While the atrocities of Stalin and Mao Ze Dong were greater in scale, they were not, as the *NS Staat* was, the product of a modern industrialized democracy that had a rich tradition of liberalism and humanitarianism.

If approaching history from that perspective gave a clearer sense of what the Hitler era was and which subcurrents in the flow of German history produced it, that would be a marvel in itself. No other construct has done that to the satisfaction of historians. Perhaps charting parameters, "initial conditions," or subtle forces that led to Hitler's rise, the outbreak of World War II, and the Holocaust might, like a photographic negative, produce a sharper image of what the true causes were. Since most history is a literary art form, it is not surprising that Nazism has often been portrayed in impressions and metaphors, for example, as "a dictatorial regime whose alleged totalitarianism was neither seamless nor inevitable . . . punctured by compromise and accommodation" whose "disjointedness and paradox" reflected "a heteromorphic nature"[43] and as a "national drama" that evolved "into permanent delirium."[44] Those images, like Virginia Wolff's description of Hitler's "baying,"[45] are wonderfully lyrical, but lie far from being science, social or otherwise. That is hardly surprising, given the enormous number of causes offered for the coming of the Third Reich. German senior officers after World War II, for example, pointed to the "significant negative impact" on the *Wehrmacht*—Nazi Germany's armed forces, 1938–1945—of von Clausewitz's and von Moltke's concepts of "absolute war and the independence of military leadership in wartime,"[46] while various historians have traced the roots of Nazism to such disparate causes as German tribalism and modern industrialism.[47]

Considering the sheer mass of proposed causes from the standpoint of chaos-complexity theory and the fact that such "causes" are only single straws in gigantic bales of causality leads to another paradox. At the same time that the concept of "sensitivity to initial conditions" puts a high premium on details, it also raises the question of whether the vast causal spiderweb of history can be mapped and its turbulent processes effectively measured. In that sense, as noted earlier, chaos-complexity may appear to overlap with deconstructionism and postmodernism and their implicit negation of meaning.[48] The intricacy of both process and analysis, then, are intimidating and can be seized upon to provide an excuse to abandon the search or to rely on lyricism, generalization, and a very broad brush. But we cannot be any more certain, no matter how refined our methods might become, that such problems will remain intractable than we can know whether, in turning away, we would lose the chance of developing techniques that might allow us to detect and prevent such horrors. If we were absolutely sure that the *Hitlerzeit* was unique and that Nazism is the only such flower of evil that will ever grow out of the compost pile of history, there would still be some value in tracing its history. That might not only give fuller dimension to the grief and horror and help to assign guilt more precisely, but remind us what human beings are capable of, if we tend to forget. But if chaos-complexity helped identify a merging of forces or elements in the future that were leading toward another cataclysm, that would look less like historical analysis and more like clinical pathology. There is no dearth of cases. Mass slaughters, after all, have occurred throughout history with all too great a frequency, from the fall of Babylon to Rwanda.

In any event, when considering the utility of chaos-complexity theory, we should keep in view the hazards of trying to use such concepts to study political and social phenomena, as well as the dangers in using history to predict the future.[49] Consider, for instance, chaos-complexity theoreticians' assertions that "Convergent, explosive, oscillating and chaotic regimes arise from [a] model depending on the choice of parameters"[50] and that "the source of chaos is missing information" and what people "observe when they lack the information to perceive the underlying order."[51] We still have a long way to go to discern just what crucial information is missing or what the underlying order is, let alone what the absolute limits may be on our ability to know such things. It seems very daunting that "in dynamical systems in nature, chaos is typical rather than the exception,"[52] but chaos-complexity concepts may offer us a faint ray of hope in seeking a way to cope with the myriad threads that comprise the tapestry of history. At the very least, it offers a check to arrogance, as Stephen Kellert suggested when he noted that "Chaos theory provides a way to understand how unpredictability happens; it tells us the way chaos limits predictability in simple systems."[53] While history is generally viewed as a very intricate process, chaos-complexity research has led to substantial improvement in control systems by using slight perturbations and one chaotic system's interaction with another, pointing to degrees of order lying beneath apparent randomness.[54] In a parallel vein, James Woodward suggested, "It is often hopeless to try to understand the behavior of the whole system by tracing each individual process. Instead one needs to find a way of representing what the system does on the whole or on the average, which abstracts specific causal detail."[55] If that allowed us to solve historical puzzles, that would be very useful indeed. It would, however, be far more valuable if it made it possible to anticipate and deal with historical pathologies like Nazism. The possibility, however remote, warrants wading further into the conceptual swamp.

NOTES

1. For other models and images, see Richard H. Priesmeyer and Kibok Baik, "Discovering the Patterns of Chaos," *Planning Review*, 17:6 (November–December,

1989), pp. 14, 15, and 47; George Johnson, "From Grains of Sand: A World of Order," *New York Times*, September 8, 1996, sec. 4, p. 106.

2. Alan C. Newell, "The Dynamics and Analysis of Patterns," in Edward D. Stein, ed., *Lectures in the Sciences of Complexity* (New York: Addison-Wesley Longman, 1989), p. 107.

3. John Allen Paulos, quoted in Faye Flam, "Mathematician: Some Events Can't Be Explained," *Houston Chronicle*, April 26, 1995, p. 3F.

4. For example, see M. Granger Morgan, "Risk Analysis and Management," *Scientific American*, 269:1 (July, 1993), pp. 32–41; and Alvin M. Saperstein, "War and Chaos," *American Scientist*, 83 (November-December, 1995), pp. 548–557.

5. Gerry Gingrich, "Simplified Complexity: Thinking in the White Spaces," *Strategic Forum*, 139 (May, 1998), p. 1.

6. Ralph A. Bagnold, *Sand, Wind and War: Memoirs of a Desert Explorer* (Tucson: University of Arizona Press, 1990), p. 190.

7. Quoted in Ronnie Manieri, "Impressions on Cycling," *Center for Non-Linear Science Newsletter*, 76 (March, 1992), p. 2.

8. See Edward Lorenz, *The Essence of Chaos* (Seattle: University of Washington Press, 1993), pp. 115–121.

9. John J. Marcus, *Heaven, Hell and History* (New York: Macmillan and Co., 1967), xv.

10. For example, Keith Robert's *Pavane*, in which Elizabeth I's assassination yields a nineteenth-century England without railways, in which technological and scientific inquiry are suppressed by the Inquisition; in Ward Moore's *Bring the Jubilee*, a time-traveler from a world in which the Confederacy won the Civil War with a victory at Gettysburg accidentally reverses the course of events, leading to Lee's defeat and a Union triumph.

11. James Marti, "Chaos Might Be the New World Order," *Utne Reader*, November/December, 1991, p. 30.

12. For example, the definition of complex systems as: appearing widely in nature, society, and technology, in a vast range of sizes; symmetrical or disordered in form; and a mix of determinism (predictable outcome) and randomness. Complexity is proportional to the number of parts; unlinked to conserving or expending energy, causes and effects, or positive or negative feedback; determined by system characteristics and setting and by interactions. Complex systems have open boundaries allowing the transfer of data, energy, and resources; cannot reverse processes; are unbalanced and unable to rest in a dynamic state; and are in transition and may be goal oriented. Their processes are usually uneven and unpredictable and often "jink," that is, change course suddenly and/or blend forms and combinations in a disorderly way; see A. B. Cambel, *Applied Chaos Theory: A Paradigm for Complexity* (Boston: Academic Press, 1993), pp. 3–4.

13. See E. C. Zeeman, *Catastrophe Theory: Selected Papers, 1972–1977* (Reading, Mass.: Addison-Wesley, 1977), p. 12.

14. Stephen H. Kellert, *In the Wake of Chaos* (Chicago: University of Chicago Press, 1993), pp. 13–15.

15. Clifford A. Pickover, *Computers, Patterns, Chaos and Beauty: Graphics from an Unseen World* (New York: St. Martin's, 1990), p. 378.

16. For a definition of disaster, see Anthony F. C. Wallace, *Human Behavior in Extreme Situations* [Publication 390, Disaster Study No. 1] (Washington, D.C.: National Research Council–National Academy of Sciences, 1956), p. 13.

17. Definitions of chaos include "an order of infinite complexity," F. David Peat, *The Philosopher's Stone: Chaos, Synchronicity and the Hidden Order of the World* (New York: Bantam Books, 1991), p. 196; "a type of randomness that appears in certain physical and biological systems . . . intrinsic to the system rather than caused by outside noise or interference," Robert Pool, "Quantum Chaos: Enigma Wrapped in a Mystery," *Science*, 243:4993 (February 17, 1989), p. 893; and a phenomenon that exceeds "the capacity of a single individual to understand it sufficiently to exercise effective control—regardless of the resources placed at his disposal," William L. Livingstone, *The New Plague: Organizations in Complexity* (Bayside, N.Y.: F.E.S. Limited Publishers, 1985), pp. 1–11.

18. Manfred Schroeder, *Fractals, Chaos, Power Laws* (New York: W. H. Freeman, 1991), p. 34.

19. Alvin M. Saperstein, "War and Chaos," *American Scientist*, 83 (November-December, 1995), pp. 548–557.

20. A useful and succinct article on fractals is S. H. Liu, *IEEE Engineering in Medicine and Biology*, 11:2 (June, 1992), pp. 28–39.

21. Thomas Whalen and Carl Bronn, "Essentials of Decision-making under Generalized Uncertainty," in Janusz Kacpyrzyk and Mario Federizzi, eds., *Combining Fuzzy Imprecision with Probabilistic Uncertainty in Decision-Making* (Berlin: Springer Verlag, 1988), p. 27.

22. N. Katherine Hayles, *Chaos Bound: Orderly Disorder in Contemporary Literature and Science* (New York: Cornell University Press, 1990), p. 11.

23. Lorenz, *Essence of Chaos*, pp. 161–162.

24. Paul Russell, Boeing aeronautical engineer, quoted in Fred Bayles, "Airline Disasters Hard to Solve," *Houston Chronicle*, May 26, 1996, p. 10A.

25. William Poundstone, *The Recursive Universe: Cosmic Complexity in the Limits of Scientific Knowledge* (Chicago: Contemporary Books, 1988), p. 198.

26. Ian Stewart and Martin Golubitsky, *Fearful Symmetry: Is God a Geometer?* (New York: Penguin, 1992), p. 223.

27. Quoted in Jeremy Harding, "No One Leaves Her Place in Line," *London Review of Books*, 20:9 (May 7, 1998), p. 31.

28. Gregoire Nicolis and Ilya Prigogine, *Exploring Complexity: An Introduction* (New York: Freeman and Co., 1989), p. 197.

29. John Horgan, "From Complexity to Perplexity," *Scientific American*, 272:6 (June, 1995), pp. 104–105 and 106–109.

30. For example, see Luther M. Boggs, "Meaningless Chaos: Pretty Pictures and Computer Paisleys—The Irrelevance of the New Nonlinear Science of History" [Contemporary History Institute, Ohio University Think Piece Series, No. 2], January 1991; John Horgan, "A Theory of Almost Everything," *New York Times Book Review*, October 1, 1995, p. 30; and Christopher Meyer's letter to the editor in response to Horgan's essay in *New York Times Book Review*, October 22, 1995, p. 3.

31. Jack Cohen and Ian Stewart, *The Collapse of Chaos: Discovering Simplicity in a Complex World* (New York: Viking Press, 1994), p. 285.

32. John A. Casti, *Complexification: Explaining a Paradoxical World through the Science of Surprise* (New York: Harper Collins Publishers, 1994), pp. 27–28.

33. Joseph Ford, "What Is Chaos, That We Should be Mindful of It?" in Paul Davies, ed., *The New Physics* (New York: Cambridge University Press, 1993), p. 354.

34. Casti, *Complexification*, p. ix.

35. James Lester, quoted in Bill Dawson, "Scientists Tell a Cautionary Tale of 2 Species," *Houston Chronicle*, November 14, 1994, p. 78.

36. For example, the argument that "Fascism (understood functionally) was born in the late 1860s in the American South," p. 12, in Robert O. Paxton, "The Five Stages of Fascism," *Journal of Modern History*, 70:1 (March, 1998), pp. 1–23.

37. Stewart and Golubitsky, *Fearful Symmetry*, p. 225.

38. Raoul de Roussy de Sales, *The Making of Tomorrow* (New York: Reynal and Hitchcock, 1942), pp. 254–255 and 282.

39. For an array of related arguments, see the bibliography in James Pool, *Hitler and His Secret Partners* (New York: Pocket Books, 1997), pp. 403–406.

40. For example, see Tomasz Kapitaniak, ed., *Controlling Chaos: Theoretical Practical Methods in Non-Linear Dynamics* (London: Academic Press, 1996).

41. Aric Hagberg and Ehud Meron, "Oscillating Reaction-Diffusion Spots," *Center for Non-Linear Studies Newsletter* 131 (November, 1996), p. 5.

42. For example, see Glenn E. James, *Chaos Theory* (Newport, R.I.: U.S. Naval War College, 1997).

43. Michael H. Kater, *Different Drummers: Jazz in the Culture of Nazi Germany* (New York: Oxford University Press, 1992), p. 202.

44. Fritz Stern, *Dreams and Delusions: The Drama of German History* (New York: Alfred A. Knopf, 1987), p. 148.

45. Anne Olivier Bell and Andrew McNeillis, *The Diary of Virginia Wolff*, vol. 5, *1936–1941* (San Diego: Harcourt Brace Jovanovich, 1984), p. 178.

46. Guenter Roth, "Field Marshal von Moltke the Elder: His Importance Then and Now," *Army History*, 23 (Summer, 1992), p. 1.

47. Victor Loefflath-Ehly, Letter to the Editors, *Chronicle of Higher Education*. February 5, 1994, p. 39.

48. For perspective on that dilemma, see Robert Artigiani, "Post-Modernism and Social Evolution," *World Futures*, 30:3 (Winter, 1991), pp. 149–161.

49. For example, see Ian Percival, "Chaos: A Science of the Real World," in Nina Hall, ed., *Exploring Chaos: A Guide to the New Science of Disorder* (New York: W. W. Norton, 1991), p. 16.

50. Murray Wolfson, Anil Puri, and Mario Martelli, "The Non-linear Dynamics of International Conflict," *Journal of Conflict Resolution*, 36:1 (March, 1992), p. 147.

51. Ford, "What Is Chaos?" p. 351.

52. Heinz-Otto Peigen, Hartmut Juergens, and Dietmar Saupe, *Chaos and Fractals: New Frontiers of Science* (New York: Springer Verlag, 1992), p. 684.

53. Kellert, *In the Wake of Chaos*, p. 83.

54. For example, see Kapitaniak, *Controlling Chaos*, esp. pp. 105–107 and 114–117.

55. Kellert, *In the Wake of Chaos*, p. 104.

2

The Third Reich as a Dialogue of Chaos and Order

The chaos of Nazism shone through its glitzy exterior throughout its brief life cycle, like a rotating glass-faceted ball above a dance floor that hypnotized some and repelled others. Its glare reflected both inner fragments and outer contradictions, and many who watched the rise of National Socialism and the Third Reich at the time pointed out the tension between the Third Reich's facade of order and discipline and the turmoil that lay at its core. As observers then and historians since struggled to sort out what was absolutely chaotic from the subtle patterns beneath apparent random turbulence, many of them, as Michael Freeman observed, tried to apply "logical reasoning to a regime which in both its leading persons and its structures was frequently illogical . . . and to combine their perspectives within statistical prisons."[1] For example, in 1935, when the full energy and horror of Hitler's regime was first coming into view, Raoul Castex, a French naval theorist, tried to make some meaning of it in the rationalist tradition of the Enlightenment. He defined Nazism as one of a series of grand historical calamities and fit it into his "Theory of Perturbation," arguing that "in the course of every century of modern times, with almost astronomic periodicity, the tranquility of Europe [and Asia] has been disturbed by a nation or political group aspiring to hegemony."[2]

Charles Lindbergh and millions of others clung to that relativist view even after the metaphorical furnace door began to swing open in the early phase of World War II, but half a decade later, with the wreckage in full view, the sociologist Hans Gerth saw Nazism as having been a "great body of religious, aesthetic, mythological, political, and historical verbiage."[3] In the early 1980s, Frank Trommler described the chaos at the core of the *NS Staat* as the result of "history proceeding by calamities" within a dynamic of "catastrophic gradualism."[4] Half a century after the fall of the Third Reich, Gerhard Weinberg noted the "administrative chaos which had been developing [in Germany,] in the years before the war, was, if anything, accentuated during the conflict."[5] At the same time, in a similar vein, others described the Third Reich as being "ruled not by systematic application of powers, but by a chaotic profusion of authorities" lacking "single jurisdiction, institution, or bureaucratic apparatus"[6] and "Hitler's rise to power . . . as the result of a chaotic mixture of nihilism and masochism, a rebellion against authority and at the same time a neurotic submission to it."[7] A historian of *UFA*, the Nazi film combine, described "the Nazi censorship offices" functioning "perfectly and irrationally at the same time . . . feverishly and at cross purposes."[8] That grand contradiction led Martin Broszat to define the Third Reich as a fragmented polity or "polyocracy" and to suggest that Nazi ideology was not "a rational proposal for the future" but "a catch-all, a conglomeration, a hodgepodge of ideas . . . nothing more than slogans."[9] Christopher Browning drew an analogy with feudalism in arguing that "Nazi Germany . . . [was] not a monolithic state in which everything was decided at the top" and flowed down "a chain of absolute obedience." He saw it, rather, as a "system composed of factions around the Nazi chieftain," which, like medieval fiefdoms, were in "a state of permanent internal war."[10] In looking at the effect of structure on behavior, George Browder defined the most rigidly centralized and coldly rational component of the *NS Staat*, Himmler's *Sicherheitdienst* (Security Service) as a "complex phenomenon" whose intricacy produced a sense of fragmented depersonalization that led people to become more easily involved in "the dutiful execution of inhumane roles."[11] Geoffrey Megargee saw the turmoil within the High Command bureaucracy, *Oberkommando des Wehrmacht*, as mirroring "the state of the entire Nazi regime."[12] In short, chaos begat chaos.

The turbulence of Nazism was not merely a product of amateurism or the distemper of the times that gave it birth. National Socialist ideology was deeply rooted in Romanticism, a fuzzy cluster of concepts that lay somewhere between religion and philosophy, based on the ideal of the strong individual acting alone to shape destiny, a role that Napoleon played on the stage of European politics for two decades. The turbulence, turmoil, and emotionalism of Romanticism that captivated German youth in the early 1800s were revived by the Nazis, leading Peter Viereck to identify the "Romantic Ego" at the heart of National

Socialism "in two words: arbitrary caprice." It suggested to him that "the ego must run the gamut of unrestricted emotional and intellectual self-expression"—and resist the imposing of standards.[13] The essence of that was caught in a Hitler-era description of the "eternal German ideal" as listening "to the beat of . . . blood and conscience" to become "capable of that superhuman greatness which is ready to cast aside all temporal bonds."[14]

In chaos-complexity terms, Romanticism was one of the "deep universal patterns concealed within the erratic behavior of chaotic dynamical systems."[15] At a more sordid level, Romanticism was also closely linked with anti-Semitism and remained so in National Socialist ideology,[16] despite such powerful countercurrents in German culture as the proverbial hunger for precision and order and humanism. The threads of that tension ran through modern German history. The philosopher Immanuel Kant, while at the University of Jena, the hub of Prussian intellectualism, produced *Critique of Pure Reason*. That tract provided a theoretical basis for the release of suppressed passions, giving students or Romanticists a lofty pretext for striking heroic poses and seeking *"sturm und drang"* (storm and stress) in battle, mountain climbing, gymnastics, and dueling. The clash between dreamy, furious ideals and eighteenth-century Enlightenment rationalism visible in the works of the Prussian military theorist Karl von Clausewitz and those of Richard Wagner and Friedrich Nietzsche half a century later ran through to the early 1900s. Romanticism flavored the "heroic realism" of the storm-troop veteran novelist Ernst Juenger and the poetry of Stefan Georg, and reached a crescendo in the Third Reich. The tension between order and chaos was visible at the very end of the Third Reich in the case of both Hitler and his nemesis, Colonel Count von Stauffenberg, who tried to blow up the *Fuehrer* in the July 20, 1944, coup attempt. The Fuehrer ranged wildly between technical preciosity and Bohemian sloppiness and tantrums, while the colonel, despite his rigorous General Staff training, was a devotee of Georg.[17]

While those contradictions help explain why some analysts of the Third Reich have seen the "bureaucratized violence" of Nazism as "an expression of contemporary Western civilization,"[18] such views of chaos and tumult run contrary to the image of the Third Reich as a monolithic pyramid in which power flowed relentlessly downward from *der Fuehrer*. It is still obvious that the Nazis' vivid stagecraft and propaganda dazzled many and diverted attention from the manifold inconsistencies and defects of National Socialism.[19] Thomas Mann, the most distinguished German novelist of that generation, who clung to his German nationalism when he emigrated to America, suggested Hitler's power was "not political" but "magic."[20] He made that the theme of his novel *Mario and the Magician.* In a similar vein, Fritz Stern described Hitler as "the greatest magician-manipulator of the aggressive, violent instincts of an outraged, perplexed people that the modern world has seen,"[21] and Albert Speer claimed that Hitler hypnotized friends and foes alike and dazzled the masses with dramaturgy and glitzy symbolism, or what Joachim Fest called "liturgical magic."

Hitler's dictum that "Non-recognition of reality is the principle of salvation"[22] underscores the difficulty of sorting out image and substance in a system whose architects and critics both knew that it was based to a substantial extent on sleight-of-hand. Of course, if that blend of persuasion and coercion produced a kind of mass psychic chaos, that provides Germans of that era with the excuse of collective insanity. That was hardly unique to Nazism. Rulers throughout history have identified dissent as a form of madness, from witchcraft to clinical mental illness. Paradoxically, the structured schizoid hypocrisy of centralism has served to induce pathologies. In any case, the reliance of modern dictators on such labels, as well as psychotropic drugs and brainwashing, reflects the special sensitivity of authoritarian systems to the smallest element of potential resistance—the human mind. Unfortunately, neither the gross statistics of Nazi Party membership, Party records, nor public opinion polls during and after World War II provide clear indices of that inner chaos, or to what degree Germans did or did not go along, and how much apparent compliance was due to carrot or stick.[23] Not only do broad statements about the susceptibility of Germans to Nazi propaganda skills and German culture as the source of certain habits of mind and of behaviors lie far from science, let alone chaos-complexity theory, but they offer no explanation of why the image of the Third Reich as a regimented, highly efficient system survived its collapse and has been widely accepted throughout the world, despite much contrary evidence. Although the Third Reich's security apparatus suppressed the writing of letters and diaries, the regime kept a relatively tight leash on the general population until 1943, when *Reichspropagandaminister* Goebbels, Nazi Germany's chief propagandist, announced that "Total War" was at hand. The full weight of repression did not come down until after the attempt to assassinate Hitler in July 1944. That substantial but immeasurable pressure and war damage erased a substantial portion of that history, making it all the more difficult to assay the always foggy domain of inner thought and motives and to determine which behaviors were due to conviction, or anger, or fear.

The massive crimes of Nazism and simplistic popular culture images have also obscured many details of the regime's workings, such as the Nazis' deft presentation of different masks to various factions and interests, first to gain money and votes and then to consolidate power and maintain support. Different Party sub-organizations brought many Germans into tangential association with Nazism, allowing different degrees of accommodation for those trying to balance their perceptions of good and evil, like the German Army chaplain who recognized that Nazis were bent on war but hoped their militarizing of society would bring order out of chaos.[24] Obviously, some supported the regime enthusiastically, or at least with apparent zeal. Others did what they saw as their duty, while others dragged their feet, worked to rule, or engaged in subtle sabotage. A few engaged in determined resistance— and those, too, for a wide range of motives. Although the latter had much to risk and little to gain by standing against the tide, the Nazi organs of state security sometimes pulled their punches when dealing with minor dissidence and used many carrots as well as sticks. From 1939 to 1943, senior officers, civilian officials, and businessmen benefitted from the looting of conquered territories, the use of forced and slave labor, and the war economy. It was clear to all sentient Germans and most observers that National Socialism promoted bullying, from gutter brawling to the idealized image of Germans as feudal overlords in the New Order. Like other European powers' imperial functionaries, some found that role repulsive, while others tolerated it or warmed to it.[25] As with imperialism in the broader sense, many Nazi instabilities and excesses did not come into clear view until after the grand spectacle was over. The intricate diversity of roles and images in the Nazi movement offers some perspective on how, despite its thuggish street fighters and coarse rhetoric, the Nazi regime was nevertheless able to gain widespread deference and respect in Germany and in other countries as well soon after Hitler became Chancellor in January 1933. The images of a tightly knit and closely controlled system, followed by apparent economic recovery and rearmament, led some to express admiration, including former British prime minister David Lloyd George. Even Winston Churchill paid some grudging tribute in the early 1930s, although he was soon alienated by Nazi cruelties.

When World War II began, the Wehrmacht's victories from 1939 to 1941 gave substance to the prewar propaganda images of National Socialist discipline, efficiency, and ruthlessness. That served to obscure such contradictions as the contrast between National Socialism's ideals of a classless society and close links with big business, and its adherence to the traditional German *Fuehrerprinzip* (leadership principle) of unquestioning deference to authority in the armed forces, civil service, schools, and families. One sharp contradiction in Nazi ideology was the divergence of Romanticist visions of individual heroism, a classless society, and a people's army. Another was *Gleichschaltung* (forced cooperation) under which nearly everyone was seduced or coerced by the regime into some kind of involvement, compliance, or at least apparent conformity. Other National Socialist disparities included coldness and ferocity; discipline and corruption; ruthlessness and sentimentality; technical prowess and atavism; creativity and philistinism; elegance and crudity; efficiency and ineptitude; and rationality and irrationality.[26] Others saw what they wanted to see. At the same time, the violent, passionate outbursts of Nazi leaders ran counter to the German ideals of self-control. Nor did all that take place in a vacuum. The Nazis clambered to power on the ornate web—or crazy-quilt—of myths, symbols, and emotions that enshrouded Germany for a generation.[27] And as we saw earlier, they did not invent anti-Semitism, but harnessed it.

In chaos-complexity terms, the broad pattern of Nazism's rise from 1919 to 1942 looked more like an earthquake on a seismograph or the tracings of a cardiogram than long, smooth waves, especially the sequence of surprises and political and military triumphs over the decade following Hitler's gaining power in January 1933, followed by a relatively rapid series of setbacks and collapse in the last two years of the war. The surges of turbulence in Europe and the Far East in the 1930s and early 1940s led many thoughtful observers to conclude that a cataclysmic transformation of the world was under way, what Anne Morrow Lindbergh deemed the "wave of the future."

As the democracies, major and minor, floundered through the Depression, appeasement, and military disasters, they appeared enfeebled and, from December 1941 to June 1942, very possibly doomed. A British Air Marshal, for example, enviously ascribed Germany's rapid rearmament to its military establishment being free of "all those factors, political, financial, bureaucratic and social, to which we in this country have become accustomed."[28] Hitler, Stalin, and Mussolini were frequently portrayed as symbols of modernism or described metaphorically as forms of natural calamities, like storms, tornados, whirlwinds, earthquakes, volcanic eruptions, and cataclysms.

The obscuring of many details of the tangle at the heart of the regime by censorship, propaganda, and wartime secrecy helped to maintain the Fuehrer's mystique until the final collapse, despite increasing awareness of Nazi ineptitude and corruption, wartime privations, mounting air raids, and the string of major defeats. Just as some victims of the 1934 *putsch* (purge) cried out "Heil Hitler" when they stood before firing squads, many Germans and the Nazi hierarchy remained loyal and deferred to the Fuehrer's whims "until the very end, when Germany was falling to pieces around them."[29] (As an index of their deference, no one in Hitler's entourage was willing to wake him early when the Allies invaded Normandy.) Until the end, many Germans expected him to reveal miracle weapons that would win the final victory. For example, Martin Bormann's wife, an ardent National Socialist, anticipated a magical turn of the tide that would lead to dissension and mutiny among the converging Allies and allow "Germany . . . [to] sally forth again, knock down what is rotten, and take possession of the chaotic space."[30]

Even amid the growing piles of rubble, Nazi mass ceremonies and symbols continued to present glittering images of order, discipline and force, masking the *NS Staat*'s malorganization, incoherent ideology, and corruption. As more and more of it became visible, many Germans blamed it on lower-level functionaries failing to stay in tune with the Fuehrer's lofty intentions. They had little sense of the fact that the regime's inner turmoil was due to Hitler's bureaucratic Darwinism. He called his stirring up of fierce rivalry in the Party hierarchy "noble competition," an ongoing vicious brawl, in which contenders struggled for power and access to the Fuehrer.[31] As a result, friction permeated all echelons and crannies of the NS Staat, military and civilian alike. In the *Waffen SS*, the combat element of Hitler's elite, black-uniformed bodyguard force, for example, the "extraordinarily heterogeneous officer structure" produced "an extraordinarily uneven level of military performance."[32] Beyond various squabbles of "revolutionary factions within the Nazi Party" were the wasteful overlaps and rivalries between the major economic programs headed by Heinrich Himmler, Hermann Goering, and Albert Speer and between the separate propaganda bureaucracies of Dr. Goebbels and Alfred Rosenberg.[33]

Some of those rivalries, which lasted until the final hours of the Third Reich, were visible in Britain and the United States during Hitler's ascendancy and in the early years of World War II. Later, many of the details faded or were erased, lost in the vortex of war damage[34] or overshadowed by Holocaust revelations and de-Nazification. After World War II, journalists and historians, most notably William L. Shirer, searched far back in German history as they tried to trace the tangled threads of Nazism's genealogy. Suggested roots included the German tribes' fending off of Roman rule and isolation from Western civilization; the brutalizing effects of medieval Germany fending off barbarian incursions; protracted tensions between intermingled Catholic and Protestant states; peasant uprisings; the truly horrific Thirty Years' War, 1618-1648; Germany being a battleground in dynastic wars for generations; its remaining divided into small feudal states longer than most European nations; and the rise of the Prussian garrison state. Ironically, the Nazis themselves had cited those ordeals as precedents and recast them as badges of honor. Even though it was a left-wing party in its social agenda, National Socialism, like Soviet Communism in 1941, resurrected images of monarchs, and especially slogans from the Napoleonic era, when Romanticism and Liberalism were alloyed with Prussian militarism after Bonaparte's defeat of the Prussian army at Jena in 1806. The Nazis' crazy-quilt ideology included the athleticism, anti-Semitism and class-leveling rhetoric of Father Jahn and his youthful gymnasts—and their ritual burning of hated books. Goebbels brought the images of those times back to the foreground when he diverted scarce resources, including troops, to the making of an epic film, *Kolberg*, which glorified the siege of a Prussian town in 1806 to urge Germans to fight on against overwhelming odds.

As we have already seen, some roots of Nazism also ran back to the traditional anti-Semitism of central Europe, and others to modernism—and antimodernism. It still remains unclear how much Hitler and the Nazis were disciples of Mussolini. Both parties' military elites wore black, and both movements gloried in force and the bullying and torture of the helpless and glorified war. Trying to sort out what was derivative and what was unique requires tracing the bizarre, murky, and often contradictory fragments of what the Nazis called their *Weltanschauung* (worldview) and the equally, or more, complicated, tangled genealogy of Fascism, properly described as "notoriously easier to describe than it is to understand."[35] Martin Broszat, for instance, traced the *"volkisch* roots" of National Socialism running back to visions of Utopian resurgence, racism, and hatred of Jews, Freemasons, and Liberals and to the *"volkisch* idea." Like Romanticism, Broszat concluded, Nazism was born of "passionate emotions," which by their "very nature defied theoretical systematization," all the more attractive to some for being vague and formless.[36] Such feverish churning also fit the description of Fascism as "Above all, action and sentiment," and an "immense driving force . . . [and an] irresistible current of national will."[37] Although various Fascist movements differed in many ways, they shared an admiration for violent impulses, and breaking down normative social boundaries.[38] That was reflected in the French Fascist Pierre Drieu La Rochelle's judgment of humanitarianism as decadent, praising "Hitlerian man . . . who rejects culture . . . [and] believes only in acts," and who lived, like the conquistadores, Puritan pioneers, Caesar and Alexander the Great, in "brutal reaction to refinement."[39]

The widely accepted image of the Third Reich as a monolithic regime and an antidote to the chaos of the Weimar era helped to obscure the divisions among National Socialists and the murkiness of its ideology. Through the 1920s, Hitler had struggled constantly to keep hostile factions and individuals in the Nazi movement from clashing. His 1934 putsch of some 4,000 dissidents briefly spotlighted the turbulence and cleavages within National Socialism, but did not end the fuzziness of

Nazi doctrine and policies or decrease the tendency of his followers to engage in personality clashes and turf battles—or Hitler's encouragement of such rivalries. That turmoil flowed into World War II and the Holocaust, reflected in differences among top Nazis over exterminating or exploiting "sub-humans," dramatized in *Schindler's List*, and the substantial number of leaders who died in accidents or suicides. The intricate texture of that vortex—a favorite symbol of proto-Fascists— was nudged out of focus by Hannah Arendt when she coined the phrase "banality of evil" during the Eichmann trial in 1961. Rather like a pathologist trying to estimate the athletic achievements of a corpse at a dissection, she generalized from the particular of the "grey man" functionary Adolf Eichmann as he appeared in captivity half a generation beyond his heyday. Of course, her view of Nazism as kitsch was not unique, nor wholly off the mark. Nazis often flaunted their anti-intellectualism, and Hitler's pedestrianism is still evident in photographs and home movies of him amid his entourage at Obersalzberg and Berchtesgaden, as it is in his flat, fastidious artistic style. But the Nazis were not all bumpkins. Speer, Schacht, Riefenstahl, von Braun, and Goebbels were all talented people; and thousands of academics, physicians, and technicians joined the Nazi Party before Hitler came to power. Some intellectuals who watched from a greater distance, like Carl Jung, saw Hitler as the embodiment of the Romanticist ideal of a determined, creative individual defining himself through bold and risky acts; and visionaries laid the philosophical foundations for the "political organization of cultural hatreds and personal resentments,"[40] calling for a Fuehrer and a *Dritte Reich*—Third Reich—to fill the vacuum created by the fall of the House of Hohenzollern and regain German honor.[41] Beyond that lay the pseudosciences of eugenics and geopolitik, whose tendrils ran through Europe and into the American heartland, and academe as well.

Soon after Hitler gained power, a small number of his supporters, both within and outside the Nazi party, found him more than they bargained for. German conservatives who set aside reservations and revulsion to pursue what they saw as a higher purpose quickly realized the new regime was no more coherent than the "class-ridden economic and political chaos of the Weimar Republic."[42] Despite the popular image of monolithic efficiency, the word "chaos" and its synonyms were increasingly used to describe the Third Reich, although to convey a sense of general disorder and disorganization, not a level of order lying within swirls of turbulence, as envisioned in chaos theory.[43] Albert Speer,[44] for example, pointed out the "havoc wreaked on the mechanisms of production by the constant arbitrary shifts in programs and priorities"[45] and the "vaguenesses" that acted as "a cancer in

Hitler's mode of governing."[46] In a similar vein, German historians
have described the "system of government in the Fuehrer state" as a
"nonsensical, chaotic and structureless . . . jungle" and the Hitler era as
"a *Walpurgisnacht* [Night of the Witches] . . . the breakdown and defile-
ment of a high culture."[47] But it would take a great deal more careful
analysis to gain a clear picture of how the NS Staat's chaos varied from
that of the other major warring powers. There were, of course, many
well-ordered sub-elements within the turmoil of the Third Reich, and
enough coherent efforts to keep Germany's numerous and wealthy foes
off balance while organizing slaughter on a massive scale.

A sense of chaos in the upper echelons of the Nazi regime flavored the
testimony of Nazi defendants at the Nuremberg war crimes tribunal in
the late 1940s[48] and the memoirs of senior German military, political,
and industrial leaders. Immediately after the war, the victorious Allies
found extensive evidence of that turmoil as they picked over the bones
of the Third Reich. A British official study of the Luftwaffe published in
1948, for example, described "unclear subordination, parallel orders
and general confusion" in its administration,[49] while inspectors discov-
ered "a great deal of duplication, waste and overemphasis on minor details" in the Nazi ordnance program at the Hillersleben Artillery and
Ammunition Center.[50] The Royal Air Force's official history of the
Luftwaffe noted the hindrance "and confusion caused by the direct intervention of Hitler . . . more and more as time went by."[51] Toward the
end of the war, the Nazi hierarchy sensed the growing chaos clearly,[52]
and half a century later, an American historian deemed the Holocaust a
"descent into chaos that the victims endured," although the death-
camps were all too well organized.[53] Albert Speer, after emerging from
twenty years in prison in the late 1960s, used the theme of a steadily
growing chaos during the twelve-year history of the Third Reich in his
memoirs. He traced a spiral that culminated in the "chaotic command
situation" in the final days of World War II "that made it possible for men
of good will to limit chaos in the future" by disobeying Hitler's order to
demolish the infrastructure of Germany.[54] Speer's appreciation of that,
however, came very late in the day. Initially attracted to National Socialism as symbol of order amid disorder, he described the *Sturmabteilung*—
storm detachments—the Nazi Party's brown-shirt street-fighting army,
in the streets in the late 1920s as a "sight of discipline in a time of
chaos,"[55] which the British sculptress Clare Sheridan, who lived in Berlin in the early 1920s, saw as a "crazy, crashed world."[56]

Among those Germans who fled the Third Reich in the mid-1930s
were former confidants of Hitler who sensed that something powerful,
primitive and formless was roaming the political landscape. In keeping
with the chaos-complexity dictum that "One must get out of a system

in order to really understand it,"[57] they recognized, long before Speer, that the Third Reich was not a carefully laid out and efficiently orchestrated regime. In 1937, for example, a veteran German bureaucrat described Hitler's regime as "provisionally well-ordered chaos."[58] In 1942, Hermann Rauschning made that case more bluntly, titling his book on the Nazi hierarchy *Men of Chaos* and proclaiming that Hitler was "born of the mental chaos of universal destruction, of a society in which all spiritual values had been effaced or shattered."[59] In a similar vein, a French diplomat who served in Germany through much of the 1930s described "Hitler's imagination" as "wildly romantic . . . fed . . . upon elements gathered pretty much everywhere . . . not uncultivated, but his cultivation was the ill-digested culture of one self-taught."[60] President Roosevelt conveyed a sense of that turbulence in his "quarantine the aggressor" speech of October 5, 1937. In predicting that events in Germany were progressing toward a cataclysm, he quoted from James Hilton's fantasy novel *Lost Horizon* to warn of a "storm . . . [that would] rage until every flower of culture is trampled and all human beings leveled in a vast chaos."[61]

The idea that Nazism and the Holocaust were satanic, insane, and neo-barbaric[62] was shared by such diverse observers as a German frontline soldier, a Field Marshal,[63] and a Holocaust scholar.[64] Such devil theories were also accepted by the Third Reich's allies as well as victims and critics. Count Ciano, Mussolini's son-in-law and Fascist Italy's foreign minister, saw the Nazis as "possessed by the demon of destruction,"[65] making it all the harder to understand Hitler's powerful attraction for many Germans until the very end. Given the minimal enthusiasm for the Fuehrer outside Germany, it is easy to understand why some Germans suggested that something was lost in translation. As Carl Jung, the psychiatrist, was being drawn toward the vortex, he suggested that "Few foreigners respond" to Hitler "at all, yet apparently every German in Germany does . . . because Hitler is the mirror of every German's unconscious" and "mirrors nothing for a non-German."[66] Undistinguished in appearance and crude in speech, Hitler had a unique rhetorical power that has been ascribed to such factors as the receptiveness of audiences, the orchestration of symbols and crowd psychology, Germanic deference to authority, and anger over the Versailles Treaty as well as the Fuehrer's own mood sensitivity, powers of observation, hypnotic abilities, and charisma. Yet until National Socialism surged in popularity in the late 1920s, Hitler was widely seen outside Germany as absurd, a slightly sinister version of Charlie Chaplin given to raving in public. His rough Austrian dialect, marginal origins, and crudity of expression were seen as debits, but there, too, complexity lay beneath apparent simplicity. Hitler was the first major politician in a democracy to multiply his presence in election campaigns by traveling in high-speed motorcars and airplanes and using television to reach large audiences. Few Americans realized that his truncated moustache, the trenchcoat he often wore in the 1920s, and the Sam Browne belts and khaki uniforms of the Sturmabteilung were derived from World War I British military fashions. Millions saw or heard only brief excerpts of his speeches, snippets that conveyed little sense of his influence or the full emotional cycle of the staged spectacles.

In making speeches, Hitler began in a flat and sometimes halting conversational monotone, sensing the mood of the audience, then built up to a shrieking, incoherent, frenzied climax, creating an "an atmosphere of fanatical mysticism" in which his "words and sounds" were "more powerful for the lack of meaning."[67] The extremes of shrieking and cold self-control in Hitler's guttural speeches became the stereotype of Nazism throughout much of the world. His political testament *Mein Kampf* was a best-seller, although few actually waded into its meandering thickets and contradictions. Despite Hitler's political canniness and substantial insight and creativity, his lack of formal education denied him a grasp of the theoretical side of technology and made him insensitive to complex processes and nuances. Fortunately, that included theoretical physics. Unlike Churchill and Roosevelt, he had no eminent scientist as an advisor; he came closer to Stalin in claiming intuitive mastery of all subjects. That arrogance and dilettantism reflected the crazy-quilt of National Socialist ideology and its myriad contradictions.[68] Although Hitler and his followers were strongly anticlerical and fascinated with the occult, they sometimes claimed he was a Messianic leader and drew parallels between him and Christ and John the Baptist. Claiming an infallibility akin to the Pope's, the Fuehrer insisted he was carrying out Christ's unfinished work in purging Germany and Europe of corrupting influences, creating a "new political faith," and preaching "a new socialist religion."[69]

To those raised in a rigidly stratified world where "birth and breeding" determined individuals' destinies, Hitler was especially perplexing. Before he entered lunatic-fringe politics, he was nondescript, quirky, self-educated, and unathletic, a ne'er-do-well meandering through life. How could a nonentity—the uneducated son of a minor customs official, marginally talented and chronically unemployed, and a mere corporal in the Army—mold a tiny political faction into Germany's dominant political party, then gain control of and revitalize the major industrial state in Western Europe, and finally dominate or conquer most of the continent? Even at the time, the stagecraft in all of that was clearly visible, as was Hitler's mugging and posturing. His dilettantism was apparent to the Party hierarchy, who, like courtiers throughout history, had to endure their master's tedious musings evening after evening, a mix of ill-informed rambling, occasional tantrums and fits and flashes of humor, based on cruel irony and sarcasm. Fascinated with technology, from fast cars and tanks to architecture,[70] he made no attempt to conceal his superstitions. When addressing Wehrmacht officers in late December 1944, for example, Hitler referred to "lucky and unlucky stars" and "omens."[71]

That lack of coherence often frustrated members of his entourage,[72] who deferred to his leadership but lived in fear of the outbursts that came in reaction to frustration or when his patience was exhausted in arguments. That unpredictability and rage, which also flavored his diplomacy, led many to speculate about possible psychopathology. He certainly had his share of personal ordeals[73]—his father's abuse, his mother's painful death from cancer, failure to become an artist, social marginality for years, and four years in a combat infantry unit in World War I. He won the Iron Cross First Class as a dispatch runner, a role requiring dexterity, initiative, and reliability, but there is no evidence of his engaging in direct combat. He was, however, often under heavy fire. In 1923, the *Reichswehr*—the troops of the Weimar Republic—fired on him during the so-called Beer Hall putsch; and in 1931, his beloved niece, Geli Raubal, was shot to death under uncertain circumstances.

Whatever the traumatic effect of those experiences may have been, Hitler's behaviors closely matched checklists of some clinical syndromes, especially fanaticism. He often claimed that he was driven by an "inner force" to carry out a great mission and deliberately rejected or ignored reality. He was explosively aggressive because of impaired affect and had phobias, including compulsive cleanliness.[74] Robert Waite, in *The Psychopathic God*,[75] set Hitler's behavior into a framework of "Private Neurosis to Public Policy," based on the key elements of private and public rage, fastidiousness, and a search for "triumphs through self-destruction."[76] That broad pattern of ascent and free-fall led Edleff Schwaab to frame a complex cyclical model[77] in which Hitler lacked the sense of a clear boundary between falsity and truth,[78] in keeping with another analyst's view of a "specific combination of irrationality and keen rationality" that characterized the Nazi regime.[79] Further out on the speculative limb are hypotheses that defeat was irrelevant to Hitler when he veered away from winning the war to launch the Holocaust[80] and that he was a rash gambler for whom "self-defeat . . . was really the principle" since his "speeches are full of dark references to his own defeat, from the earliest years . . . to the final defeat."[81] Other psychiatric and physical pathologies and syndromes offered as causes of Hitler's cycle of success and failure include an Oedipus complex, various phobias, and tertiary syphilis, gallstones, hypermedication,[82] temporal lobe epilepsy, and Parkinson's disease.[83] While the observation of a former physician of Hitler's that he was "a sick man and Germany [was] a very sick country"[84] seems like an empty generalization, the Nazis also followed the semantic fashion of the times in using medical and epidemiological metaphors to assail their enemies. The regime's propagandists drove home the image of *untermenschen* (subhumans) by portraying Jews as the "bacillus" of revolution and cultural degeneracy, as spiders spinning a web of a "world conspiracy," or as akin to rats and lice in spreading contagious diseases.[85]

Whatever may have ailed Hitler over the years from January 1933 to late 1941, he was widely acclaimed or feared as a master politician, diplomat, and warlord. During that interval, he rarely seemed to put a foot wrong in his diplomatic and military maneuvers. Speer marked the crucial turning point in the waning of Hitler's powers as his ordering the panzers not to close in on the British forces encircled at Dunkirk in late May 1940, while others set the watershed in the Fuehrer's deterioration in judgment closer to the invasion of Russia, or even later. Despite the apparent decline in his powers, many at the time—and some historians and journalists afterward—continued to weigh Hitler's personality and decisions as a primary factor, reinforcing his claims of special, virtually magical demagogic influence, a theme invoked by the editors of *Time* in naming Hitler "Man of the Year" for 1938. At the same time, they discounted the way in which Hitler's belief in his unique powers of foresight and his gambling impulse and a long series of wins led him to double his stakes again and again, despite the sharply steepening odds and increasing probability of reversal. The emphasis on his paramount centrality, then and since, has discounted major shifts in the balance of power during World War II, especially the forming of the Anglo-Soviet-American alliance, the mobilizing of the Allied nations' economies, the improvement in the military techniques of Germany's foes, and the arousal of their peoples against Fascism. None of those seemed likely before the war, nor even in its early phases. In any case, historians, despite hindsight and access to far more data, have not been able to determine how and when the balance shifted any more than those who lived through those times—but the concept of sensitivity to initial conditions offers a fresh perspective.

A close examination of Nazi military methods shows how the problem of chaos in war, long a matter of concern to military professionals and theorists, was addressed in the Reichswehr and the Wehrmacht. Their battle tactics were designed to maintain momentum in the chaos of modern mechanized war and to impose a sense of chaos on their foes. Recognition of the increasing disorder and diffusion of combat in the industrial age was reflected in catchphrases of the Weimar Republic's army, the Reichswehr, which were retained by the Wehrmacht—and ultimately, by the Bundeswehr. Those included such slogans as *Kriege ohne Feldherrn* (war without generals), *Angriff ohne befehl* (if lacking orders, attack), and *Feuer und Bewegung* (fire and maneuver). In Spain in 1936–1939 and during the first half of World War II, the Nazis generated chaos among their foes through rapid, diffuse penetrations by tanks, armored cars, and motorcycles, mounting sirens on Stuka dive-bombers, and launching air and armored attacks in rolling waves. Such orchestration of turbulence and confusion contrasted sharply with academic concepts developed by the Kaiser's general staff on the basis of phasing, linearity, and symmetry, such as "surface-and-gap" theory, which attempted to reduce the chaos of trench warfare to an an abstract geometric construct.

In the opening phase of World War II, as Germany's enemies strove vainly to find patterns in the turbulence of what became known as *Blitzkrieg* ("lightning war," a term invented by foreign journalists, not the Nazis), they failed to recognize that they were looking at an anti-doctrine, or a doctrine that rejected doctrine in the orthodox sense. Reichswehr and Wehrmacht officers, like some of their counterparts in other armed forces, recognized how mechanization had made aerial and ground combat more like the mixing of gas clouds or liquid flows than the clash of blocs that dominated trench warfare and was embodied in France's Maginot Line and in most of the Allies' tactics during the first three years. To add to the confusion, some observers saw blitzkrieg as derived from the German "infiltration" tactics of World War I, methods developed by non-Regular officers experienced in fire-fighting in which small teams of elite "storm troops" penetrated weak spots in the enemy front, then maneuvered independently, bypassing strong points to attack key communication and command nodes. The use of the storm-troop motif by the Sturmabteilung added to the confusion. Nor did Germany's foes realize initially that the chaos of combat was often as perplexing to the Wehrmacht as it was to them. That was visible during the great *panzer* drive across France during the assault in 1940, when the German Army's High Command, jittery at the lack of clarity and the slushy feel of control, ordered a pause for "regrouping." A similar concern led Hitler, after he took direct command of the Army in late 1941, to suspend fluid "operations." His growing conservatism clashed with his artistic pretensions and tolerance for loose ends and the left wing of Nazism and contrasted with his edict to Nazi Party security forces following in the wake of the armed forces at the beginning of the war in Poland that "Total disorganization must be created! The Reich will give the Governor General the means to carry out this devilish plan."[86]

He was not misguided in applying the brakes. By late 1942, the balance began to shift from chaos on the fighting fronts in Europe and the Mediterranean, in the form of positional warfare. The fusion of antitank guns, land mines, and the Allies' development of superior close air support systems vastly reduced the Wehrmacht's ability to carry out the grand sweeping arcs, penetrations, and envelopments as they had done in the early campaigns. Many German commanders as well as Hitler became concerned about the lack of coherence in Wehrmacht operations, even some who had formerly urged crashing ahead without concern for forms and patterns, like Rommel and Guderian.[87] Another major source of chaos in the German war machine was reflected in the bewildering organization chart of the Wehrmacht, which, as Gerhard Weinberg observed, "no normal person could be expected to understand."[88] The entrainment of chaos as an instrument of terror also lay at the heart of the *Nacht und Nebel* ("Night-and-Fog) decree issued by Oberkommando des Wehrmacht (OKW) on December 12, 1941, which was designed to inflict anguish in occupied areas by having people suddenly disappear, usually in the middle of the night, under the logic that "Efficient . . . intimidation can only be achieved either by capital punishment or by means by which relatives of the criminal and the population do not know the fate of the criminal. This aim is achieved when the criminal is transferred to Germany."[89] Such well-honed, deliberate cruelty was no surprise to those watchers of the Third Reich who, from the early 1930s on, discerned the dark forces at work and patterns within the vortex. Walter Langer, for example, foresaw Hitler's suicide, and Peter Viereck predicted that the Nazis would use poison gas for mass executions.[90]

From the standpoint of chaos-complexity theory, various points along the path of National Socialism's rise and fall suggest "sensitivity to initial conditions," that is, the wide yawing of a complex system due to very slight forces, such as Hitler's overriding his advisors, field commanders, and the OKW staff. Better-known examples of that include his canceling plans to invade Britain, deciding to attack the USSR, obsessing on seizing Stalingrad, holding back on committing reserves against the Normandy landings, and expending the Wehrmacht's last major reserves in the Ardennes in 1944.[91] The results of his interference were not always negative, however. As one of Hitler's most eminent biographers, Sir Alan Bullock, pointed out, the Fuehrer's military micromanaging sometimes led to substantial success, such as his involvement in designing the airborne assault on Fort Eben Emael, his support of von Manstein's attack plan in 1940, and his insistence on standing fast in Russia in the winter of 1941, when many generals urged a massive retreat. On the other hand, less dramatic decisions also had significant results. One was keeping consumer goods production close to peacetime levels, to shield German civilians from the privations that led to riots and mutinies in 1918. Another was allowing the middle and upper classes to employ domestic servants well into the war, while not mobilizing women for war industry and military auxiliary roles, in contrast with Britain and Russia and, to a lesser extent, the United States. Other choices by the Fuehrer that produced unexpectedly major destabilizing effects were:

imposing a "one year" limit on the development-to-deployment interval of weapons systems in 1941, thus blocking or delaying such projects as long-range bombers and jets

rejecting proposals for an airborne assault on Malta

halting effective Luftwaffe intruder raids against British air bases in 1941–1942

requiring jet-propelled Messerschmidt 262s to be built as fighter-bombers rather than as interceptors

dismissing nuclear research as "Jewish physics"[92]

The failure of historians of the NS Staat to agree on just how bad things were organizationally is understandable, since Hitler avoided rational procedures and formats, like structured cabinet meetings with agendas and schedules, which would have defined unpleasant issues clearly and force him to make clear choices.[93] Nor should we overlook the substantial turbulence in other major nations' war machines in World War II—or any major modern war.[94] That is partly due to the simple fact that while Axis systems were open to scrutiny afterward, the victors kept some of their successes and failures under wraps. Beyond that, the Allies' military and industrial systems in 1945 would have looked pretty chaotic to outside inspectors and did seem that way to participants like Bruce Catton, whose book *The War Lords of Washington* threw some light on the "mess in Washington"—a major Republican slogan after the war. Although there is no way to be certain whether records of some German secret projects were destroyed by the Nazis or by war damage, or looted or captured and kept secret by any of the Allies, enough evidence survived the war to show that Nazi science and technology often fell far short of the propaganda images of coherence and brilliance. Hitler recognized the mess in 1942 when he attempted to straighten out the Nazi scientific-industrial nexus by naming his chief architect, Albert Speer, as Minister of Armaments. Things improved in many respects, but the results were uneven, and his efforts were resisted in many quarters. Despite continuing chaos and hostility, Speer was able to disperse industry and massively increase weapons production in the face of mounting Allied bombing and vigorous in-fighting among Nazi leaders and agencies. His substantial efforts fell well short of the orchestration of science and industry in Britain and in the United States. There were no equivalents of the National Defense Research Council or the Office of Scientific Research and Development, or scientist "czars" to determine the feasibility and priority of military concepts and project proposals, like Vannevar Bush in America and F. E. Lindemann, "the Prof," later Lord Cherwell, in Britain. Although each of the Wehrmacht's armed services, pursuing its own business "without much thought about what anybody else might be doing along the same lines,"[95] mirrored the Third Reich's tangled administrative structure, that too was not wildly different from the interservice rivalry and bureaucratic tangles in Japan, Britain, the USSR, and the United States.

Looking closely at such details may give us a better sense of the intricacy of history as a process, but it falls short of absolute historical truth. The chaos is diminished, but not fully erased. How much does that matter? Not much, if we visualize history as a mighty river or "a tide in the affairs of men." In that case, slight differences or "initial conditions" would make little or no difference, as mere twigs and ripples that have no effect on the grand flow. If we use chaos-complexity terms to explain Nazism as a partly evolutionary and partly revolution-ary process or describe Germany history as a series of phase-transitions from 1870 to 1945 or as a series of chaotic states, of which the Weimar Republic was one and the Nazi era another, what does that really mean? Scrutinizing history through chaos-complexity theory's lenses may give us new metaphors and make us more sensitive to its intricacy and to the possibility that the range of possible outcomes may be greater than common sense or linear thinking leads us to believe. That certainly helps explain why it has been so unpredictable. But how much closer does that lead us to understanding how Hitler fit into the grand flow of German, European, and world history? If his rise and fall was a case of a complex system being influenced by subtle forces, that is also true of a host of historical cases, from King David to Joan of Arc and from Napoleon to John Kennedy. Just as physicists aren't sure whether light consists of particles or waves, historians are uncertain whether history is a massive flow of events that follows a certain course and shapes everything in its path or a boiling pot of large and tiny forces that spills over from time to time. Such searching for meaning and causes may seem to be "merely academic," and the question of whether Nazism was unique, inevitable, or one of many possible by-products of the tumult of German and European politics and culture irrelevant. That leads us to the shadowy realm of "what-ifs."

In his fantasy novel *Iron Dream*, Norman Spinrad described an "alternative future" world in which Hitler emigrated to America and became a science fiction writer and artist, presenting Nazism as a marginal science-fiction cult. However fanciful such "alternative futures" are, they suggest the hall of mirrors of paradoxes and possibilities that confront those trying to make some sense out of Nazism and have led some historians to frame such hypotheses in the crafting of "nonfactual history." That does not lie all that far from speculating on whether the Nazis rode to political triumph because a sufficient—or critical—number of Germans pursued "nihilism as an end in itself"[96] or viewing Weimar Germany as a charged battery waiting to be discharged by a charismatic leader along the lines of Anthony Wallace's "revitalization theory."[97] Was Hitler like Dr. Miracle in *The Tales of Hoffman*, a charlatan, hypnotizing a Germany afflicted with a fatal malaise as the evil doctor mesmerized the fragile Antonia, inducing her to sing forbidden songs that doomed her?[98] Or was it inevitable, as the physicist Leo Szilard predicted in 1931, that "Hitler would get into power, not because the forces of the Nazi revolution were so strong, but rather because . . . there would be no resistance whatsoever"[99] in the spirit of Edmund Burke's adage that "the only thing necessary for the triumph of evil is that good men do nothing"? If Hitler was the key actor, the crucial catalytic sine qua non, would all the rage, resentment, and frustration of millions of Germans after World War I and throughout the Weimar era not have led to a political explosion if he had not appeared on the scene? Was the "river of time" running toward World War II? Would it have broken out or raged with much the same destructive intensity if Hitler was never born, or if he had fallen in Flanders in 1916, or if the United States had stayed in the League of Nations, or if Chamberlain had been killed in combat—and so on?

Over the years since the collapse of the NS Staat, the Socialist revolutionary dimension of Nazism has been overshadowed by its nationalist elements. Few today have a sense that class-leveling was a primary goal, one which the conservative German officer corps tolerated, although many of them in the higher ranks of the Army and Navy held the Nazis in contempt. They went along with such programs as the *Hitlerjugend* (Hitler Youth) and the replacement of the old Army and its feudal trappings and traditions with a National Socialist force. That was only one facet of what Alan Beyerchen called a "maze of mutually canceling contradictions,"[100] as, despite the Nazis' hostility toward aristocrats, civil servants, officials, businessmen, and officers—the residue of the old order whom the Nazis openly insulted in education and propaganda—the vast majority of the old guard set aside whatever contempt they felt privately and served Nazism when the Party usurped power after aban-

doning the electoral process.[101] In a supreme irony, German elites helped
the Nazis help the regime negotiate and keep government functioning
and "get things done." Ultimately, the top Nazis grudgingly acknowl-
edged how much the "old school" provided the superstructure beneath
the facade of the Third Reich. Even so avid a National Socialist as Martin
Bormann, after maneuvering his way to the key role of Chancellery secretary, found that cheerleading and posturing could not compensate for
the amateurism and ineptitude of Party officials. Unable to develop a
cadre of effective Nazi civil servants to replace those of the old system,
Bormann became increasingly frustrated when he realized that administering the NS Staat and armed forces was a complex and tedious business that required such non–National Socialist traits as patience,
cooperation, and competence. That makes it all the more perplexing that
military commanders like von Rundstedt, who could barely conceal
their disdain for Nazi hacks and blusterers, deferred to them nevertheless, trapped by their sense of duty. As Hjalmar Schacht, the "old wiz-
ard," used his skills in high finance to help the Third Reich rearm and
economically influence eastern Europe far beyond Germany's resources
and productive capacity, he lamented that "Nazi policy encouraged inefficient production in order to promote employment."[102] But he served
the Nazis well all the same.

The National Socialists' highly touted *Weltanschauung* (worldview)
was not a coherent catechism, but a mishmash of images, ideas, and
slogans including sizable chunks of militarism, Romanticism, Prussian
nationalism, and anti-Semitism. How, then, did they gain enough support to make the system work despite its massive defects? Beyond
seeking revenge for Versailles, economic dislocation, or searching for
order, many Germans turned to National Socialism to escape the drab
or painful realities of life in a bureaucratic industrialized society, as
their forebears had flocked to the Wagnerian operas that Hitler loved
so passionately. The ultimately irony was that it led to far greater chaos
in the end. While many Germans were giving way to powerful and
savage impulses, others saw that the scenery was fake. There were
grave dangers in peeking backstage, as the investigative reporter Carl
von Ossietsky found out. After revealing secret details of German
rearmament, some of which predated the Hitler regime, he was thrown
into a concentration camp and murdered after winning the Nobel Peace
Prize. As a counterpoise to their thuggery, the Nazis displayed a wide
array of what they saw as positive images, including statues and por-
traits of rosy-cheeked *Bauerntum* (peasantry) as the touchstone of folk
values and racial purity upon which an all-Aryan, classless society—the
Volksgemeinschaft—was to be built. That, too, like Romanticism, they
drew from the past. As Richard Noll suggested, "the National Socialists

constructed their ideology out of the elements of German *Volkisch* thought that had been popular for several generations among the educated middle classes."[103] The ideological mishmash of the National Socialist Weltanschauung was visible in the widely differing perspectives of the Nazi leaders. It encompassed such extremes as the murky and convoluted racial theories of Alfred Rosenberg, the Nazi Party's premier intellectual, and the crude, sensationalist anti-Semitic and sadomasochistic pornography of Julius Streicher. The most sinister panel in that crazy-quilt was Heinrich Himmler's bizarre fiefdom, in which threads of medieval nostalgia, occultism, and Jesuit imagery were entwined to indoctrinate the security apparat and the SS. The rageful bravado, brutality, and racialism that were instilled in German youth to imbue them with a sense of mastery over servile underclasses bolstered their individual pride and self-confidence but ignored Von Clausewitz's warning that tact was an antidote to the friction of war. Fortunately for the Third Reich's enemies, all the time spent on ceremonials, self-congratulation, and implanting mythology was at the expense of building technical, administrative, and military skills. Toward the end of World War II, when the Nazi hierarchy tried to imbue the armed forces with National Socialist ferocity, much military training time was given over to cheerleading and sloganeering and instilling those virtues seen as underlying the Party's political victory—the lust for power, ruthlessness, and blind determination, all in the spirit of the *SS Junkerschulen* (cadet schools), "to remove emotional and rational barriers to action."[104]

The utility of burning zeal had been driven home to Germans in 1918 when morale crumbled under the combined blows of the Allied offensives and their propaganda campaigns. The tables were turned in the opening phase of World War II, when the harnessing of powerful, primitive emotional forces in their youth, including the use of amphetamines, gave the Wehrmacht a powerful edge. On the other hand, Nazi admiration for imperialism, particularly that of Rome and Britain, blinded them to the fate of those empires and how slavery, as Jefferson and many travelers in the American South had noted, debased masters and slaves alike. The Nazis' arrogance at the pinnacle of triumph also blinded them to the possibility that the advantages gained by their thrustful boorishness might be transitory. They were not inclined to attribute their political triumphs to random processes or complex forces, or to consider that they had been won regardless of—or even in spite of—their brutal posturing. In 1942–1943, that arrogance and anger prevented them from realizing that they were no longer dealing with the fumbling, timid leaders whom they had bullied and deceived in Europe since 1933 or with indifferent masses in timid and self-indulgent democracies. They were also slow to appreciate how much of the Wehrmacht's edge had been taken off and how sharp their foes' had become. The Allies were no longer the poorly led, marginally trained, and dispirited forces that had been so easily defeated during the blitzkrieg era. By mid-1943, the Third Reich was ringed by growing hordes of well-provisioned foes, led by men enraged by Nazi excesses and also bent on victory at all costs.

Thus was further chaos layered upon chaos—but it did not become total chaos until the very end. The newsreels of the vast destruction and confusion during that final phase were followed by films and histories portraying the surrealistic state of affairs in the *Fuehrerbunker*, Hitler's underground shelter complex, beneath the ruins of Berlin in the spring of 1945 during the Nazi *Gotterdammerung*—literally, "Twilight of the Gods," the Wagnerian final collapse. The surreal and gloomy scenes of bombed-out cities and conditions in the concentration camps in the last days reinforced the general sense of the war having been "a vast natural cataclysm which had swept over friend and foe alike." That left out of focus the fact that the National Socialist regime functioned almost to the end and that many Germans continued to comply and serve,[105] which brings us to the heart of German agony since World War II—how many went along with Nazism, and how much, and why? Some did so eagerly, others sluggishly, and many swam against the current now and then, or very subtly. But there chaos lay, at the very center, as Victor Klemperer, after the Nazis ransacked his apartment, recorded in his diary having seen "that same chaos, that bestial devastation by cruel, drunken apes . . . which I often heard described."[106] And that had long been visible. From the outset, Nazi savagery had alarmed or alienated many who had initially been attracted to National Socialism by one or another of its seductive masks. More and more horrors became visible throughout the 1930s and World War II,[107] as the Gestapo (the secret state police) and other state security organs grew in scale and influence, direct and indirect. Although they were less efficient and powerful than they seemed at the time, their menace stemmed from the uncertain limits of the reach of their surveillance and informers, as well as from the bullying and swaggering demeanor of Party officials and the distant but more terrifying menace of the concentration camps. Pressures grew in German society as the war lasted longer than anyone had hoped or feared. After Christmas 1941, with Russia unconquered, America in the war, and British bombing raids increasing, many Germans began to withdraw into themselves in what was called "inner migration," to reading, hobbies, or whatever activities occupied the mind and which were far from the war and politics.[108] It was hard to ignore the signs of the turning tide as increasing numbers of German soldiers, airmen, and sailors were lost in battle, and those on leave from the fighting fronts or recuperating showed the wear of battle to a nation whose cities were under growing air attack. Reichspropagandaminister Goebbels compounded the sense of weirdness by bending Allied policies and actions to stiffen Germans' resolve to fight on, including Roosevelt and Churchill's "unconditional surrender" proclamation at the Casablanca Conference in early 1943, U.S. Secretary of the Treasury Henry Morgenthau's plan to "pastoralize" Germany after the war, the devastation of German cities by strategic bombing, and the growing likelihood of Soviet vengeance. The first two weakened the cause of those who tried to resist Hitler, and the last two made increased numbers of Germans dependent on the Nazi regime for rescue and survival.

While all of those fed the growing sense of chaos noted by Speer in his memoirs, the aura of strangeness was also heightened by the regime's attempts to keep German civilians' quality of life at prewar levels. Hitler, like Bonaparte, kept a close eye on the public mood and refused to put the German economy on a full war footing until mid-1943, following Wehrmacht defeats in North Africa and at Kursk, the collapse of the U-boat campaign in the Atlantic, and the surge in strategic bombing. Goebbels's call for "Total War" in his carefully staged *Sportspalast*—Sports Palace—speech later in the year marked the major shift from seduction to intimidation. A large symbolic carrot was withdrawn in September of that year, as Allied armies reached Germany's frontiers, when the Reichspropagandaminister shut down opera and stage performances and ordered actors and theater workers into war production or the armed forces. The challenge of mapping the overwhelming details of that vast and intricate process has forced historians of the NS Staat to focus on particular details of it, rather like using a jeweler's eyeglass to paint miniatures, which has left the painting of large, sweeping canvasses to novelists and popularizers.[109] The sense of chaotic ruin carried on into the postwar period. Some films, like *The Big Lift* and *A Time to Love and a Time to Die*, caught the chaotic essence of a landscape littered with paradoxes, with the irony noted by James Diehl that Wehrmacht "veterans did not return *from* a no man's land, but *to* one—a moonscape of skeleton cities and massive destruction."[110] The scenes of ruin also served to blur the fact that many Nazis survived, even though little of the regime did. In the late 1940s, it was easy to conclude that all the gamblers, the Nazi Party principals, militarists, and industrialists, had lost their personal stakes as well as Germany's, perhaps for generations. As the discovery of Hitler and Speer's plans for colossal monumental architecture provided a mocking contrast to the reality of vast tracts of featureless ruins, basic recovery let alone a return to a pre-war standard of living seemed very unlikely.

Although some Germans viewed that ruination as a grim kind of justice,[111] in general it caused a numbing rather like the wartime "inner migration," along with widespread denial and rationalization. There was little indication of the impending *Wirtschaftwunder*—economic miracle—that followed the easing of the western Allies' occupation or of the reunification that came a generation later.

Another dimension of ruination lay beyond the hollowed-out cities—the reversal of almost every cause that Hitler and the Nazis championed. For example, as Gerhard Wilke pointed out, even though Nazi rhetoric ennobled the peasantry, their policies had "effectively destroyed the 'traditional' structure of village life" before World War II.[112] Italian Fascism vanished for a generation, and the major Fascistoid outworks, Franco Spain and Peronist Argentina, were shunned, while Germany—ravaged, divided, occupied, and "de-Nazified"—was dominated by those whom the National Socialists deemed racially and socially inferior. Germany was rebuilt in a bland and unheroic format by the Nazis' most hated class-enemies—by the bourgeoisie and industrialists in West Germany and in a more stunted form in the East by their ideological nemesis—Marxist bureaucrats. In especially exquisite twists of fate, Germany's postwar armed forces, East and West, were led by the least National Socialist remnants of the Wehrmacht, while the victims of the *Endloesung* (final solution) became martyrs, their fate giving impetus to the founding of a Jewish nation whose soldiers, in a further irony, gained an estimable martial reputation by refining the blitzkrieg. As a capstone to those ignominies, National Socialism and the Third Reich were denied even a crypt in the mausoleum of history. As with the American Tories, there was no faded glamor, tattered banners lovingly displayed, statues, expatriate colonies, or popular culture heroes like those left in the wake of other lost causes like the Jacobites, Bonapartists, and American Confederates. Despite the fact that the Third Reich's official linking of sadism with political power made "Nazi" the most insulting of political epithets, traces of the inner chaos persisted, like coals from a scattered fire. "Nazi ideological policies" that Norman Rich described as "so grotesque, so perverse, and so self-defeating that they defy credulity and seem to belong to a realm of sadistic fantasy"[113] were treasured here and there throughout the world by alienates and sexual pathologues.

The chaos stirred up by the Third Reich set new benchmarks in history. From 1939 to 1941, the Wehrmacht used mechanization and a high operational tempo to accelerate the pace of military operations and function amid wild turbulence, with the highest effect-to-loss ratio seen in a major modern war. The Endloesung, later deemed the Holocaust, vied with Soviet "collectivization" for the record in murdering large numbers of people in a short period of time. In the aftermath, the recovery of Germany from the object of the heaviest sustained air bombardment up to that point to an unprecedented level of prosperity showed remarkable resilience and regenerative capacity. In each case, degrees of order were found lying beneath apparent chaos. The massive scale of devastation raised the question of not only where all that fury and horror came from but of how much the destruction and defeat was a goal. The Nazis rejected Freud, of course, and his theories of the subconscious, but that granted them no immunity to them, to the extent they were valid. There is no need to wrangle over the soundness of the concept of the subconscious here, or to try to link the concept of inner chaos to definitions of mental illness. There is more than enough evidence of Hitler's impulse to exult in catastrophic turbulence and the echoes of the frenzy of German Romanticism and nationalism in Nazi leaders' rhetoric—and private lives. Those reached a zenith—or nadir— in April 1945, when the Fuehrer ordered his minions to create total chaos by completely demolishing Germany's infrastructure. Only at that point did his most loyal lieutenants, including Albert Speer and various generals and administrators, finally disobey him.

What are the roots of the recurrent cycle of rashness, defeat, humiliation, and resurgence in modern German history? Why, in Shakespeare's words, did the Germans, mainly but not exclusively the Prussians, end up lying "at the foot of a proud conqueror" four times over two centuries? Was that due to "bad luck" or geographical determinism, or did some powerful collective psychic impulse to create chaos lead to Gotterdammerung again and again? It is far easier to ask such questions than answer them, and we could also ask them about France and Russia as well as other nations. Did the cataclysmic collapses of 1806, 1919, and 1945 reflect an underlying pattern in the unfolding of history, like Mark Twain's suggestion that history does not repeat itself, but rhymes? Or were they just the fall of the figurative cards, or coincidental straws in a very large of bale of probability? It was German philosophers and nationalist historians, after all, who held so firmly to the propositions that nations have souls and that history is the product of the working out of a larger design.[114]

NOTES

1. Michael Freeman, *Atlas of Nazi Germany* (New York: Macmillan Publishing Co., 1987), p. 1.

2. Raoul Castex, "The Theory of Perturbation," in Eugenia C. Kiesling, ed. and trans., *Admiral Raoul Castex, French Navy: Strategic Theories* (Annapolis: Naval Institute Press, 1994), pp. 403–409.

3. Hans Gerth, "The Nazi Party: Its Leadership and Composition," *American Journal of Sociology*, 45:1 (January, 1940), p. 521.

4. Frank Trommler, "Between Normality and Resistance: Catastrophic Gradualism in Nazi Germany," *Journal of Modern History*, Supplement (December, 1982), pp. S82-S101.

5. Gerhard L. Weinberg, *The World in Arms: A Global History of World War II* (Cambridge: Cambridge University Press, 1994), p. 477.

6. Leni Yahil, *The Holocaust: The Fate of European Jewry, 1932-1945*, trans. Ina Friedman and Haya Galai (New York: Oxford, 1990), p. 59.

7. Amos Elon, "The Jew Who Fought to Stay German," *New York Times Magazine*, March 24, 1996, p. 54.

8. Klaus Keimeier, *The UFA Story: A History of Germany's Greatest Film Company, 1918-1945* (New York: Hill and Wang, 1996), p. 233.

9. Quoted in Martyn Housden, *Resistance and Conformity in the Third Reich* (London: Routledge, 1997), pp. 2–4.

10. Christopher Browning, *The Final Solution and the German Foreign Office* (New York: Holmes and Meier, 1978), p. 2.

11. George C. Browder, *Hitler's Enforcers: The Gestapo and the SS Security Service in the Nazi Revolution* (New York: Oxford University Press, 1996), p. 227.

12. Geoffrey P. Megargee, "Triumph of the Null: Structure and Conflict in the Command of German Land Forces, 1939-1945," *War in History*, 4:1 (January, 1997), p. 80.

13. Peter Viereck, *Metapolitics: The Roots of the Nazi Mind* (New York: Capricorn Books, 1961), pp. 92–93.

14. Friedrich Alfred Beck, quoted in Selected Members of the Philosophy Department, University of Colorado, *Readings on Fascism and National Socialism* (Chicago: Swallow Press, 1952), p. 70.

15. Jack Cohen and Ian Stewart, *The Collapse of Chaos: Discovering Simplicity in a Complex World* (New York: Viking Press, 1994), p. 218.

16. Some historians have traced the disjointedness and inconsistency of the Nazi *Weltanschauung* (world outlook or philosophy) to the nihilistic neo-Romanticism fashionable in Germany after World War I, and others to structural ambiguities in German literature and language. For example, see Ralph Manheim, "Translator's Note," to Adolf Hitler, *Mein Kampf* (Boston: Houghton Mifflin, 1971), pp. xiii–xiv.

17. Albert Speer met Stefan Georg and followed the German Romantic tradition in taking nature tours, cf. Albert Speer, *Inside the Third Reich: Memoirs, by Albert Speer*, trans. Richard and Clara Winston (New York: Macmillan, 1970), p. 10.

18. Richard L. Rubenstein, *The Cunning of History: The Holocaust and the American Future* (New York: Harper Torchbooks, 1975), p. 94.

19. Martin Broszat, *The Hitler State: The Foundation and Development of the Internal Structure of the Third Reich*, trans. John W. Hiden (London: Longmans, 1981), pp. 280–294.

20. Quoted in Raoul de Roussy de Sales, *The Making of Tomorrow* (New York: Reynal and Hitchcock, 1942), p. 268.

21. Fritz Stern, *National Socialism and the Drama of the German Past* (New York: Vintage Books, 1987), pp. 121–122.

22. Quoted in Stern, *Dreams and Delusions: The Drama of German History*, p. 145.

23. For example, see Francis L. Loewenheim's review of Daniel L. Goldhagen, *Hitler's Willing Executioners: Ordinary Germans and the Holocaust* (New York: Alfred Knopf, 1996), in *Houston Chronicle Zest* magazine, April 14, 1996, pp. 21 and 16.

24. Quoted in Ladislas Farago et al., eds., *German Psychological Warfare: Survey and Bibliography* (New York: Arno Press, 1972), p. 98.

25. For a discussion of the role of plunder in the postwar Wirtschaftwunder, see Avraham Barkai, *Nazi Economics: Ideology, Theory, and Policy*, trans. Ruth Hadass-Vashitz (New Haven: Yale University Press, 1990), p. 240.

26. Karl A. Schleunes, *Twisted Road to Auschwitz* (Urbana: University of Illinois Press, 1970), pp. 260–261.

27. Daniel Jonah Goldhagen, "The People's Holocaust," *New York Times*, March 17, 1996, sec. 4, p. 15.

28. Wesley W. Wark, *Ultimate Enemy: British Intelligence and Nazi Germany* (Ithaca, N.Y.: Cornell University Press, 1985), p. 238.

29. Gordon Craig, "Under an Evil Star," *New York Review of Books*, 42:15 (October 5, 1995), p. 26.

30. H. R. Trevor Roper, ed., *The Bormann Letters: The Private Correspondence* (London: Weidenfeld and Nicholson, 1981 [1954]), p. 117.

31. For example, see Macgregor Knox, "Expansionist Zeal, Fighting Power, and Staying Power in the Italian and German Dictatorships," in Richard Bessel, ed., *Fascist Italy and Nazi Germany: Comparisons and Contrasts* (Cambridge: Cambridge University Press, 1996), pp. 126–127.

32. Bernd Wegner, *The Waffen SS: Ideology, Organization, Function* (New York: Basil Blackwell, 1990), p. 182.

33. Erhard Bahr, "Nazi Cultural Politics: Intentionalism vs. Functionalism," in Glenn R. Cuomo, ed., *National Socialist Cultural Policy* (New York: St. Martin's, 1995), pp. 13–17.

34. Rudolf Hoess, *Commandant of Auschwitz: The Autobiography of Rudolf Hoess*, trans. Constantine Fitzgibbon (Cleveland: World Publishing Co., 1959), pp. 190–191.

35. Robert O. Paxton, "The Uses of Fascism," *New York Review of Books*, 43:19 (November 25, 1996), p. 48.

36. See Broszat, *Hitler State*, pp. 17–18.

37. Alfred Rocco, quoted in *Readings on Fascism*, p. 27.

38. A recent useful bibliographical essay is Paxton, "The Uses of Fascism."

39. Robert Soucy, "Drieu La Rochelle and Ascetic Aestheticism," *South Central Review*, 6:2 (Summer, 1989), pp. 54–55.

40. See Fritz Stern's essays on Paul la Garde, Arthur Moeller-Bruch, and Julius Langbehn, in *The Politics of Cultural Despair: A Study in the Rise of the Germanic Ideology* (Berkeley: University of California Press, 1961).

41. Erich Kahler, *Man the Measure* (New York: George Braziller, 1956), pp. 587–590.

42. Hermany Rauschning, *Conservative Revolution* (New York: G. P. Putnams, 1941), p. 279; and Dick Geary, "Image and Reality in Hitler's Germany," *European Historical Quarterly* 19:3 (July, 1988) pp. 385–390.

43. For example, see James M. Diehl, *The Thanks of the Fatherland: German Veterans after the Second World War* (Chapel Hill: University of North Carolina Press, 1993), pp. 85 and 231.

44. For example, Albert Speer, *Infiltration*, trans. Joachim Neugroschel (New York: Macmillan, 1981).

45. Speer, *Inside the Third Reich*, p. 182.

46. Ibid, 207.

47. Harold Kaplan, *Meditations in a Museum of the Holocaust* (Chicago: University of Chicago Press, 1994), pp. 1 and 118.

48. For example, Otto Ohlendorf said that Hitler "not only denied the state as a purpose in itself but totally destroyed it, so that it was no longer available to him as an instrument; the state was superseded by arbitrary action on the part of the multiplicity of authorities"; quoted in Heinz Hohne, *Order of the Death's Head: The Story of Hitler's SS*, trans. Richard Barry (New York: Ballantine Books, 1967), p. 11.

49. N.a., *The Rise and Fall of the German Air Force, 1933-1945* (London: Arms and Armour Press, 1983 [1947]), p. 418.

50. See "Technical Notes," *Ordnance*, 29/153 (November–December, 1945), pp. 420–422.

51. N. a., *Rise and Fall of the German Air Force*, p. 415.

52. For example, Trevor Roper, *Bormann Letters*, pp. 163 and 190.

53. Hohne, *The Order of the Death's Head*, p. 385.

54. Albert Speer, *Inside the Third Reich: Memoirs by Albert Speer*, trans. Richard and Clara Winston (New York: Macmillan, 1970), p. 460.

55. Ibid., p. 18.

56. Clare Sheridan, *Naked Truth* (New York: Harper and Brothers, 1928), p. 357.

57. John L. Casti, *Complexification: Explaining a Paradoxical World through the Science of Surprise* (New York: Harper Collins Publishers, 1994), p. 17.

58. Quote in Hans Mommsen, "Reflections on the Position of Hitler and Goering in the Third Reich," in Thomas Childers and Jane Caplan, eds., *Reevaluating the Third Reich* (New York: Holmes and Meier, 1993), p. 86.

59. Hermann Rauschning, *Men of Chaos* (New York: G. P. Putnam's, 1942), p. viii.

60. Andre François-Poncet, *The Fateful Years: Memoirs of a French Ambassador in Berlin, 1931-1938* (New York: Harcourt Brace, 1947), p. 292.

61. Quoted in Frederick L. Schuman, *Night over Europe: Diplomacy of Nemesis, 1935-1940* (Westport, Conn.: Greenwood Publishing Co., 1970 [1941]), p. 600.

62. Ronald Aronson, "Why? Towards a Theory of the Holocaust," *Socialist Review*, 11:4 (July–August, 1981), pp. 63–82.

63. For example, Guenter von Scheven's "out of terror I am building piece by piece concrete pictures," quoted in Stephen G. Fritz, *Frontsoldaten* (Lexington: University of Kentucky Press, 1995), p. 101, and Field Marshal von Leeb's description while testifying at Nuremberg of Hitler as "a demon . . . a devil," *Trials of War Criminals*, vol. X, p. 551.

64. Gerald E. Markle, *Meditations of a Holocaust Traveler* (Albany: State University of New York Press, 1995), pp. 78–84.

65. Quoted in Norman Rich, *Hitler's War Aims* (New York: W. W. Norton, 1973), p. 126.

66. Quoted in de Sales, *Making of Tomorrow*, pp. 266–267; for a recent perspective on Jung's much-debated links to Nazism, see Richard Noll, *The Aryan Christ: The Secret Life of Carl Jung* (New York: Random House, 1997).

67. T. C. Jarman, *The Rise and Fall of Nazi Germany* (New York: New York University Press, 1956), p. 167.

68. For a broad-ranging essay on Hitler's worldview, see Eberhard Jaeckel, *Hitler's Weltanschauung*, trans. Herbert Arnold (Middletown, Conn.: Wesleyan University Press, 1972).

69. Hitler proclaimed, "I am not the Messiah. He will come after me. I have only the will to shape the foundation for a people's society"; quoted in Enrico Syring, *Hitler: Seine politische Utopie* (Berlin: Propylaen Verlag, 1994), p. 255; for a detailed discussion of such pseudo-religiosity, see *idem*, pp. 244–255.

70. For example, n.a., *Hitler's Secret Conversations, 1941-1944* (New York: Signet Books, 1953).

71. Felix Gilbert, ed., *Hitler Directs His War* (New York: Oxford University Press, 1951), p. xxiii.

72. D. Jablon Hershman and Julian Lieb, *A Brotherhood of Tyrants: Manic Depression and Absolute Power* (New York: Prometheus Books, 1994), pp. 77 and 151.

73. For example, George Victor, *Hitler: The Pathology of Evil* (Washington, D.C.: Brassey's, 1998).

74. For example, see Josef Rudin, *Fanaticism: A Psychological Analysis*, trans. Elizabeth Reinecke and Paul C. Bailey (Notre Dame: University of Notre Dame Press, 1969), pp. 161, 172–177.

75. Robert G. L. Waite, *The Psychopathic God* (New York: Basic Books, 1977).

76. Ibid., pp. 403–405, 445–451, and 478; a rather more poetic but vague prophecy was Ludwig Wagner's, that "Hitler willed and created war, and in the end war will devour him," in Ludwig Wagner, *Hitler: Man of Strife* (New York: Norton, 1942), p. 334.

77. Of dormancy-incubation-fermentation-disintegration.

78. Edleff H. Schwaab, *Hitler's Mind: A Plunge into Madness* (New York: Praeger, 1992), pp. viii and 156.

79. Kahler, *Man the Measure*, p. 598.

80. Sebastian Haffner, *The Meaning of Hitler*, trans. Ewald Osers (New York: Macmillan Publishing Co., 1979).

81. Peter Hoffman, *Hitler's Personal Secretary* (Cambridge: The MIT Press, 1979), pp. 264; and Hiden and Farquarson, *Explaining Hitler's Germany* (Totowa: Barnes Noble, 1983), pp. 27–29.

82. For a contemporary perspective, see Burnet Hershey, "Something Has Happened to Hitler," *Liberty*, 20:22 (May 29, 1943), pp. 1 and 54–55.

83. For example, David Irving, ed., *The Secret Diaries of Hitler's Doctor* (New York: Macmillan, 1983).

84. Kurt Krueger, *I Was Hitler's Doctor* (New York: Biltmore, 1943), p. 316.

85. See Norman Cohn, *Warrant for Genocide: The Myth of the Jewish World Conspiracy and the Protocols of the Elders of Zion* (New York: Harper and Row, 1967), esp. pp. 213–215.

86. Quoted in William L. Shirer, *The Rise and Fall of the Third Reich* (New York: Fawcett Crest, 1989), p. 872; the term "demonic" has often been used to describe Hitler and the Nazis, for example, D. Jablow Hershman and Julian Lieb, *A Brotherhood of Tyrants: Manic Depression and Absolute Power* (Amherst, N.Y.: Prometheus Books, 1994), p. 74.

87. Werner Maser, *Hitler: Legend, Myth*, trans. Peter and Betty Ross (New York: Harper and Row, 1973), p. 218.

88. Gerhard L. Weinberg, *A World at Arms: A Global History of World War II* (Cambridge: Cambridge University Press, 1994), p. 686.

89. That a legal critic of the Nuremberg Tribunal process found it hard to understand why the decree was deemed criminal offers some perspective on the question, cf. August von Knierim, *The Nuremberg Trials* (Chicago: Henry Regnery, 1959), pp. 212–214.

90. Walter C. Langer, *The Mind of Adolf Hitler: The Secret O.S.S. Wartime Report* (New York: Basic Books, 1972), p. 211.

91. For a concise list, see n.a., *The Rise and Fall of the German Air Force, 1933–1945* (London: Arms and Armour Press, 1983 [1947]), p. 416.

92. See Albert Speer, *Infiltration*, trans. Joachim Neugroschel (New York: Macmillan Publishing Co., 1981), pp. 5 ff. Speer judged Hitler as too technically unsophisticated to grasp nuclear dynamics, cf. Speer, *Inside the Third Reich*, pp. 227–228.

93. For example, for a critique of the position articulated by John Kenneth Galbraith et al., see Peter Hayes, "Polycracy and Policy in the Third Reich: The Case of the Economy," in Thomas Childers and Jane Caplan, *Reevaluating the Third Reich* (New York: Holmes and Meier), pp. 190–210.

94. For example, Eliot Janeway, *The Struggle for Survival* (New York: Weybright and Talley, 1951); and Bruce Catton, *The Warlords of Washington* (New York: Harcourt and Brace, 1948).

95. Ian V. Hogg, J. B. King, John Batchelor, and Bernard Fitzsimmons, *German and Allied Secret Weapons of the Second World War* (London: Phoebus, 1976), p. 11.

96. John Strawson, *Hitler's Battle for Europe* (New York: Scribner's Sons, 1971), p. 246.

97. Anthony F. C. Wallace, "Revitalization Movements," *American Anthropologist*, 58:2 (April, 1956), pp. 264–281.

98. For an analysis along those lines, see Fritz Stern, *National Socialism in the Drama of the German Past* (New York: Vintage Books, 1987), pp. 121–122, 128, 141, and 148.

99. Quoted in Alan Beyerchen, *Scientists under Hitler: Politics and the Physics Community in the Third Reich* (New Haven: Yale University Press, 1977), p. 209.

100. Ibid., p. 140.

101. For an overview, see Raul Hilberg, "The Establishment," in *Perpetrators, Victims, Bystanders: The Jewish Catastrophe, 1933-1945* (New York: Harper Collins, 1992), pp. 20–26.

102. Edward L. Homze, *Foreign Labor in Nazi Germany* (Princeton: Princeton University Press, 1967), p. 7.

103. Noll, *The Aryan Christ*, p. 273.

104. Wegner, *Waffen SS*, pp. 178–179.

105. T. C. Jarman, *The Rise and Fall of Nazi Germany* (New York: New York University Press, 1956), p. 343.

106. Victor Klemperer, "The Klemperer Diaries," *New Yorker* (April 27 & May 4, 1998), pp. 129–134.

107. For example, John Milfull, *The Attraction of Fascism: Social Psychology and Aesthetics of the "Triumph of the Right"* (New York: St. Martin's Press, 1990).

108. Herman Stresau, as quoted in George L. Mosse, ed., *Nazi Culture: Intellectual, Cultural and Social Life in the Third Reich* (New York: Schocken Books, 1966), pp.

383–384; and Glenn R. Cuomo, *National Socialist Cultural Policy* (New York: St. Martin's, 1995), pp. 89 and 176.

109. For example, William L. Shirer's *The Rise and Fall of the Third Reich*, Herman Wouk's *Winds of War* and *War and Remembrance*, and the films of Stanley Kramer, Sam Peckinpah, and Stephen Spielberg.

110. James M. Diehl, *The Thanks of the Fatherland: German Veterans after the Second World War* (Chapel Hill: University of North Carolina Press, 1993), p. 231.

111. For example, see Frank Clark, "The 36th Mission," *American Heritage*, 46:3 (May/June, 1995), pp. 52, 54–56, 58, and 60.

112. Gerhard Wilke, "Village Life in Nazi Germany," *History Today*, 35:12 (October, 1985), pp. 23–26.

113. Norman Rich, *Hitler's War Aims* (New York: W. W. Norton, 1973), p. 249.

114. Ten to 15 percent of Germans polled in the Federal Republic continued to rate the *Hitlerzeit* favorably, and neo-Nazi parties failed to gain even substantial minorities, but less than 15 percent of those queried from 1959 to 1967 ascribed Germany's losing the war to Hitler and National Socialism. Richard L. Merritt, *Democracy Imposed: U.S. Occupation Policy and the German Public, 1945-1949* (New Haven: Yale University Press, 1995), pp. 110–112 and 129.

3

Facades over Chaos:
The Mystique of Nazi
Technology

While chaos in the theoretical sense may be a degree of order within apparent turbulence, the converse was true in the Third Reich, where a facade of order was placed over inner chaos. The regime's propagandists worked very hard at projecting an image of disciplined order, much of it in the gleaming metal and spare stonework fashionable in that age of Art Deco—and it worked. Since World War II, the Nazis have been widely viewed as paragons of technical and military practice, as symbolized in film clips of the Messerschmidt 262 jet fighter plane, the *Vergeltungswaffen* (vengeance weapons)—the V-1 cruise missile and the V-2 stratospheric rockets—and the *autobahnen* (superhighways), which stand as the only surviving trace of their monumental handiwork half a century later. Many other technical triumphs have been forgotten, like the Grand Prix triumphs of 1934 to 1939, now known to relatively few motor racing buffs. In the early 1950s, the image of Nazi technical prowess gained some momentum from West Germany's dramatic postwar economic revival. That and the rise to prominence of German scientists in the American space program served to obscure many of flaws and the chaos within the Third Reich's scientific and technical establishment, like wasteful organizational duplication and the diversion of talent and resources to dead-end projects.[1]

The techno-triumphs of the 1930s were not unique products of National Socialism. German manufacturers had claimed a special degree of excellence in precision manufacturing in international business competition since the mid-1800s. That continued during the Weimar era, but contrary winds were blowing when the Nazis began their march to political power in the early 1920s. The mass slaughters and protracted stalemate of World War I were widely seen as the grim results of harnessing science and technology to the service of nationalism. Winston Churchill's reference to "the lights of perverted science" was made in much the same spirit as former storm-troop officer Ernst Juenger's complaint of being "overcome by nausea" by the fact that "wars are waged by technicians."[2] Many hoped that total disarmament or static defense might prevent a recurrence of such bloodletting, while others who saw such expectations as naive were drawn to a perverted humanitarianism as they sought to harness mechanization and aviation to the waging of rapid, decisive warfare that would minimize casualties—on their own side, at least. German military professionals sought to circumvent the constraints of the Versailles Treaty that denied them submarines, tanks, airplanes, and heavy guns and reduced the Reichswehr and navy to mere constabulary forces. They devised rapid, free-flowing maneuvers and tactics, searched open literature, helped industrialists deceive inspectors, and watched tank maneuvers in Britain. Some resigned or took leave to serve as advisors in China and Bolivia or became stunt fliers or mail pilots in the Americas. Exile factories carried on military research and development and developed production expertise, while those in Germany maintained the capacity for conversion and expansion. From 1925 to 1935, German troops trained covertly at Lipetsk in Russia under a special agreement with the Soviets. Many weapons and military methods wielded by the Wehrmacht were products of those cryptic efforts.

After Hitler gained power, it was hard to tell, and would be later, just what in the NS Staat's array of science and technology was Nazi and what was German. We have also seen how Hitler used an amalgam of technologies in his election campaigns, as he would when he governed and conducted foreign policy both by persuasion and intimidation and then in waging war. Although the tradition of claiming unique German technical excellence continued, that did not mesh with reality in every case, but there was enough substance, along with propaganda imagery, to convince friends and foes that it might be true. The effects of that mystique were most visible in the last phase of World War II in Europe, when Allied leaders feared and many Germans hoped Nazi super-weapons might suddenly appear and turn the tide of battle.

But however unique the Nazis' style in harnessing and brandishing technology was, it was more of a variation on a theme than wholly original. Their well-publicized Grand Prix racing victories and break-ing of land and air speed records were part of a broader pattern of international technological rivalry that appeared in the late nineteenth century, peaked in the late 1930s, and then rose to another pinnacle during the Cold War in the Space Race. When Hitler became chancellor in late January 1933, the world was being covered with expanding networks of telephone, telegraph, teletype, television, radio, motion picture theater distribution, and transportation. Although most seg-ments of that vast technical evolution were created by private initiative, in Germany, under the Weimar Republic, many such systems were brought under government control.[3] At the same time, in democracies and dictatorships alike, less visible and secret technologies were woven into the apparatus of power. Dozens of regimes run by "strong men" in the 1930s, including Hitler and Stalin, used modern technology to propagandize, impress, monitor, control, and intimidate, including tape recorders, shredders, and special data-processing and encryption-decryption machines. At the same time, their security forces used myr-iad sinister devices to monitor, arrest, torture, confine, and in some cases, carry out mass murder.

Nor were the Nazis unique in using propaganda and psychology in politics and war. Modern democracy marched in step with the printing press, mass literacy, and advertising. In World War I, the western Allies, and especially the British, employed propaganda techniques with great success, and the United States followed suit with the forming of the Committee for Public Information.[4] The Red Army's commissars became vivid symbols of the Bolsheviks imposing their ideology on their armed forces, followed by the bombastic posturing and sloganeering of the Italian Fascists. Between the world wars, journalistic and academic interest in propaganda grew in the democracies, and several European powers used mass media and expositions to put the best face on their imperialism. At the same time, revisionist historians and journalists in the United States claimed that Allied propaganda had seduced America into World War I, while weakening the Central Powers' civilian and armed forces' morale. Isolationists and pacifists in all the western democracies used such means to influence politics, including propaganda films, which first showed their powerful potential early in World War I, reaching large audiences in the 1930s in such diverse forms as sound newsreels; the documentaries of John Grierson in Britain, Leni Riefenstahl in Ger-many, and New Deal filmmakers and the *March of Time* in the United States; and epic films glorifying the regimes in Italy and the USSR. The hyperpatriotic flavor of totalitarian cinema contrasted sharply with such pacifist commercial films in Western democracies as *Grand*

Illusion, The Big Parade, All Quiet on the Western Front, Westfront 1918, Tell England, and *What Price Glory?*

A rising concern about those trends was visible throughout the industrialized world in both high and popular culture, including pulp magazines, film,[5] and science fiction plots, and in serious treatises as well.[6] Technical advances were judged both sinister and thrilling, since some of them were seen as stereotype images of authoritarian regimes, like "Mussolini modern" architecture, Soviet dams, and Nazi Grand Prix cars. At the same time, major public works projects in the United States, even those begun under Republican administrations, became symbols of the New Deal. Some found them awe-inspiring, but others viewed them as boondoggles, or symbols of excessive federal government power. The wave of Art Deco fantasy in the United States crested in the 1939 New York World's Fair's futuristic technology displays, whose themes of hopeful progress clashed with the outbreak of war in Europe. The divergence of views over the promise of technical evolution in America was a fainter version of a major schism in the Nazi and Fascist movements. As Umberto Eco noted, Hitler and Mussolini's regimes both praised and reviled technical modernism.[7] That was especially paradoxical since several early twentieth-century modernist writers and artists were Fascists, or admirers of Fascism.[8] As both regimes also competed with other industrial powers in a kind of ongoing techno-Olympics, the Nazis played a counterpoint as they played to strong fears of modernity by stressing themes of agrarian Romanticism and staged grotesque pageants that blended medieval and pagan images.

It is impossible to tell what braking effect that nostalgia had on German technical momentum. As we have already seen, Nazism was many things to many people and was deliberately pitched to different and contrary viewpoints. As suggested in Hans Fallada's novel *Little Man, What Now?*, National Socialism presented hopes of a bright future and upward mobility to many in the lower and middle classes who were afflicted or threatened by unemployment or limited career prospects. Fallada portrayed the Nazis' capitalizing on the frustration and hopelessness of the Weimar era as they recruited a disparate array, from the unemployed to doctors, professors, technicians, and engineers. Some Nazi-era technical attainments were clearly due to the creative visions and efforts of Nazi leaders, including Hitler, Todt, and Speer, but others were products of the German engineering tradition, epitomized by such maestros as Dornberger, Porsche, and Messerschmidt. Wherever the boundaries lay, German-Nazi technical prowess hinged on the efforts of vast numbers of technicians and functionaries throughout industry and science, despite the fact that, as Arnold Krammer noted, by mid-1933, just a few months after the Nazis gained power:

[t]he government had already become a maze of overlapping and often conflicting bureaucratic fiefdoms. . . . Rivalries ranged from small bitter wars to frontal confrontations . . . complicated by Hitler's practice of allowing his subordinates to engage in . . . rivalries . . . to prevent their forming alliances against him. The result was bureaucratic chaos.[9]

Historians have traced that turmoil through many tiers and crannies of the NS Staat. It did much to impair the working of the Nazi regime, as Albert Speer found during the last third of World War II as he tried to rationalize armaments production and grappled, often in vain, with the flamboyance and spontaneity of Nazi Romanticism and its antimodernist undercurrents. Some of the tumult was due to the amateurs and bumpkins who had gained power through the "Brown (shirted) Revolution" and some to Hitler's encouraging of rivalry, but also, as Edward Homze pointed out, to a tendency of the Nazis to "transpose . . . economic problems into political ones."[10] As a result, the islets of technical excellence in the Third Reich were lumps of modernism in a soup of Romanticism and amateurism. After World War II Schacht noted how Hitler had begun rearming "in complete disregard of the practical possibilities," without "the slightest idea what was necessary from the financial and economic point of view to wage a modern war."[11] Yet it was people like Schacht who used their talents and skills, acquired under the old order that the Nazis derided, who helped the Nazis rule and to forge their new weapons. Again, whether or not the innovations of that era were more the products of German traditions of rigor and efficiency,[12] if not longer and deeper waves of history,[13] we cannot reduce that differential to percentages. Nor can we trace it through the messy tangle of modernism and regression, inefficiency, corruption, and brutality, including slave labor and the Holocaust, that led a historian to ask how much beneath the gleaming facade of the NS Staat was "machine or morass?"[14] In chaos-complexity terms, what kind of order was embedded amid what many saw as virtual chaos?

Some patterns were clearly visible. The "Brown Revolution" used high technology during the Weimar election campaigns, arrays of motorcars and motorcycles, aircraft, and television that presented facades of dynamic modernist power to Germans. A further irony in all that was the fact that the Versailles Treaty limits, by clearing the decks of old weapons and methods, made it easier for the Reichswehr's officer corps to think about alternatives and a chance to build a wholly modern force when Hitler began openly rearming in 1936. They were also aided by strong pacifist sentiment in the democracies and then by the Great Depression, which constrained military development in all major industrial nations except the USSR until Hitler's most likely foes in the West made a major effort to catch up after the Munich crisis of 1938.

Nevertheless, some nations gained a substantial lead in various technologies—Britain in radar, France in nuclear weapons, Japan with torpedoes, and the USSR, in tank quality and numbers. Despite the Nazis' apparent head start, inner complexities and contradictions offset the apparent advantages. When enthusiastic and skilled German engineers and technicians drawn to Nazism by the prospect of being able to "do their thing" in the mid-1930s went to work on rearmament,[15] many were dismayed when they encountered the corruption, arrogance, stupidity, and organizational confusion of the Nazi Party.[16] More and more Germans came to see that the Third Reich was not an efficient, tightly orchestrated monolith, but despite that, most Germans and foreign observers continued to see the NS Staat as a well-disciplined symphony orchestra directed by a maestro.[17]

The enduring power of the image of Nazi technical supremacy is hardly surprising, given how strongly Hitler and his propagandists played that card, first in diplomacy and then in war. He held his hand very close at first while consolidating power and moved toward rearming in stages, first withdrawing from the League of Nations in 1935 and then announcing military expansion the next year while re-occupying the Rhineland and dispatching ground and air forces to fight in the civil war in Spain. At the same time that Germany was hosting the Olympics with great hospitality and efficiency, Nazi air and armored forces were fighting in Spain. It was there that the Fascists won a significant propaganda victory by creating the "fifth column" myth. A Francoist general claimed that a "fifth column" (additional to the four military columns) of sympathizers and agents behind Republican lines had prepared the way for Nationalist military attacks with rumors, agitation, espionage, and sabotage. Although it was a fabrication, belief in it grew rapidly, feeding on the anxieties of the enemies of Fascisim, and haunted the Allies throughout World War II. Used by Ernest Hemingway as the title of a play, "fifth column" became a popular expression, demonstrating the intrinsic power of making a threat. That concern was visible in the major Allied powers' creation of special programs to counter Nazi influence among the vast numbers of German prisoners of war that fell into their hands.[18] It was in Spain that Nazi propagandists and Western intelligence analysts and journalists began exaggerating the quality and quantity of German weaponry, which did not impress those in the Wehrmacht, who saw glitches and shortfalls not reported in the media or discerned by enemy intelligence services.[19]

Sometimes the inflation of Nazi potential and prowess was deliberate, as when the Luftwaffe passed inflated figures to Western contacts on the eve of Munich,[20] and sometimes unintentional, like the aura of special deadliness that grew around the 88 millimeter antiaircraft / anti-tank gun.

As the Wehrmacht won victory after victory from 1939 to 1941, it became clear to Germany's enemies that the Nazis had gained much through boldness, bluff, and the skillful use of propaganda, as Hitler promised in *Mein Kampf*. At the same time, however, images of over-weening Nazi technical prowess and cleverness became deeply rooted and would long outlive the defeat and collapse of the Third Reich. That was partly due to newsreels and photographs that conveyed glimpses of Stuka dive bombers and panzers, which, as they became the visual stereotype of the blitzkrieg after World War II, weakened the appreciation—much stronger at the time—of how the Nazis had softened up their victims with propaganda before the war.

A major instrument of that effort was the *Nationalsozialistische Kraftfahr Korps (NSKK)* (National Socialist Motor Corps). After Hitler came to power, the NSKK became a pseudo-governmental entity, like several other Nazi Party sub-elements, such as the *Organisation Todt*, the Nazi Party's heavy construction corps, headed by Fritz Todt, which oversaw major construction projects, and the SS. Hitler unhinged the arms control talks at Geneva by insisting that such paramilitary forces be excluded from discussion of force reductions. The Motor Corps, especially visible until World War II, allowed many of its quarter-million members, who otherwise would have had no access to motor vehicles, to receive training and gain experience as drivers and mechanics.[21] In the election campaigns of the late 1920s and early 1930s, it became a major symbol of Nazi power and presence, projecting an aura of paramilitary verve and velocity as Hitler criss-crossed Germany by plane and car,[22] a novelty at that time.[23] The NSKK's sleek black cars and leather-clad and helmeted motorcyclists were emulated by French prewar Fascists, while the Nazis blended them imagistically with their major public works project, the autobahnen that ringed the Third Reich.[24] That system became a major Nazi political goal in the late 1920s, when Josef Goebbels translated Hitler's desire to free travelers from the congestion and delays of the railways[25] into a proposal for knitting existing fragments of intercity controlled-access roadways into a national network.[26] As autobahn expansion began soon after Hitler became chancellor, its military utility was muted in official propaganda,[27] while its value as a public works program was emphasized.[28]

The NSKK was headed by Korpsfuehrer Adolf Huhnlein, a stolid veteran of World War I and a former Reichswehr officer. Holder of Nazi Party card No. 31, he ranked just below Himmler in the hierarchy in the mid-1930s.[29] His especially high status stemmed from his having risked his army career by joining Hitler in the Munich coup attempt in 1923 and being arrested.[30] Despite his peasant origins and reputation as a stolid plodder, Huhnlein managed to hold his own in Nazi inner-circle political skirmishes.[31] With Hitler's support, he fended off charges by some left-wing Nazis that the autobahnen were "rich men's roads," but the major sop to that populism,[32] the *Volkswagen* (people's car) program, proved disappointing. Due to a long lag between subscription and delivery, orders were about a third of those expected,[33] especially ironic in view of the VW's military and postwar commercial success as a mainstay of the Wirtschaftwunder—economic miracle—of the 1950s and the purchase of Rolls-Royce by BMW in 1998.

Although the NSKK staged mass motor tours of Germany to display Nazi power and gave the lower echelons training and experience that dovetailed with mechanizing the German ground forces,[34] the Motor Corps' most visible and glamorous activity was overseeing Germany's racing-car teams. There was a Fascist precedent for that too. The Italian dictator Mussolini had subsidized and encouraged Alfa-Romeo's racing efforts to hype Fascism in the major international spectator sport.[35] Hitler, a motor-racing enthusiast and member of the German Auto Club,[36] approached Mercedes-Benz and Auto-Union[37] before he came to power with plans to use international motor sport racing to dramatize German technical prowess.[38] Proposing that each firm design, build, and field a Grand Prix car team, he offered very small subsidies immediately, but prospects of arms contracts[39] and access to scarce materials in the long run. The two firms accepted, and their engineers, including Dr. Ferdinand Porsche, began work on the project under the aegis of the NSKK,[40] an especially challenging effort, since the international association that controlled motor racing in Europe had just created a Grand Prix car formula designed to undercut German supremacy.[41]

Like the limits of the Versailles Treaty, that formula stimulated creativity, as the German engineers exploited the new rules to gain dominance in motor racing, the major spectator sport in Europe at that time.[42] In a nearly unbroken string of victories from 1934 to 1939, crowds of over a quarter of a million watched the races. When German cars placed first, the Nazi flag was raised, and the national anthem, *Deutschland uber Alles*, was played, usually by a military band. The German cars bore the swastika flag insignia, and the Fuehrer created a special trophy—a bust of himself. At races in Germany, the NSKK directed traffic, controlled crowds, and orchestrated ceremonies, while Huhnlein and other senior Nazi functionaries often attended races in other countries. Journalists and spectators alike were amazed when Mercedes-Benz and Auto-Union cars exceeded 200 miles per hour despite the formula's limiting of all-up weight to 750 kilograms. The modernist side of National Socialism came to the fore in the crisp, paramilitary organization of their teams' logistics, signaling, and disciplined, efficient pit work that became a special attraction for racing fans. But here, too, as with other aspects of National Socialism, substance did not always align with reality. The Grand Prix triumphs overshadowed the fact that popular car ownership in Germany was only half that of Great Britain on the eve of World War II.[43] Although the NSKK officially controlled the teams and basked in their reflected glory, it also bore the burden of the victories. As success followed success, and the limelight became brighter, Huhnlein, his subordinates, and the team managers came under close scrutiny and pressure, especially from Hitler and Goebbels. At the same time, Huhnlein was struggling to maintain his influence over the German automobile industry as other Nazi Party elements encroached on his turf, in keeping with Hitler's divide-and-rule bureaucratic style.[44] Although several top German Grand Prix drivers held high NSKK ranks,[45] not all were ardent National Socialists. Some were playfully disdainful,[46] and a few were openly hostile.[47]

There was another layer of chaos underneath that facade of order. The demands of the unique racing cars ran athwart the Nazis' racialist fantasies. Since the vehicles were very unstable and broke traction very easily, and the rear-engine Auto-Unions tended to oversteer, very few drivers could master them. The racing managers resorted to recruiting motorcycle racers, but not enough German nationals could be found to man the teams. When the National Socialist tenet of "racial purity" was compromised by the hiring of French champion Louis Chiron, Hitler tried to block it and became furious when the Italian maestro, Tazio Nuvolari, the "flying Mantuan," drove an Auto-Union to victory at the Nurburgring in 1935—even though "Taz" was from Fascist Italy.[48] Ecstatic when Bernd Rosemeyer won the Vanderbilt Cup in the United States in an Auto-Union in 1937,[49] the Fuehrer lost his temper again when Mercedes-Benz signed a British driver, Richard Seaman. His fury peaked when Seaman won the 1938 German Grand Prix.[50] At that point, the wild ride was almost over. The Munich crisis in late 1938 disrupted the racing schedule, and the coming of war in September 1939 ended competition in Europe. After a final German victory at Tripoli in 1940, Grand Prix competition ceased for a decade as the Wehrmacht mobilized and expanded. The NSKK quickly shrank and declined in status as most members entered military service[51] and others were assigned to Organisation Todt construction units and panzer training duties.[52] There were no more attempts to break various land speed records, one of which took the life of Grand Prix ace Bernd Rosemeyer. Huhnlein was assigned to bureaucratic duties related to logistics and died in 1942 at age 60, after a long illness.[53] A few fragments of the Nazi Grand Prix heyday survived the war. Some surviving prewar apparatus was used when Mercedes-Benz resumed racing in the late 1940s, and the Soviets displayed some captured cars in technical institutes.

The Grand Prix triumphs reflected the peculiar fusion of German technology and Nazism that led Erich Kahler to point out in 1933, as Albert Speer did a generation later, German engineers' "high organizational capacity and complete color-blindness towards values, faith without content, and discipline without justification" for whom "technics and ethics [had] become, in a curious way, synonymous."[54] Most civil servants, technicians, and military professionals bore the ever-heavier yoke dutifully, and some enthusiastically, as they applied their talents to compensate for Nazi shortfalls and ineptitude amid the organizational vortices of the NS Staat.[55] A British postwar report noted how professional values and norms blunted the effect of *Gleichschaltung* (forced coordination imposed by the regime):

> In secondary features, German equipment was often superlative . . . [and] the German engineer generally very good, but . . . not able or allowed to get to grips with the real operational problem. . . . their scientists as a class had more prestige than our own. But they were weak in collaboration. Each . . . felt that he had to be individually brilliant . . . [resulting in] a great deal of independent and isolated effort.[56]

Such was the chaos that one historian concluded that "Any attempt to read so much logic into actions of the Third Reich . . . misses the point that the system of National Socialist rule was inherently structureless and contradictory,"[57] and another observed that when the war began, "chaos reigned in German education and science."[58] That offers some perspective on the Third Reich's failure to capitalize on its early victories and to exploit the vast amounts of talent and resources it commanded from 1940 to 1944. It is difficult to trace patterns of order amid the chaos on either side in World War II and precisely to measure out how much the Nazis fell far short of the western Allies in organizing for war because of flaws and errors, as opposed to the aggregate manpower and resource superiority of Russia, China, Britain, and the United States. Understandably enough, both observers at the time and those looking back at that turbulence have tended to fall back on lyricism and generalization. Kahler, two-thirds of the way through World War II, saw Nazi atrocities being committed in "a rational, systematic, administrative way"[59] while Hermann Rauschning concluded that "Hitler's emphasis on brutality and ruthlessness" was based on "a desolation of a forced and artificial inhumanity."[60] A generation later, Jeffrey Hert saw the Nazis as "reactionary modernists" whose ideology spanned the conflicting themes of "romanticism and technology" and who put "cultural provincialism and chauvinism" ahead of the spirit of the Enlightenment. He, too, puzzled over the "intoxication and irrationality" of engineers and technicians "whom we might expect to champion sobriety and technical reason."[61]

That exalted creativity took many forms during the Nazi era, across a range from the V-2 rocket to the lowly "jerry can." On the other hand, many ingenious projects led nowhere, were produced in small numbers, or went into production too late to have a significant effect, much in the spirit of the title of Max Hoffman's World War I memoir, *The War of Lost Opportunities*. Major braking and distorting forces were exerted by over-organization, referred to in the popular use of *organisierte*—to organize—as a sarcastic reference to bureaucratic confusion. While Hitler's assumption of a quick victory in Russia led him to proclaim in early 1941 that no weapon or system should go into production that could not be delivered to the Wehrmacht in less than a year slowed the momentum of various projects, including jet-propelled aircraft and long-range heavy bombers, there was little enthusiasm for jets in the Luftwaffe hierarchy until May 1943. Even after Adolf Galland, chief of fighter forces and a top ace and apathetic up to that point, test-flew a Messerschmidt 262, his excitement was not contagious. A year elapsed after the first test flights before General Erhard Milch, overseer of Luftwaffe production, authorized a limited production effort. Delays and technical problems resulting from the early disinterest included a lack of support elements for field operations and the engines' short service life and tendency to fail in flight. Another obstacle appeared just as limited production began in late mid-1943, when Hitler insisted that Me 262s be produced as fighter-bombers, not interceptors. Although the Fuehrer's intrusion was later cited as a crucial lost opportunity, it had little practical effect, since the main snags were chronic engine failures, production problems, and Allied bombing damage. In the end, the Luftwaffe jets' operational impact was marginal,[62] and German jet development served mainly as the technical baseline for British and American postwar developments.[63] U.S. Army Air Force official historians described the "British and Germans . . . actually more nearly abreast" than differences in the dates of their respective first flights suggested.[63] Some experimental Me 262s saw combat briefly while test-flying in the late spring of 1944, but the RAF's first jet squadron flew against V-1 "buzz-bombs" in July, three months before the Luftwaffe's first squadron of 262s entered service.[64] By early 1945, almost a year after production began, on the eve of the Third Reich's collapse, about 200 German jets were operational. Fueled by kerosene, they were relatively unaffected when aviation fuel stocks and distribution plummeted because of Allied air attacks on synthetic oil production sites and transport nets and the Red Army overran natural petroleum sources.

The fitful course of Nazi jet development reflected the broader chaos within the Luftwaffe's upper echelons. Created as a brand-new, separate service under Goering's authority in the mid-1930s and the most National Socialist of the Third Reich's armed services, the new air force was mainly intended to support ground forces. Its doctrine and tactics were shaped by the Condor Legion's experiences in the Spanish Civil Wars and by Ernst Udet, head of Luftwaffe technical development in 1936-1941. The top surviving German fighter ace of World War I, he had toured America as a stunt-flying "barnstormer" during the 1920s and became aware of U.S. Marine Corps glide-bombing developments. Impressed by German experiments in the early 1930s that showed dive-bombing to be far more accurate than other air attack modes, Udet's insistence that all Luftwaffe bomber types should be able to glide-bomb, later labeled "Stukamania,"[65] warped force balance, doctrine, and procurement throughout World War II, leading Werner Baumbach, a senior Luftwaffe commander, to later accuse Udet of having "brought our air service into complete chaos"[66] by thwarting development of German long-range bomber forces, which gave Soviet factories in the Urals and bomber bases in Britain immunity and awarded the Allies a special edge in the Battle of the Atlantic.[67] The suicides of Udet in 1941 and Jeschonnek, Luftwaffe chief of staff, in 1943 were attributed to their realizing the results of their earlier decisions,[68] but that did not bring an end to the confusion. Baumbach later depicted the Air Reichsministerium as an epicenter of "plotting and scheming by interested aircraft firms," whose functionaries stifled or delayed many promising systems, while concocting bizarre schemes.[69]

In 1943, as Albert Speer, Minister of Armaments, struggled to sort out the techno-feudal tangle of German war production and development, he was able to rationalize and streamline some elements of the system, but fresh swirls of chaos arose as others subsided. Those fresh vortices were due to the Allied air offensive, the rise of Himmler's SS industrial empire, and the Fuehrer's dabblings and vacillations. Speer encountered widespread personal and organizational rivalries and found many lines of effort uncoordinated or unaligned with future research and development or the *Wehrmacht*'s operational needs. Some crucial weapons and systems had not been converted to mass production and were soaking up vast amounts of skilled labor in fabrication. While much of the disjointedness that Speer encountered was a product of National Socialism, some of it was due to traditional German fixation on labor-intensive methods and traditions of artisanship. As he focused resources on operationally feasible projects, Speer halted "pure" research and suspended development of "neat" ideas with slim prospects of yielding practical results. He also pooled resources, personnel, and concepts, ordered that trade secrets be shared, and tried to show how silly and irrelevant many projects were.[70] Those reforms yielded many improvements, but they did not offset the major dislocations stemming from Himmler's parallel SS industrial fiefdom, the turbulence in the upper echelons of the regime, and interservice rivalry.

Does chaos-complexity provide us with a clearer perspective view on such bewildering disarray and confusion? Ideally, appraising failures in the Nazis' military and foreign policy and determining how much that was due to their conflicting and murky ideology and frenetic style, which led to their diverting much energy and attention to dead-end projects of all kinds, requires a scale that would allow comparison with adversaries, allies, and other cases. Some of the chaos that Speer was trying to cope with was generic to the waging of a major war, which generates massive internal dissonance because of such interlocking dilemmas as balancing innovation against operational needs, choosing lines of development for mass production, and matching materials and labor to tasks. In both world wars and in many smaller ones in the twentieth century, each side was constantly changing or modifying methods and equipment in response to rapidly changing conditions in various theaters of war. In the future, more sophisticated analytical methods may allow a more precise mapping of the tangled patterns of the NS Staat. It is hard to anticipate how that would help make greater sense of aberrations like the Nazi fascination with occultism or the dreams of some right-wing Nazis and German Nationalists of restoring the Kaiser's empire in Africa and the Far East. The latter was a goal of Nazi foreign policy well into World War II and led the armed forces and Foreign Office to prepare for regaining the lost colonies, including allocating scarce aluminum stocks to build prefabricated buildings that would be immune to termites in sub-Saharan Africa. More aberrant but more profound in its effect was Hitler's imperial vision of making German farmers into feudal landholders in Eastern Europe and Russia, set forth in *Mein Kampf* and based on his crude view of the British Empire. It would appear all the more ludicrous if it had not led to the deaths of millions. Such absurdities seemed to feed on themselves, like the Italian Fascist and Nazi regimes encouraging higher birth rates while demanding colonies as an escape valve for their growing populations, invoking as justification the geopolitical rubric of *Lebensraum* (living space). However, fantasies of the viability of imperialism also warped French, British, and even American strategic thinking, and all the major powers turned to the pseudo-science of geopolitics. In a further irony, as the Nazis wasted time, attention, and resources on such futile imperial schemes, they overlooked how fast the tide of anti-colonialism was rising in the world at large—and how much their Japanese allies' early victories had unhinged that system. In a further inanity, Nazi eugenicists and racists rationalized the contradiction of Germany having Asian allies and overlooked scientific findings regarding Caucasian genetic diseases, while Nazi economists ignored the drain of European empires on their mother countries. They meandered far from their socialist roots by blending German imperialism and Social Darwinism with imperialist-capitalist methods, while inverting mass production techniques to mass slaughter of those they defined as *untermenschen* (subhumans).

That tangle of Nazi illogicalities led many to judge Hitler and Nazism as insane, although that was not allowed as a defense in the Nuremberg war crimes tribunal. But if Nazism was so flagrantly and unashamedly vicious, and its leaders insane, why were so many Europeans, Germans and others, attracted to it, as others were by Stalinism? How could madhouse inmates gain power over the largest western European nation by democratic processes and establish a hegemony over the Continent that transcended Bonaparte's conquests? Was most of European civilization in the generation collectively demented, making it a kind of psychological wobbling top, easy for someone to nudge and send careening into a dark corner? Did Hitler see patterns in that turbulence that he was able to bend to his cruel purposes? Are such instabilities and artful mountebanks always present in society that might align under rare but not wholly impossible circumstances? The hypothesis of National Socialism as a symptom of a potentially recurrent pathology adds gravity to that especially grim model of proto-war, the "ideological struggle" of Soviet theory, or what Edmond Taylor in looking at Nazi propaganda in the 1940s labeled the "pre-military phase of war,"[71] elements of which have endured for half a century—despite defeat and all the revelations of the Third Reich's crazy-quilt structure, corruption, and uneven scientific and technical efforts.[72]

It is not hard to identify factors that contributed to that turbulence. During World War II, beyond the invincibility and technical excellence claimed by Nazi propagandists, the mystique of Nazi technical prowess received a boost from the democracies' tendency to self-criticism. Some Allied techno-triumphs were concealed by wartime censorship, others muted by interservice or international rivalry. That was visible in the shifting attitudes of Americans, most of whom enthused over the Battle of Britain, Alamein, and Stalingrad early in the war but, as the conflict progressed, became less and less inclined to credit their Allies' successes, or how much of the burden China and Russia had borne, or the technical aid the United States received from Britain.[73] Such parochialism was echoed in the half-century World War II commemoration ceremonies, when the U.S. media portrayed the 1944 Normandy invasion as primarily an American achievement, even though British and Canadian troops had comprised over half of the assault forces and the U.S. Navy had provided a fraction of the warships involved. After the war, American, British, French, and Soviet technicians searched the Third Reich's ruins for technical apparatus and found exotic technologies, from tape recorders and computers to rockets. At the same time, as the Cold War intensified, the former Allies revealed some of the wartime technical successes but kept others secret. They also recruited a host of German technicians and engineers. In the West, as de-Nazification was eased and then dismantled, the Nuremberg war crimes tribunals were scaled back, and many convicted war criminals' sentences were reduced or commuted. During the Nuremberg trials, the Allied prosecutors had drawn sharp distinctions between the Nazi and top military leaders and German society. Intentionally or not, that meshed with the Western democracies' attempts to woo West Germany into becoming a Cold War ally in the mid-1950s, something which German elites anticipated and prepared for during the war. In the last months of that struggle, military and industrial leaders at lower tiers of the NS Staat hierarchy considered what they might salvage from the ruins of the Third Reich and how to deal with the victors.[74] Because of Cold War secrecy, much of that postwar era lies in the shadows, closer to true than to theoretical chaos. It is difficult to tell, for example, whether the failure of the much-feared Nazi "Werewolf" resistance movement to materialize was due to a deliberate move toward conciliation or whether it was an index of Germans' disillusionment and exhaustion or a weaker commitment to National Socialism than was estimated at the time—or since.[75]

As East-West tensions mounted in the late 1940s, some unsavory deals were cut. Western diplomats and intelligence services began to work closely with veterans of the Third Reich's intelligence organs and the Wehrmacht.[76] Such linkages were strengthened after a Communist coup in Czechoslovakia in the spring of 1948 led to the forming of a Western military alliance in Europe and to the creation of NATO in 1949 and a self-governing republic in West Germany in the mid-1950s. In the course of that, some remnants of the Third Reich were discarded and others were retained, or transformed. To make Germany's transformation less menacing in Britain and the United States, book publishers selected works that soft-pedaled the Wehrmacht's links with Nazism and portrayed the officer corps as apolitical *nur Soldaten* (only soldiers). Harsh critiques, like Geyr von Schweppenburg's *Gebrochene Schwert* (Broken Sword) were left untranslated. The best-selling, praiseful biography of Field Marshal Erwin Rommel, *The Desert Fox*, by a former British officer, Desmond Young, depicted a cleavage between the Wehrmacht and Nazism and left Rommel's prewar links to Hitler and National Socialism out of focus. So did the film version, which portrayed German officers as frustrated, duty-bound, and politically neutral professional warriors.

In the mid-1950s, as German forces became the mainstay of NATO defenses in Central Europe over the next generation, Western defense planners lived in fear of a massive Soviet assault in Central Europe. Admiration for the Wehrmacht's military performance and Nazi-era technical achievements replaced the shock and condemnation that followed revelations of the Holocaust. The lines of continuity between National Socialism and the Bundesrepublik's bureaucracy and armed forces were not easily visible in the Anglo-American media in the mid-1950s, nor was there public reaction in the Western democracies when the West German government began paying veterans' pensions to Waffen SS veterans. Some of the latter, leaving the 1939 Nazi-Soviet Pact and Holocaust out of focus, now claimed they had been precursors of NATO and "premature anti-Communists" when they fought on the eastern front in World War II. Former paratroop general Hermann Ramcke took revisionism several steps further in labeling Roosevelt, Churchill, and Eisenhower the "real war criminals" and predicted that "the Waffen SS will again have the first place on history's honors list as the defenders of Europe."[77] Far more visible in Britain and the United States was the *Wirtschaftwunder*. Here, too, lines of continuity with the Nazi era were blurred. In the United States, Volkswagens were mass-marketed, Mercedes-Benz filled the niche left by the failure of the Packard Motor Car Company, and German cameras and radios became popular.

Against that backdrop, West German military and civilian leaders were trying to sort out what to keep and throw away from the Hitlerzeit. In struggling to chart a respectable genealogy for the Federal Republic of Germany's armed forces, they softened the Wehrmacht's image by fitting pieces of its traditions and practices and many veterans as well into its new armed forces, the Bundeswehr. As a counterbalance, leaders were to be imbued with civic values and a spirit of independent judgment through indoctrination—*Innere Fuehrung* (inner leadership)—designed to weaken traditional German deference to authority, which many Germans and others saw as a fundamental source of Nazism. Links between the American and German military systems were also being strengthened by propinquity and common purpose. The largest single concentration of U.S. forces overseas in peacetime was deployed in West Germany. Bundeswehr and Luftwaffe units trained at sites in the United States, and American servicemen saw duty in Germany as highly desirable until the mark gained ground against the dollar in the early 1960s.

Other close American-German ties came into public view soon after the Soviets launched the first earth-orbiting telemetry satellite, *Sputnik*. That triggered a space race, part of it military and secret and part of it open, in the United States at least. The sensation of *Sputnik* led to the creation of the National Air and Space Administration (NASA) in 1958; and in 1961, other Soviet cosmic triumphs led President John Kennedy to initiate the Apollo project, aimed at landing Americans on the moon within a decade. Over the next decade, some German rocket scientists and engineers who had worked on Nazi V-2 strategic rocket develop- ment under Walter Dornberger became celebrities in the United States, most notably Wernher von Braun. (Little note was made of his once being a special favorite of the Fuehrer.) American respect for Nazi technology was reflected in a *Star Trek* episode portraying a marooned starship captain who used Nazism to stimulate a backward culture's advance and in the slang term for genius—"rocket scientist."

As the Cold War approached the final zenith of intensity in the early 1980s, a major collector's market in Nazi era memorabilia had devel- oped in the United States and western Europe, and neo-Nazism gained ground in several countries. Former Wehrmacht commanders were hired as tactical consultants by the U.S. Department of Defense; and in 1984, President Ronald Reagan honored German war dead at a military cemetery at Bitburg that included Waffen SS graves. In the early 1990s, following German reunification, the United States withdrew the bulk of its forces from what had been the Federal Republic; and by the end of that decade, German firms were the largest foreign employer of American workers. The hardihood of the image of German technical superiority and the merger of Chrysler and Daimler-Benz and BMW's purchase of Rolls-Royce raised the question of just what kinds of order was embedded in what appeared to be chaos during the Hitler era—and afterward.

NOTES

1. For a compendium, see Rudolf Lusar, *Die Deutschen Waffen und Geheimniswaffen des 2 Weltkrieges under ihre Weiterentwicklung* (Munich: J. F. Lehmann, 1962).

2. Alistair Hamilton, *The Appeal of Fascism: A Study of Intellectuals and Fascism, 1919-1941* (New York: Macmillan, 1971), p. 168.

3. Arnold P. Krammer, "The Nazification of Germany's Industrial Economy," *Red River Historical Review* 3:2 (Spring, 1979), p. 343.

4. An overview of the American experience in World War I and afterward is Christopher Simpson's *Science of Coercion* (New York: Oxford University Press, 1994), pp. 16–22.

5. For example, *Modern Times* and *Things to Come*.

6. For example, Siegfried Giedion's *Mechanization Takes Command* and Lewis Mumford's *Technics and Civilization*.

7. Umberto Eco, "Ur-Fascism," *New York Review of Books*, June 22, 1995, pp. 12–15.

8. Some useful perspectives are Hans Mommsen, "National Socialism: Continuity and Change," in Walter Laqueur, ed., *Fascism: A Reader's Guide* (Berkeley: University of California Press, 1976), pp. 179–210; and A. James Gregor, *The Fascist Persuasion in Radical Politics* (Princeton, N.J.: Princeton University Press, 1947).

9. Krammer, "The Nazification of Germany's Industrial Economy," p. 344.

10. Edward L. Homze, *Foreign Labor in Nazi Germany* (Princeton, N.J.: Princeton University Press, 1967), pp. 4–5.

11. Hjalmar Schacht, *The Magic of Money*, trans. Paul Erskine (London: Oldbourne, 1967), pp. 100–101.

12. For an excellent overview, see Chapter 1 of Laurence Moyer, *Victory Must Be Ours: Germany and the Great War, 1914–1918* (New York: Hippocrene Books, 1995), pp. 14–38.

13. For example, the controversy among Holocaust scholars over whether or not the Holocaust fits into a historical continuum of genocide, for example, Steven T. Katz, *The Holocaust in Historical Context*, vol. 1, *The Holocaust and Mass Death before the Modern Age* (New York: Oxford University Press, 1994).

14. Michael Geyer, "The Nazi State: Machine or Morass?" *History Today*, 36:1 (January, 1986), pp. 35–39.

15. Hermann Rauschning, in tracing the technocratic aspect of National Socialism, pointed out "how many engineers Hitler drew into his select circle," in *Men of Chaos* (New York: G. P. Putnam's, 1942), pp. 230–234; while Albert Speer held that Nazism's retarding effect on technical developments was compensated for by "the cooperation of those echelons from the days of the Kaiser and the Weimar Republic . . . under coercion or from a sense of duty . . . not the veteran Party members," in *Infiltration*, trans. Joachim Neugroschel (New York: Macmillan, 1981), p. 4.

16. Douglas Culligan, "The Nazi Papers," *Omni*, October, 1980, p. 52.

17. See *Time* magazine's "man of the year" cover for 1938.

18. Arthur L. Smith, Jr., *The War for the German Mind: Re-educating Hitler's Soldiers* (Providence, R.I: Berghahn Books, 1996).

19. For example, the British Joint Intelligence Committee's 1942 estimate of German tank production as 1,000 a month versus the actual output of 345; F. H. Hinsley, E. E. Thomas, C. F. G. Ransom, and R. C. Knight, *British Intelligence in the Second World War: Its Influence on Strategy and Operations*, vol. 2 (London: Her Majesty's Stationery Office, 1981), p. 147.

20. See Charles Lindbergh, *The Wartime Journals of Charles Lindbergh* (New York: Harcourt Brace Jovanovich, 1970), pp. 95–141.

21. For an overview, see Alfred Vagts, *Hitler's Second Army* (Washington, D.C.: Infantry Journal Press, 1943), pp. 96–103.

22. N.a., *Adolf Hitler: Pictures from the Life of the Fuehrer 1931-1935* (New York: Pebbles Press, 1978), pp. 5–16 and 85–95.

23. For a contemporary view of the role of mechanization and motor sport in Hitler's electioneering, see Hans Ernest Fried, *The Guilt of the German Army* (New York: Macmillan, 1943), pp. 347–348.

24. James D. Shard, "The Reichsautobahn: Symbol for the Third Reich," *Journal of Contemporary History*, 19:2 (April, 1984), pp. 189–200.

25. See Werner Maser, *Das Fruehgeschichte de NDSAP: Hitler's Weg Bis 1925* [The Early History of the National German Socialist Workers' Party: Hitler's Path to 1925] (Frankfurt am Main: Atheneum Verlag, 1965), p. 460; Erich Kern, *Adolf Hitler und Seine Bewegung* [Adolf Hitler and His Movement] (Gottingen: K. W. Schatz, 1970), pp. 145 and 224; and Jeremy Noakes and Geoffrey Pridham, *Documents on Nazism, 1919–1945* (New York: Viking Press, 1975), p. 382.

26. Curt Reiss, *Joseph Goebbels* (Garden City, N.Y.: Doubleday, 1948), p. 141.

27. See n.a., "Grossnung der Reichsautobahnestrecke" ["Expansion of the Nation's Superhighway Route"], *Volkischer Beobachter*, May 10, 1935, p. 1.

28. A. Mueller, *Hitler's motorisierte Stoss Armee* [*Hitler's Motorized Shock Army*] (Paris: Editions du Carrefour, 1936).

29. For example, Gerd Ruhle, *Das Dritte Reich: Dokumentarische Darstellung des Aufbau der Nation* [*The Third Reich: Documentary Evidence of the Rebuilding of the Nation*] (Berlin: Hammerverlag, 1933), pp. 216–217; and Baldur von Schirach, *Die Pioniere des Dritten Reiches* (Essen: Zentralstelle fur der deutschen Freiheitskampf, n.d., c. 1933), pp. 114–115.

30. Alan Bullock, *Hitler: A Study in Tyranny* (New York: Harper and Brothers, 1958), p. 99.

31. For example, the absorbing of Hitler Youth motor formations by the NSKK in 1936.

32. See Fritz Thyssen, *I Paid Hitler* (London: Hodder and Stoughton, 1941), pp. 173–175.

33. Guenter Reiman, *The Vampire Economy: Doing Business under Fascism* (New York: Vanguard, 1939), pp. 133–134; also see Walter Henry Nelson, *Small Wonder: The Amazing Story of the Volkswagen* (Boston: Little, Brown, 1967).

34. See Rudolf Absolon, *Die Wehrmacht in Dritten Reich* [*The Wehrmacht in the Third Reich*], vol. 4 (Boppard am Rhein: Harold Boldt Verlag, 1979), pp. 45–46.

35. Joseph M. Wherry, *The Alfa-Romeo Story* (Philadelphia: Chilton, 1967), p. 71.

36. See David Irving, *The War Path: Hitler's Germany, 1933-39* (London: Michael Joseph, 1978), p. 23.

37. For numerous comments on designs and proposals for motor vehicles and highways, see Henry Picker, ed., *Hitlers Tischgesprache im Fuehrerhauptquartier* [*Hitler's Table-Talk in the Fuehrer Headquarters*] (Stuttgart: Seewald, 1976), esp. pp. 37–54 and 130.

38. David Scott-Moncrieff, St. John Nixon, and Clarence Paget, *Three-Pointed Star* (New York: W. W. Norton, 1956), p. 254.

39. Ian Ward, ed., *The World of Automobiles: An Illustrated History of the Motor Car* (Milwaukee: Purnell Reference Books, 1977), p. 137.

40. For details on the building of the team structure, see L. J. K. Setright, *The Designers* (London: Weidenfeld and Nicholson, 1976); for technical details, see Laurence Pomeroy, *The Grand Prix Car*, vol. 2 (London: Temple Press Books, 1964);

and Robert W. Nitske, *Mercedes-Benz: A History* (Osceola, Wis.: Motorbooks International, 1978), pp. 62–85.

41. L. J. K. Setright, *The Grand Prix, 1906–1972* (London: Thomas Nelson, 1973), pp. 109–111.

42. For a succinct survey of the period, see Rodney Walkerley and Rodney Fellowes, *Grands Prix, 1934–1939* (Abingdon-on-Thames: Motor Racing Publications, 1950).

43. See Richard Grunberger, *The 12-Year Reich: A Social History of Nazi Germany, 1933-1945* (New York: Holt Rinehart Winston, 1971), pp. 215–216; also see Michael Burleigh, "Beetles in Brown Shirts?" *History Today*, 42:11 (November, 1992), pp. 11–13.

44. Johann Heinrich von Brun, *Ein Mann Macht Auto Geschichte* (Stuttgart: Motorbuch Verlag, 1972), pp. 249–250.

45. For example, Hermann Lang and Manfred von Brauchitsch, brother of the Field Marshal who headed the Army from 1938 to 1941.

46. For example, Bernd Rosemeyer, later killed in a land speed record attempt, inserted a cigarette between the lips of the "Goddess of Speed" trophy statuette during a Huhnlein speech, cf. George Monkhouse, *Motor Racing with Mercedes-Benz* (Los Angeles: Floyd Clymer, 1945), p. 70. Huhnlein, angry at young British and French women frequenting the German pits and kissing drivers, forbade public osculation. At the next race, drivers awaited the NSKK official contingent, then all kissed their wives; cf. Alfred Neubauer, *Speed Was My Life*, ed. and trans. Stewart Thompson (New York: Clarkson N. Potter, 1960), p. 103.

47. For example, revelations that Hans Stuck's wife was Jewish, Bella Fromm, *Blood and Banquets* (New York: Harper and Brothers, 1942), p. 70, led to Nazi anti-Semitic posters appearing at the Feldburg Hill Climb in 1935, William Court, *Power and Glory: A History of Grand Prix Racing, 1906-1951* (London: MacDonald, 1966), p. 234. When Rudolf Carracciola (a German) refused to entertain Axis troops, his pension was blocked. He lived in Switzerland and was warned not to visit Germany, cf. Rudolf Carracciola, *A Racing Car Driver's World* (New York: Farrar, Strauss and Cudahy, 1961), pp. 168–169; also see David Hodges, *Great Racing Car Drivers* (New York: Arco Publishing, 1972), pp. 117–122.

48. Giovanni Lurani and Luigi Marinatto, *Nuvolari*, trans. John Eason Gibson (London: Cassell, 1959), p. 128.

49. The German pit stops averaged half the time of the best American cars; for details see Monkhouse, *Motor Racing with Mercedes-Benz*, pp. 51–54.

50. For details, including the row between Huhnlein and Neubauer, see Neubauer, *Speed Was My Life*, pp. 121–126. Seaman considered leaving the team, but was encouraged to stay after polling various British racing and government officials; for biographical data on Seaman, who was killed in an accident in 1939, see Chula Chakrabongse, *Dick Seaman: A Racing Champion* (Los Angeles: Floyd Clymer, 1948).

51. Dietrich Orlow, *The History of the Nazi Party, 1933-1945* (Pittsburgh: University of Pittsburgh Press, 1973), p. 308.

52. Franz Neuman, *Behemoth: The Structure and Practice of National Socialism* (Toronto: Oxford University Press, 1944), p. 530.

53. Max Domarus, *Hitler: Reden und Proklamation 1932-1945*, 2 vols. Munich: Verlagsdruckerei Schmidt, Neustadt und Aisch, 1962), pp. 623, 1762, and 1892.

54. Erich Kahler, *Man the Measure* (New York: George Braziller, 1956 [1943]), p. 596.

55. Krammer, "The Nazification of Germany's Industrial Economy," p. 352.

56. J. G. Crowther and R. Whiddingdon, *Science at War* (New York: Philosophical Library, 1948), p. 88.

57. Heinz Hohne, *The Order of the Death's Head*, trans. Richard Barry (New York: Ballantine Books, 1967), p. 373.

58. Michael J. Neufeld, *The Rocket and the Reich: Peenemuende and the Coming of the Ballistic Missile Era* (New York: Free Press, 1995), p. 82.

59. Erich Kahler, *Man the Measure* (New York: Georges Braziller, 1956), p. 660.

60. Quoted in Walter C. Langer, *The Mind of Adolf Hitler: The Secret Wartime Report* (New York: Basic Books, 1972), p. 206.

61. Jeffrey Hert, "The Engineer as Ideologue: Reactionary Modernists in Weimar and Nazi Germany," *Journal of Contemporary History*, 19:4 (October, 1984), p. 652.

62. Jeffrey Ethell and Alfred Price, *The German Jets in Combat* (London: Jane's Publishing Co., 1979), p. 24.

63. Frank Wesley Craven and James Lea Cate, *U.S. Army Air Forces in the Second World War* (Chicago: University of Chicago Press, 1955), p. 246.

64. See Matthew Cooper, *The German Air Force, 1933-1945: The Anatomy of a Failure* (New York: Jane's Publishing Co., 1981), pp. 350–351.

65. He was portrayed as the stunt flier Ernst Kessler in the film *The Great Waldo Pepper*.

66. Werner Baumbach, *The Defeat of the Luftwaffe*, trans. Frederick Holt (New York: Dorset, 1992), p. 29.

67. Werner Held and Holgar Nauroth, *The Defense of the Reich: Hitler's Nightfighters and Pilots*, trans. David Roberts (New York: Arno Publishing, 1982), p. 190.

68. See Richard Suchenwirth, *Historical Turning Points in the German Air Force's War Effort* (New York: U.S. Air Force Historical Division, 1968) [Monograph No. 189], pp. 38–39.

69. Baumbach, *Defeat of the Luftwaffe*, p. 29.

70. Leslie E. Simon, *German Research in World War II: An Analysis of the Conduct of Research* (New York: Wiley, 1947), pp. 102–107.

71. Edmond Taylor, *The Strategy of Terror: Europe's Inner Front* (Boston: Houghton Mifflin, 1941), p. 71.

72. Albert Speer, *Inside the Third Reich: Memoirs, by Albert Speer*, trans. Richard and Clara Winston (New York: Macmillan, 1970), pp. 8 and 23–33.

73. For example, the first phase of nuclear weapons research (code-named "Tube Alloys"), the cavity magnetron radar component, napalm, proximity fuzes, the quick-release parachute harness, skip-bombing, aerial photography interpretation techniques, and the "Phantom" concept.

74. Fear of the Wehrmacht hard core holding out in a "National Redoubt" in south Germany and Austria persisted until the last weeks of the war in Europe, for example, see Alfred D. Chandler, Jr., et al., *The Papers of Dwight David Eisenhower: The War Years: IV* (Baltimore: Johns Hopkins Press, 1970), pp. 2560 ff.; and Chester Wilmot, *The Struggle for Europe* (New York: Harper and Brothers, 1952), pp. 690–695.

75. See the report of the Strasbourg meeting of August 10, 1944, in Harry C. Butcher, *My Three Years with Eisenhower* (New York: Simon and Schuster, 1946), pp. 708–710.

76. For an account of American recruiting of a former Wehrmacht intelligence "asset," see Reinhard Gehlen, *The Service,* trans. David Irving (New York: World Publishing Co., 1972), pp. 119–148.

77. T. H. Tetens, *The New Germans and the Old Nazis* (New York: Random House, 1961), p. 89.

4

Riding the Tide of Chaos: *Auftragstaktik* and the Law of the Situation

While considering the German military's longstanding concern with functioning amid the chaos of battle, it is useful to remember that war has often been described as a form of chaos, not only in journalism and history, but in mythology and religion as well. Both the Hindus and Romans believed that the wild disorder of battle reflected deep chaotic forces in nature, a view not too far in spirit from a D-Day veteran's reflecting on how: "the near catastrophe of June 6 diminished forever the credibility of the concepts of strategic planning and of tactical order [but] provided me instead with a sense of chaos, random disaster, and vulnerability."[1]

In a similar vein, Ernie Pyle, the dean of American war correspondents in World War II, described a theater of war as "colossal writhing chaos shaped into something that intermeshed and moved forward with efficiency. . . ."[2] That sense of some kind of pattern lying beneath the surface of apparent turbulence runs through military history and thought, since the essential art of generalship and of military theory lies in discerning patterns in and imposing them on the chaos of war. If we visualize the dialogue between order and disorder in battle over the centuries as a series of peaks and troughs, then the deeper valleys include, for example, Viking melees, the pell-mell assaults of "wild Irish" regiments, and submarine warfare, while summits of coherence include such cases as the articulated blocs of the Roman legions and the geometrical fortifications, siegecraft, and battle arrays on land and sea of the seventeenth and eighteenth centuries. Some commanders and visionaries have foreseen impending turns in those cycles. Marshal de Saxe, for example, in the mid-1700s correctly anticipated the impending increase in the size of armies and their dispersion in battle. Anticipating the impending "light infantry revolution," he called for increasing lightness and flexibility in tactics, equipment, and organization.[3] Soon afterward, the Comte de Guibert framed his detailed prophecy of the nations-in-arms, which was soon realized in the French Revolution and Napoleonic Wars.

Both of those changes fueled the sense of growing chaos in war over the last two centuries, along with waves of inventions that churned and reshaped the dynamics of warfare, in a virtually continuous military-technical evolution. Any single major technical advance—railways, steam power, telegraphy, mass production, the application of chemistry to industry, the internal combustion engine, lighter-than- and heavier-than-air flight—might have altered the military balance significantly by itself, but so could any one of a host of less significant inventions, like the machine gun and proximity fuze. To further complicate that tangled ongoing fusion, some inventions were conceived with military applications in mind while, conversely, military and naval weapons and systems were derived from devices originally intended for peaceful uses. On a parallel course, early industrialization gave impetus to the concept of *Volk im Waffen* (people in arms) in the late 1700s, while refinements in technology forged it into a new alloy a century and a half later in the form of *Totalenkrieg* (total war), a titanic, all-consuming struggle drawing deeply on the physical and moral resources of the nations engaged. The first glimpses of that monstrosity appeared in the American and French revolutions, loomed larger in the Napoleonic era, then seemed to fade until it flowered again in America in 1861. By 1900, all major industrial nations except the United States had raised large active and reserve conscript armies, armed with increasingly destructive weapons. The problems of raising, training, and deploying them preoccupied military professionals and theorists, as did the mounting scale, cost, and tempo of battle on land and sea and, then, in the air. Time and time again, in spite of the blistering pace of technical evolution, the high commands held on to familiar forms when facing the chaos of war. For example, the British Army's linear tactics and equipage were held on to from Waterloo until the Crimean War in the mid-1850s. On the other hand, military careerists' firm devotion to archaic forms was sometimes a reaction to the also often ludicrous blind faith of inventors and theorists in their favorite device or concept.

Along that grim pathway, various warriors and theorists grappled with the increasing problems of the chaos in combat being produced by the repeated convergence of technical innovations and social forces. In the French Revolutionary and Napoleonic wars, for example, ideological fervor, the *levée en masse* (mass conscripted armies), new map-making techniques, improved road systems in Europe, logistical improvements, and novel weapons and tactics created a new matrix of war. Battles, unlike the ponderous engagements of linear forces, now coalesced like crystals in freezing water, growing out of chance encounters of scattered elements as dispersed units of armies came together on extended road nets, like the blending of clouds of smoke or gas. To deal with that, Bonaparte relied on his marshals, selected for their verve and initiative, to exercise independent judgment when out of immediate touch with him. They acted under general orders, remaining flexible as they engaged the enemy closely, while Napoleon orchestrated the convergence of the elements of the *Grande Armée* and committed reserves at the crucial points. Boldness and intuition were crucial, since Napoleon recognized, as his most able opponent, the Duke of Wellington, did as well, that battles had a momentum of their own.

The erosion of the tactical symmetry and linearity were brought home to the Prussians dramatically in 1806, when Bonaparte defeated their traditional rigid formations at the Battle of Jena-Auerstadt and showed the obsolescence of their dependence on orders flowing from high-level commanders, hallmarks of the Prussian Army since the time of Frederick the Great. Although that humiliating defeat did not totally destroy the Prussian aristocracy's obsession with hierarchy and discipline or their reverence for the memory of *der Alte Fritz*, Queen Louise ruefully admitted that "we fell asleep on the laurels of Frederick the Great." Following that calamity and the fall of several Prussian fortresses, the French occupation brought further humiliations and a social and political revolution that included the military reforms of Scharnhorst and Gneisenau. The rise of patriotic enthusiasm and Romanticist liberalism brought hordes of youthful volunteers to the colors as a revamped Prussian Army used more flexible tactics and light infantry to play a major part in Allied victories over Bonaparte at Leipzig in 1814 and at Waterloo in 1815.

The tides of reform were reversed in peacetime, however, as reactionary elements around the king maneuvered to scrap and undermine the reforms, especially those that had liberalized Prussian politics. Despite that, two principal military reforms endured, both of them reactions to the growing turbulence of war and to the widening technical gap between military professionals and the king and his noble functionaries who formally commanded the Army as feudal overlords. The first was a strengthened Prussian General Staff, whose officers became the elite advisors to commanders. Their expertise and right of direct access to the Chief of the General Staff made them virtual battle managers, an arrangement that preserved the fiction of military competency being related to hereditary feudal rank. Traditional forms of deference to the monarch were retained, but actual control of troops in war passed into the hands of a small corps of carefully selected and trained intellectuals in uniform. In the mid-nineteenth century, the Great General Staff, as a key institution of state—royal—power in Prussia played a main role in undermining liberalism, much as its successors helped Hitler gain power in 1933 and destroy the Weimar Republic, providing him with the structure and precedents that he used to become dictator of the state and, ultimately, command the army.

The second reform, the doctrine of granting lower echelon commanders substantial discretion in commanding their units, was based on the recognition of the chaos of battle. Commanders of combat forces, both in garrison and in maneuvers and war, often had need to adapt quickly to the specifics of the local situation and to make decisions on the basis of overall guidelines, within certain limits of procedure and responsibility, without using up precious time in asking for permission.[4] Long referred to as *Selbstaendigkeit*—individual commanders' independence in operations—that doctrine of operational latitude was re-labeled *Auftragstaktik* (mission tactics) in the 1950s.[5] (The term *auftrag* [mission] had often been linked with the concept of local tactical option before and during World War II).[6] Walter Goerlitz, historian of the German General Staff, deemed *Auftragsweise Fuehrung* (mission-mandated leadership) "the great masterpiece of the Moltke school." In contrast to American enthusiasts' freewheeling visions of the concept after the Vietnam War,[7] Goerlitz defined Auftragsweise Fuehrung as a practice based on "a rigidly uniform course of instruction" that allowed "each individual senior commander . . . complete liberty, within the framework of the general plan, to carry out the task allotted to him as he saw fit" and consonant with the "old Prussian General Staff . . . set up by Scharnhorst and Gneisenau . . . [a] child of that liberal and civic age which inscribed the freedom of the individual and the ideal of universal education as the crest on its banner."[8]

After the German victory in the Franco-Prussian War in 1870-1871, Prussian practices and doctrines became popular in British and American military circles and in other nations as well, as those of the Wehrmacht would a century later, despite defeat and the stain of the Holocaust. Translations of German military writings and enthusiastic derivative essays[9] reflected widening concern over centralization-decentralization in industry, government, and organization theory as well as warfare.[10] While the British and U.S. armies adopted some Prussian practices to increase war mentality in peacetime, like staff colleges, war games, and staff rides, they did not adopt the Great General Staff (GGS) model to the extent that many other nations did. Some critics in both countries feared that such elite centralism threatened time-proven methods and informal social systems, or democracy itself. In the early twentieth century, however, general staff enthusiasts in Britain and the United States minimized such concerns and stressed efficiencies when rudimentary versions of the GGS were created in both countries in 1903. Amid all that discussion, few paid attention to an inner contradiction that concerned some German military professionals. Despite the use of telegraphy and railways and very rigorous staff work, widespread turbulence had occurred in the German forces during their campaigns against Denmark, Austria, and France. The highly acclaimed maestro of those victories, *Feldmarschall* Helmut von Moltke the Elder, chief of the Great General Staff, had warned about the fragility of war plans. The essence of his dictum, that "No general plan survives contact with the enemy for more than twenty-four hours," often misquoted as "no plan survives contact with the enemy,"[11] was borne out by Field Marshal Count von Blumenthal's comment in his diary after the fall of Sedan that:

> there set in the wildest confusion in the communications of orders . . . the written orders of Moltke and Podbielski did not tally with the orders communicated verbally; in short, it looked as though they had intended to bring chaos and confusion into our counsels, then to withdraw and let the thing work out its own salvation. . . . In a word, it was a most dreadful chaos.[12]

His concern was echoed by the Prussian military critic Verdy du Vernois, who attributed the widespread operational disorder to "the tendency of our leaders, so praiseworthy in the abstract, to carry out action independently" and questioned the value of the new open order tactics, which prevented maintaining a well-delineated *ordre de bataille*.[13] While that discounted the effects of the growing volume and accuracy of firepower on linear and massed formations, he and others recognized that enhancing the higher echelons' ability to gather information and transmit orders to widely dispersed elements did not lead to certainty as to where optimal control lay on the hierarchical ladder. Paradoxes abound. Widely varing local differences seemed to heighten the need for Selbstaendigkeit, while improved communications flow amplified commanders' strengths and weaknesses alike, conveyed error as well as truth, and allowed higher authorities of lesser ability to closely control subordinates. That turbulence was addressed obliquely in the Prussian concept of *der Gesetz der Sache* (the Law of the Situation). In keeping with the Victorian maxim, "circumstances alter cases,"[14] that was a kind of wisdom, but it lay far from being a practical method for dealing with the quandary.

The most dramatic attempt of the Great General Staff to impose order on a strategic plan was the *Schlieffenplan*, designed in the late 1800s to defeat France quickly by rapidly deploying the bulk of the German Army in a grand envelopment or pincers movement and then turning on Russia. That elaborate scheme, honed to a fine edge over a generation, was derived from rigorous study of Hannibal's victory over the Romans at Cannae by the plan's prime architect, Chief of the Great General Staff Graf (Count) Alfred von Schlieffen. When it was put into action in 1914, the intricate phasing and control needed to maintain coherence and momentum proved to be beyond the Germans' reach despite all their careful preparations. Despite initial German successes in northeastern France, friction and dissonance brought their massive advance through Belgium into northern France in the heat of the late summer to a halt. The Russians were held at bay but not knocked out of the war. Throughout the opening phase of the war, as later, chaos begat chaos.

From the perspective of chaos-complexity, the Schlieffenplan's failure looks rather like its precursor, the *Titanic* disaster, which did—or could—not encompass all the crucial shaping elements, let alone assign them the proper relative weights. The "obvious" causes of the debacle include the General Staff's chief, Helmut von Moltke the Younger, who oversaw the execution of the Schlieffenplan, and who was widely judged to be far less gifted than his famous uncle. Thrown off balance by growing chaos in the West and the unexpected speed of Russian mobilization, he followed the classic Prussian hands-off doctrine of command when he decided not to override the five Army Group commanders as their forces drifted out of phase and the French mounted a counterattack. Did he grant too much leeway to those at the "cutting edge"? Why then did he interfere with the balance of the plan and withdraw two corps from the crucial right wing? That question arose again a year later during the Allied amphibious assault at Gallipoli. The British ground forces commander, Sir Ian Hamilton, adhered to the hands-off principle in rejecting the urging of his staff that he give direct orders to commanders ashore, who were clearly fumbling a prime opportunity to seize crucial high ground.

There were, of course, many other factors, including the hot weather that wore down all the forces involved, the unexpected advantages provided to the Allied commanders by the first extensive use of aircraft for reconnaissance, the initiative of junior French officers in forming the "taxicab army," and so on. When the question of sensitivity to initial conditions is rung into the equation, the causal model becomes very unwieldy indeed. In any case, even before the massive slaughters at Verdun and on the Somme, the failure of either side to gain a clear advantage in the opening weeks of World War I made it clear that the struggle had become a blind collision of forces, which went on and on because it had begun. As British troops sang to the tune of *Auld Lang Syne*, "We're here because we're here because we're here." From the outset, the mechanization of the war cut the social pyramid to shreds and turned the dynamics of battle into literal mayhem. The fragmentation of close combat on land and sea and in the air placed the control of operations in the hands of very young men, more and more of whom were being selected from all social classes on the basis of their capacity to operate and maintain mechanical devices. That had a powerful effect on the social fabric of all the major combatants during the war, and afterward. The chaos of the war fed chaos in the societies involved, as mutinies abounded and thrones were toppled, and patterns of order crystallized out of the chaos after the war.

As Communists, Fascists, and Nazis each struggled to realize their respective visions of a new social order, they did not share pacifists' hopes of perpetual peace, at least in the immediate future, but like various military professionals and analysts in the democracies, searched for ways to reduce casualties and damage in combat by developing new techniques for waging war. In Britain, the United States, and France, the search for "new ways of war" was driven by humanitarianism and by funding strictures. In Germany, in 1919-1933, as covert attempts were being made to rebuild military capacity under the tight strictures of Versailles, the officers of the Weimar Republic's tiny army, the Reichswehr, developed ways to fight against great odds in case of invasion, especially from Poland. On a parallel track, Hitler also sought ways to win victories cheaply and quickly, hoping to avoid the prolonged ordeal that eventually wore down the German public's morale in World War I. Such military modernists as Felix Steiner in the Nazi Party and the Reichswehr's tank enthusiast Heinz Guderian encountered substantial resistance, not only from pacifists and economy-minded politicians but from military professional traditionalists as well.

A central focus of the reformers' concern was the chaos of battle. In World War I, despite commanders and staffs' attempts to exercise control over coherent formations, telephone and telegraph networks provided very tenuous links between advancing elements and higher echelons, and chaos was the norm once units left the trenches. Wires often broke or were cut by shells or bullets, and messages carried by runners—like Corporal Hitler—provided generals with a blurred picture of operations, often incomplete and far out of phase with the actual position and condition of the units that dispatched them, hours and sometimes days earlier. On the eve of World War I, some German military writers, with that turbulence in view, echoed earlier calls for a return to close order formations to overcome fragmentation and "organize the necessary disorder of the attack."[15] Amid such tumult, independent initiative in combat was as much a response to the wild disorder as a product of doctrine, but it was not clear how much it really yielded an advantage, as opposed to careful planning, when that was done thoroughly and sensibly by such commanders as Plumer and Monash. The views of Erich von Ludendorff, Chief of the General Staff, reflected the uncertainties and contradictions posed by the turbulence of battle. On the one hand, he complained, the proliferation of telephones and a dearth of experienced NCOs and junior officers had weakened the authority of small unit leaders, but on the other, he regularly used telephones to override the authority of lower echelons.[16] On the other hand, while combat veteran Erwin Rommel stressed the bewildering chaos of war as he developed new techniques to cope with it, he emphasized the utility of a "well-prepared telephone net."[17] Hitler's vision in *Mein Kampf* of winning quick victories at low cost with a fusion of mechanization and elite troops was very much in tune with those of some Reichswehr officers, including its commander, Hans von Seeckt, as well as such junior leaders as Karl von Rundstedt and Heinz Guderian. On a similar track was Felix Steiner, who later played a key role in creating the Waffen SS. Reichswehr and Nazi reformers differed on some issues, but both were wrestling with the same basic strategic problem: fighting a delaying action against great odds in the first phase of a war. Throughout the 1920s and into the early 1930s, von Seeckt and other senior commanders knew that because of the Versailles Treaty limits and lean funding, German ground forces, without armor or air cover, would have to cover mobilization by fending off a converging circle of foes and against especially heavy odds, especially if all the guarantors of the Locarno Pact in 1925 joined in.

Most top Nazis were World War I combat veterans who had experienced the chaos of modern warfare. In keeping with chaos-complexity theory or not, the novelist Ernst Juenger, a veteran storm troop commander, saw "sublime order . . . concealed in the manifold"[18] and "a pattern in the chaos of battle."[19] A recognition of that turbulence lay at the heart of the German Army's World War I infiltration tactics noted earlier: small detachments of elite storm troops, who advanced independently through gaps and weak points in the enemy front, avoiding strongholds and pitched battles while probing for key "nerve centers" in the rear areas. (The Nazis based their brown-shirted street army—the Sturmabteilung or SA—on the storm-troop model, just as the Italian elite *arditi* shock squads' uniforms were copied by the Fascist Blackshirts.) They were highly effective when first used, but did not give the German army the overall victory it strove for. Infiltration reflected the tendency, also noted in the case of German and Nazi technology, to fixate more closely on small mechanical components and craftsmanship than on logistics and grand strategy, certainly more so than their foes in the world wars. Thus the shadows of Frederick the Great, Napoleon, von Clausewitz—or at least certain interpretations of von Clausewitz— von Moltke the Elder, and von Schlieffenfailed to darken the faith of the Reichswehr and, later, the Wehrmacht that winning battles quickly at the outset of a war would lead to victory. They were undaunted by the fact that infiltration, like the Schlieffenplan, the U-boat campaign, the zeppelin raids, poison gas, and flamethrowers, won a major tactical success at first, but failed to yield a decisive victory.

Just as Juenger echoed the military reformers' views when he proclaimed that "all success springs from individual action"[20] and observed that "now and then . . . a man in the rear, overtaken by sudden frenzy, appears among the leaders . . . taking the foremost place,"[21] senior German officers in the early 1930s, including Ludwig Beck, chief of the Army's shrunken general staff, attempted to recast the old Prussian-German practice of giving junior commanders a free hand within the framework of a larger design. Their ideas gained momentum from Hitler's enthusiasm for mechanizing the armed forces, as he began rearming Germany and named Heinz Guderian, a panzer enthusiast, as Inspector General of armored forces. Following the Prussian style, Guderian coined pithy tactical catchphrases[22]—"*Klotzen, nicht kleckern*" (punch, don't tap); "*Ohne Befehl zu Kampfen . . . zu Siegen*" (without orders, fight . . . and win); and "*Vorwaerts*" (in all situations, advance).[23]

Such ideas, along with the forming of large armored units, were not widely accepted in the Reichswehr's upper echelons, even though von Seeckt and his colleagues recognized the need for tactical mobility and flexibility and hoped agility and operational skill would compensate for inferior strength. They also remained committed to von Schlieffen's methods, including careful planning and detailed orders and tight control of operations from the top. Von Seeckt had recognized the evolutionary nature of military doctrine and practice when he cautioned against mistaking the momentary state of an army for what might follow. His warning was borne out as the landscape shifted dramatically throughout the 1930s amid the cross-currents of increasing Nazi influence, the tripling of the Army, and the retirement, year after year, of officers who had served at higher command and staff levels in World War I and then of those with combat command experience above the company level. The long labors of the Reichswehr bore fruit in 1933 in the form of *Truppenfuehrung* (troop leadership), a major revision of German Army

Field Service Regulations that presented a fresh battle doctrine. Closely studied in several foreign armies, it was novel in content and format and modernist in tone, blending elements of psychology with tactics and principles and ranging over the complex problems of leadership in modern warfare in a terse and racy style, while stressing the uncertainty and chaos of combat. Truppenfuehrung offered no clear answer to the old dilemma of where the optimum locus of battle management lay. It listed as desirable leadership traits creativity, independence, responsibility, mutual trust, will, physical toughness, courage, steadfastness, and coolness, but left some matters unaddressed.

Those doctrines and various concepts developed in peacetime maneuvers, map exercises, and at the secret testing site at Lipetsk in Russia in 1925-1935 were proof-tested in the Spanish Civil War, including refined concepts of Selbstaendigkeit. Again, not all German officers or military intellectuals favored that practice.[24] The expectation of chaos in combat was realized when the German army went to war in 1939. The wild fluidity and turbulence in the opening campaigns tore apart many of the Wehrmacht's doctrines, along with many senior commanders' and staff officers' expectations based on their personal experience and/or analysis of World War I operations.[25] That, of course, was even more of a problem for Germany's foes during the opening campaigns. In any case, despite recognition in German Army doctrine of the likelihood of massive disorder, its command processes in World War II remained technically complex, and Selbstaendigkeit was kept within clear limits. The tactical portion of Truppenfuehrung recognized the ambiguity, fluidity, and unpredictability of battle and identified mission and situation as the key elements in the command process. Urging commanders to maintain a clear objective and organize forces in depth depending on the situation, its authors recognized that the situation would often be obscure and made no plea for brevity in writing orders,[26] although they did stress the need for simplicity in field orders, which, especially in armored units, often took the form of terse fragments and simple overlays. While the need for simple formats in fast-moving or tight situations was recognized,[27] that was not general Wehrmacht practice.[28] At the Nuremberg Tribunal, Field Marshal von Rundstedt testified how he routinely requested from one to three detailed reports daily from subordinate headquarters in response to such questions as "How are things going; how are you doing; are you advancing or retiring?"[29]

Although delegating command option was common in free-flowing motorized operations during the so-called blitzkrieg era of World War II—late 1939 to late 1941—Guderian and other senior commanders often intervened at the "cutting edge" in the heat of battle. Outcomes resulted from relative, not absolute, advantages, especially the Wehrmacht's edge in communications and the high operational tempo—augmented by the use of stimulants. In the opening campaigns, opposing forces accustomed to a much slower operational pace were often paralyzed, bewildered, and panicked. To further complicate matters, many senior Allied commanders were superannuated, even by the standards of the time. Bewilderment of various kinds afflicted not only different levels of the Allied chain of command but the political leaders and diplomats as well. Germany's ring of foes proved less coordinated and more timid than von Seeckt had feared, which allowed Hitler to take them on one or a few at a time from 1938 to 1942. There was no "Locarno War," with a ring of powerful foes quickly converging on Germany, nor a "Grand Alliance" like those that thwarted the Bourbons, brought down Napoleon, and toppled the Kaiser. The announcement of the Nazi-Soviet Non-Aggression Pact on the eve of the Russo-German invasion of Poland in September 1939 stunned the world, as did the speed and brevity of the campaign, which most observers in the Western democracies expected to last several months. As the Nazis, with passive assistance from the Soviets, flattened Poland, Britain and France stood by and did little to interfere with the Wehrmacht's redeployment during the winter of 1939-1940 to launch a major attack in the West. Despite many German officers' deep concerns about the problems encountered in combat, the *Wehrmacht* gained a nearly mythological status that survived over half a century, some of it, as noted earlier, from the Third Reich's psychological softening up of potential foes and victims before the war. The long hiatus, known as "the Phoney War," allowed the German Army and Luftwaffe to make corrections, although some analysts noted the widespread confusion among German forces during the Polish campaign and concluded that the "so-called Blitzkrieg"—not a Wehrmacht term, but the creation of Western journalists—"was . . . not a coherent operational concept consciously evolved by the military leadership" but was "much more a reflection of Hitler's demands" and of "developments . . . in the domestic and . . . armaments economies."[30]

As Edward Luttwak and others pointed out a generation later, German tactical dominance in 1939-1942 was due more to a state of mind and style than to a doctrine, but it also hinged on the inadequacies of Germany's foes. During the opening campaigns, enmeshed in the doctrinal webs that they later discarded, Allied military professionals, along with journalists and analysts, searched for patterns in the free flow of German operations. They were puzzled by the way in which the Wehrmacht, in keeping with von Moltke the Elder's view of strategy as a sequence of ad hoc responses, mixed various types of weapons in battle without regard to symmetry or format, striving to maintain momentum, move quickly, and outflank, encircle, and intimidate foes, while avoiding duplication and static warfare. Over time, some patterns of German reflex and method became visible, beyond the impulse to advance, practices and routines like phase-line defenses and infantry retreating to reverse slopes when attacked, then counterattacking enemy forces as they tried to consolidate position. In stages, the Allies formulated counter-blitzkrieg stratagems. The first setback to the Nazis' momentum came in the aerial Battle of Britain in late 1940 and a year later, on a much larger scale, when the Wehrmacht's sweeping encirclements and grand maneuvers in Russia in the summer of 1941 fell short of winning a decisive victory. After the setback at Moscow, the freewheeling, modernist Wehrmacht began to look more and more like the old Army, revealing the fact that two-thirds of it was not mechanized, but remained dependent on horse and rail transport throughout the war. Nor had breaking loose from linear and rigid tactical formats and democratizing leadership styles eliminated the powerful adherence to Fuehrerprinzip (deference to authority) in German culture.

Although the Nazis in their socialist mode had attempted to abandon rigid "Prussian barracks square" methods, strong traces of traditional iron discipline were retained in Wehrmacht training and command-and-control.[31] The ramrod came back into view more and more as the war dragged on far beyond what Hitler and most Nazi and Wehrmacht leaders had expected. At the same time, the concept of Selbstaendigkeit was being eroded by Hitler and the OKW as they increased their direct control of the armed forces. Despite many postwar claims to the contrary, that was not wholly the result of the Fuehrer's hunger to dominate the generals. Even during the heyday of the *blitzkrieg*, Army commanders retained the concept of *schwerpunkt*—the image of an ideal "hardpoint" at which a concentration of forces seemed most likely to yield positive results in battle.[32] In Russia, the German Army's High Command found itself facing the same dilemma that von Moltke the Elder confronted in 1870, the fact that reserves were limited, many wanted them committed in their sector, and someone at the highest echelon had to decide where and when.

A schwerpunkt had been designated in the campaign of May–June 1940 by the German Army High Command—the crossing of the Meuse at Sedan, where success led to the dash to the Channel and a smashing victory, despite a running debate throughout the operation between Guderian and the High Command over his maintaining momentum. The 1940 campaign's coherent format sharply contrasted with Operation Barbarossa, the invasion of Russia a year later, in which three vast arrays of Axis forces advanced along diverging vectors, with no clear strategic objective. From the very outset, that splayed effort generated tensions and confusion in the High Command that spread down the chain of command. On June 25, three days into the campaign, a debate erupted among the senior commanders over whether Minsk or Smolensk should be the operational goal of Army Group Center; soon afterward, von Brauchitsch, the Army Chief of Staff, began to show the signs of irresolution and fatigue that ultimately led Hitler to assume full authority over the army.[33] The Fuehrer took the first steps in that direction in 1938 when he created OKW, then took a firmer hand during the Polish campaign in 1939 and played a substantive role in planning the assault in the West.[34]

While the decline in sweeping blitzkrieg maneuvers from late 1941 was partly due to Hitler's insisting that the basic nature of the war had shifted from free-flowing offensive to static defense, others shared that point of view. Wehrmacht commanders did not wholly abandon such methods, and several of them became concerned along the way about the lack of coherence in concepts and command. After the war, Hermann Hoth, a veteran senior German tank commander, pointed out the contrast between the strategic success of 1940 and the shambles in Russia in 1941. He concluded that the greatest German tank victories stemmed from massing several *Panzerarmees* to carry out a single mission, while the lack of a "unified operative concept" in the East resulted in the wasteful dispersal of forces and failed to win a strategic victory despite spectacular encirclements.[35] Other German generals also favored strong central control in defensive operations, including Field Marshal Gunther von Kluge, Army Group Center commander, who, in late 1941, still "believed he could still exercise direct personal control over his old army by telephone and wireless from Smolensk."[36] So did *General der Flieger* (Air General) Wolfram von Richtofen. At Stalingrad in late 1942, he complained that a lack of "clear thinking and a well-defined primary objective" had produced a fragmented effort.[37] Verdy du Vernois's critique of selbstaendigkeit after the Franco-Prussian War was echoed by a senior Wehrmacht commander, General Frido von Senger und Etterlin, who faulted *Auftragsbefehlgebung* (mission order methods) for fragmenting initiative and hampering the complex coordination of adjacent units essential in combined arms operations and withdrawals. Pointing out that such tactics required vast reserves, he saw little practical value in commanders' staying well forward, since it virtually abandoned authority to the chief of staff.[38] Debates over such issues reflected the tendency of German military professionals and analysts to focus on tactics at the expense of strategy and the complex administration of war. [39]

Throughout World War II, the Fuehrer went through field marshals and army chiefs of staff like facial tissues. Some, like von Leeb, von

Rundstedt, and von Manstein, were dismissed after clashing with Hitler over issues of strategy and tactics, while the departure of others was ascribed to illness (including von Brauchitsch, von Bock, and the stridently pro-Nazi von Reichenau). The top functionaries at OKW, Keitel and Jodl and later Model, complied with Hitler's micromanaging and oversaw its implementation. In doing that, they were complying with authority but also adhering to the principle that lower echelon units' independence was appropriate in the attack, but not in the defense. An academic variant of that argument based on the "Law of the Situation"[40] closed a logical circle. Infiltration tactics had evolved from tactics designed to launch counterattacks against Allied assaults without waiting for approval from higher headquarters. As the campaign in Russia became more and more static and defensive, many Wehrmacht officers resented the sophisticated communications nets that linked OKW and Hitler's field headquarters in East Prussia with forward units and allowed them to micromanage them. By late 1943, the loss of initiative in the East after the massive Battle of Kursk and the string of defeats on other fronts led many Germans, and others as well, to conclude that the Third Reich was losing the war because of Hitler's intransigence. While Army generals, including some close to the National Socialist entourage, like Rommel, and stalwart Party members like Felix Steiner, an SS general, became disillusioned, most were not inclined to take direct action. Some did, however, and joined the conspirators of various political hues in the July 1944 bomb plot. But they were swimming against the tide. Whatever anyone in the armed forces thought privately, the vast majority honored their personal oaths to the Fuehrer. After the coup attempt, the continued allegiance of most officers made it possible for Hitler to retain power through the telephone and teletype networks and quash the conspiracy. (Curiously, no serious attempt was made by the conspirators to disrupt or commandeer the communications system.) That led the Nazi security apparatus to crack down far more fiercely on Germans than it had up to that point, although Hitler, like Bonaparte, still saw himself as a politician and tried to curry public favor until the final days of the war, although with less and less consistency and effect.

The postwar complaints of both former Wehrmacht officers and Allied military critics about Hitler's and the High Command's micromanaging put the compliance of higher-ranking German officers in the shadow and bolstered their claims of having been "*nur Soldaten*" (only soldiers), that is, professionals without political views. Very few took active steps against Hitler (like von Kluge, who paid for his resistance with his life), although some, like von Manstein and Guderian, later claimed they had stood up to Hitler.[41] True, they had squabbled with the Fuehrer over some military issues, but they had also sanctioned some of the regime's more grisly undertakings, and knew of others.[42] Critics of Hitler's oversupervision steered around what it would have really meant if Hitler had given the officer corps a freer hand that led to a German victory or at least a peace more favorable to the Third Reich and that allowed Nazism to survive. Although some critics asked why the officers fought on after realizing that the Fuehrer's meddling imperiled the nation's and the troops' welfare, none discussed what Germany or Europe would have looked like and what would have happened to Hitler, his entourage, the Nazi Party, or the Holocaust if the military had been allowed to "do its thing." That picture is further clouded by the fact that the 1944 plotters did not plan to fully de-Nazify the government they meant to form after killing Hitler.

The strands in the web of Hitler's dominance over the Wehrmacht included the compliant senior Army officers whom he selected to administer OKW, the power of his personality, the officer corps' personal oath to him, his popularity with the masses, and his role as head of state. Although the OKW command structure appeared to be a Nazi modernist concoction, it was in essence a variation of the old Prussian system. It blended the political, technical, and military elements identified by von Clausewitz and recreated the role of the chief-of-state as overseer of the armed forces in wartime. That structure, however, failed to close the chasm between front and rear that caused so much difficulty in the German Army during World War I and that Hitler and many of his lieutenants hoped to avoid through National Socialist class-leveling socialization and training. In the German Army, 1914-1918, that gap had been aggravated by keeping German General Staff officers away from the fighting front, since they were seen as being too precious a resource to expose to the hazards of battle. As a result, they were deprived of a reality reference, and their theoretical habits of mind led them to devise schemes far out of phase with conditions in the trenches, adding to the hostility that frontline troops felt toward the *Etappe* (rear services) who did not share their misery and horror.

In late 1942, when some OKW officers urged the assigning of young combat-experienced officers to the General Staff to inject realism into top-level planning, a debate erupted in the High Command over reforming the system.[43] Despite some tentative steps in that direction, many fighting troops continued to see themselves as being at the mercy of distant and impersonal authorities. Tinkering did not alter Hitler's power or inclination, as *Feldherr* (master of the field), to micromanage, even as his health and powers declined visibly. The officer corps conformed to his dicta on matters great, small, and even trivial; and by

1944, Germans sarcastically referred to the bewildering bureaucratic tangle of the Third Reich by using the verb "organisierte." At the same time, many clung to the belief that the widespread error, confusion, and ineptitude were due to corrupt or stupid lower-echelon functionaries keeping Hitler in the dark, in keeping with the cliche: "If the Fuehrer only knew." Despite the attempts to attribute defeat to Hitler's meddling, his intervening in military matters was not universally disastrous, even after his powers began to wane. Most senior officers agreed, for example, that the Fuehrer's "no retreat" order in the winter of 1941, issued against the advice and urging of many commanders, had prevented a mass rout in Russia.

In the mid-1950s, as the Bundesrepublik took form, West Germans, tracing the roots of Nazism to rigid discipline and deference to authority, sought to weakening traditional rigidity and obedience in family and society. In keeping with that trend and the reluctance of many Germans to rearm, the Bundeswehr instituted the Innere Fuehrung program, whose chief proponents, Count Wolf von Baudissin and Ulrich de Maziere, attempted to strengthen servicemen's sense of conscience and personal responsibility by sensitizing them to moral issues, including the weighing of orders against personal values. Innere Fuehrung, based on an assumption of the value of indoctrinating leaders, dovetailed with the recasting of Selbstaendigkeit as *Auftragstaktik*, now proclaimed to be a keystone of German military tradition and theory, with a lineage drawn to the liberalism of Scharnhorst, Gneisenau, and von Clausewitz through von Moltke the Elder to von Schlieffen.[44] Both Innere Fuehrung and Auftragstaktik served as counters to the *nur-soldaten* mythos.[45] The term Auftragstaktik was derived from a panzer tactical command method developed on the Eastern Front in World War II.[46] Aimed at brevity of orders and quick decision making, it grew from a descriptive reference in the 1950s to become a mainstay of Bundeswehr doctrine by the early 1970s.

At the same time, a variant of the concept became popular in American military circles and gained momentum to become part of U.S. Army doctrine in the late 1980s.[47]

The principle of chaos begetting chaos was visible in that case. The popularity of Auftragstaktik in the U.S. Army had much to do with what had happened in Vietnam, where many junior and field-grade officers saw senior officers summarily relieve and browbeat their subordinate commanders. Beyond tantrums and flagrant careerism, the junior leaders especially resented the "squad-leader-in-the-sky," the practice of generals and colonels hovering over combat operations in helicopters and taking direct command by radio of small units. As a symbol of anti-micromanagement, Auftragstaktik looked very attractive to those who had had their command authority diminished by such intrusions, as did the stereotype of the Prussian cool and detached style and von Clausewitz's view of tact as an antidote to friction. Its implications for the principle of civilian authority over the military, the discipline and command process, and the potential for generating complexity were left in the shadows by enthusiasts, who saw it as a way to maintain operational initiative amid the wild disorder of a massive Warsaw Pact assault in Central Europe.[48] That became the prime focus of senior U.S. Army officers and defense analysts who, as American forces withdrew from Vietnam in the early 1970s, strove to develop a new body of combat doctrine. The product of that exegesis, *Field Manual 100-5-Operations*, included elements of Bundeswehr and Wehrmacht doctrine and practice[49] and, like the old Prussian concept of Selbstaendigkeit and the Reichswehr's Truppenfuehrung manual, was based on the inevitability of chaos in battle. The enthusiasm for Auftragstaktik[50] under the rubric "general mission–type orders" in American defense circles led in 1981 to former Wehrmacht generals serving as maneuver commanders in a Department of Defense–sponsored war-game using a "flexible, self-confident style of maneuver" in which they thrashed vastly superior Eastern Bloc invaders.[51] That experience and books like Trevor DuPuy's *A Genius for War* and Martin Van Creveld's book *Fighting Power*[52] fed the rising enthusiasm of junior and middle-level officers for the Wehrmacht mystique, although critics better versed in German military history suggested that the "mission order" concept was being misinterpreted. Some critics suggested that the new concepts failed to take into account the full complexities of "maneuver warfare," along with Germany's defeats in World War II and the close links between National Socialism and German-Prussian militarism. Others saw Auftragstaktik as unique to the German culture and military system and not transferable to the U.S. and British armies, given the differences in culture, politics, officer selection, and vetting methods. Both the new U.S. Army battle doctrines and Auftragstaktik reinforced a view of land warfare as primarily infantry-armor-artillery combat and tended to minimize the complexities of high-level planning, phasing, orchestrating, and coordinating ancillary elements and logistics.[53] The close focus on Wehrmacht triumphs early in World War II tended to obscure how battle losses and massive expansion had eroded its quality. As the war progressed, German staff and command training was devoted more and more to low echelon tactics and, as noted in greater detail later, to ideological indoctrination.

Auftragstaktik was also harnessed to other purposes. While it dovetailed with Innere Fuehrung as a symbol of independent judgment, it was also the antithesis of Hitler and OKW's micromanaging of lower echelons in World War II. It also gained strategic significance in the context of West German defense policy. FRG *White Papers* in the late 1980s promised—or threatened—that in case the Eastern bloc attacked on the Central front, Bundeswehr units would be free to act independently and aggressively if their communications with higher headquarters were cut off, a clear contrast with the Wehrmacht of World War II. That also assured the Federal Republic's civilians that the Bundeswehr would immediately strive to push the battle zone as far east and away from West Germany as possible. The political and diplomatic dimensions of Auftragstaktik were not of much concern to enthusiasts in the United States and Britain, nor were cases in military history where a "hands-off" command approach had yielded disaster, like Jeb Stuart's ride at Gettysburg, Custer's last stand, and Gallipoli. The "Law of the Situation" was also left out of sight, as were German critiques of Auftragstaktik in its earlier forms, like a draft field manual on small unit operations prepared under a U.S. Army contract in the early 1950s by former senior Wehrmacht commanders directed by Air Marshal Albert Kesselring. After analyzing World War II operations, they recommended a command hierarchy that allowed subordinate units some independence, but far less in defense than in attack, assuming that the flow of operations would conform to higher echelons' plans and directives, and that commands at various levels would engage in a vigorous ongoing dialogue on the signal net.[54]

There were other contradictions in respect to Innere Fuehrung and Auftragstaktik as well. Both precepts were based on military officers having an implicit right and/or obligation to weigh orders against conscience. Affirmed in war crimes trials in the late 1940s and deemed the "Nuremberg Precedent," that tenet clashed with the principle of civilian control of the military in the major democracies. Nevertheless, the Bundeswehr managed to stay upright on that tightrope throughout the Cold War, despite occasional incidents where the old ways flashed into view and the ongoing debate in the German officer corps and Bundesrepublik defense ministry over which Prussian, German, and Nazi era elements should be blended in the Bundeswehr's tradition. That process was complicated by the fact that its leaders were selected from lower tiers of the Wehrmacht, since many veteran senior officers were unacceptable in the new scheme of things, including most Army and Luftwaffe generals, all Waffen SS officers, and those who were blatantly pro-Nazi and unapologetic in defending the NS Staat. Those included the militarily capable but politically unacceptable Waffen SS general Felix Steiner, who, after Hitler ordered him to defend Berlin, refused to comply with Hitler's scorched-earth edicts in the last days of the war. Another was Guderian, a much respected combat commander, but loyal to Hitler after the July 1944 coup attempt as Army Chief of Staff during the grisly "cleanup" of the officer corps by Nazi security elements and unrepentant after the war.[55] The cases of Guderian and von Manstein highlighted the blurred boundaries between military professionalism and Nazism in the Wehrmacht. Many and perhaps most Germans saw the July 20 plotters as traitors, during the war and afterward, attitudes visible in the squabbles over commemorating Marlene Dietrich a generation later.

Such echoes of the Hitlerzeit and the resurgence of interest in the complicity of Germans and others in the Holocaust make it all the perplexing that so little note has been made of the extensive overlap of the Wehrmacht with National Socialism. There was more than one kind of chaos in all of that, some inadvertent, some deliberate. It is unclear how Selbstaendigkeit affected lower-echelon commanders' tactical performance during the freewheeling operations early in World War II or to what extent it may have hindered or aided the exercise of conscience of individuals when the Army became involved later in the war in security operations. Were Army atrocities, more and more of which have come to light over the years, due to allowing too much latitude at lower echelons? With the highest civilian authorities and later the military leadership thundering Nazi bullying and master-race polemic, how often were ordinary soldiers inclined apply the brakes to the horrific momentum? There is no way to measure how often officers or soldiers complied with Nazi directives or looked the other way, refused to go along, or acted against the regime. Nor is it clear how much the loosening or tightening of the command system at various points increased or decreased chaos versus effectiveness.

Chaos-complexity theory offers another perspective on Auftragstaktik. In sharpening awareness that there are few universal truths, it offers little comfort to those searching for panaceas. But if there are levels of order embedded within the apparent randomness of war that could be measured or mapped, that might lead to being able to determine the optimum level for monitoring and directing operations on the chain of command in various situations. It might also allow the measurement of ratios of order to disorder in combat and lead to a constant, or a range. The basic paradox here arises from the tension between finding simple solutions to problems in war and the intricacy highlighted by chaos-complexity theory. It not surprising then that Auftragstaktik enthusiasts shaped a very spare version of what were intricate processes in der Alte Heer and the Wehrmacht. The Germans' disagreement on such matters was dramatized at the Nuremberg Trials, when Field Marshal Paulus, captured with his Sixth Army at Stalingrad in early 1943, responded to Hermann Goering's condemnation of his lecturing at a Soviet military college while a prisoner of war: "Soviet strategy has turned out so much above ours that the Russians could hardly want me to lecture even at a school for noncommissioned officers. The best proof of this is the outcome of the Battle on the Volga, as a result of which I found myself a prisoner, as well as the fact that you, gentlemen, are sitting here in the dock."[56]

At the end of the twentieth century, the Law of the Situation still stands unchallenged. Despite many attempts to measure the dynamics of war and devise formulas, very few military operations have aligned closely with their designers' and commanders' plans and intentions. Until the utility of non-linearity in military affairs becomes clearer, we should keep in mind that the conceptual boneyard of military theory is littered with failed constructs, like the "angle of attack" theory of the late eighteenth and early nineteenth centuries, the Napoleonic tactics of the American Civil War, and the French offensive school in World War I. Those, like the Wehrmacht's experiences in World War II, suggest how attempts to cope with turbulence or reduce it may actually generate further complexity.

NOTES

1. William Preston, Jr., "On Omaha Beach," *New York Review of Books*, July 14, 1994, p. 46.

2. Ernie Pyle, *Here Is Your War* (New York: Henry Holt, 1943), p. 296.

3. In the ritualized battles in Europe, from the late seventeenth to the mid-eighteenth century, infantry usually marched and fought in well-drilled and tightly massed formations and lines and fired volleys on command. Their smooth-bore muskets had an effective range of about a hundred yards and were often not aimed at a particular target. Light infantry, evolving from hunting and mountain warfare in central and southeastern Europe and North America, were selected for agility and initiative and deployed in small detachments as raiders or skirmishers or to screen, harass, and demoralize large enemy formations. (Light companies of the British army that Minutemen clashed with at Lexington-Concord were speed-marching from Boston to capture rebel arms.) Such *jaegers* (hunters), *chasseurs a pied* (dismounted hunters), and rangers often used rifles' advantage in range and accuracy over standard infantry muskets. Such troops' higher intelligence and independent operation posed a political threat to orthodox military discipline, as they came to symbolize the ideological fervor of French revolutionary armies. Their independence was especially threatening to authoritarian states like Prussia.

4. So suggested the Bundeswehr's Inspector General, Ulrich de Maiziere, in *Bekenntnis zum Soldaten: Militarische Fuehrung in unserer Zeit—reden, vortrage, ansprachen* [Profession to the Soldiers: Military Leadership in Our Time—Talks, Lectures, Addresses] (Hamburg: R. v. Dreckers Verlag, 1971), p. 59.

5. Often translated by referring to a related term, *Auftragsbefehlgebung*, or general mission–type orders.

6. For example, in Justus Scheibert, ed., *Illustriertes Deutsches Militar-Lexikon* [Illustrated German Military Lexicon] (Berlin: W. Pauli's Nachf. [H. Gerosch], 1897).

7. For essays providing a range of perspectives and definitions, see Richard D. Hooker, Jr., ed., *Maneuver Warfare: An Anthology* (Novato, Calif.: Presidio Press, 1993).

8. Walter Goerlitz, *Paulus and Stalingrad* (New York: Citadel Press, 1963), p. 40.

9. For example, Bronsart von Schellendorff, *The Duties of the General Staff*, 3rd ed., trans. W. A. H. Hare (London: Her Majesty's Stationery Office, n. d. [c. 1896]), esp. pp. 285-291; and Rudolf von Caemmerer, *The Development of Strategical Science During the Nineteenth Century*, trans. Karl von Donat (London: Hugh Rees, 1905), pp. 172-173; also see U.S. Army Colonel Arthur L. Wagner's *Organization and Tactics*, 7th ed., n. trans. (Kansas City: Franklin Hudson, 1906), pp. 196-199. On the eve of U.S. entry into World War I, an American officer saw the "idea behind the German system" as, "Give an officer all the assistance he wants and needs, but trust him to command in his own way," A. W. Bjornstad, *The German Army* (Fort Leavenworth: Department of Military Art, 1916), p. 23. For British perspectives on the German system in the same era, see then Royal Engineer captain, later General Sir Frederic Maude, *Military Letters and Essays* (Kansas City: Hudson-Kimberly, 1895), p. 271; and Colonel G. F. R. Henderson, *The Science of War: A Collection of Essays and Lectures, 1891-1903* (London: Longmans Green, 1912), pp. 4–5, 123–126, 137, and 164.

10. For example, Carl Hans Hermann, *Deutsche Militargeschichte: Eine Einfuehrung* [German Military History: An Introduction] (Frankfurt-am-Main: Bernard and Graefe Verlag, 1966), p. 265.

11. He actually said, "No general plan survives in its entirety contact with the enemy more than twenty-four hours."

12. Albrecht von Blumenthal, ed., *Journals of Field-Marshal Count von Blumenthal*, trans. A. D. Gillespie-Addison (London: Edward Arnold, 1903), pp. 115–116.

13. I. von Verdy du Vernois, *Studies in Troop Leading*, trans. H. J. T. Hildyard (London: Henry S. King, 1872), p. 24.

14. As in Mary Parker Follett's applying of the Law of the Situation to management theory. Prime apposite examples are the Battle of Santiago in 1898, in which, while their commander was ashore, individual U.S. ship commanders lunged at the Spanish fleet attempting to exit the harbor, and the first day at Gallipoli in 1915, when the Allied ground forces' commander, General Sir Ian Hamilton, rejected subordinates' urgings that he prod a sluggish commander to seize an opening and cross the peninsula. Hamilton was not widely criticized for that, and the British military critic B. H. Liddell Hart held that he acted "somewhat naturally" in that case.

15. Andrew Hilliard Atteridge, *The German Army in War* (London: Methuen, 1915), pp. 85–87.

16. Erich von Ludendorff, *Ludendorff's Own Story, August, 1914-November, 1918* (New York: Harper and Brothers, 1919), p. 468.

17. Erwin Rommel, *Infantry Attacks* (Vienna, Va.: Athena Press, 1979), p. 293.

18. Quoted in J. R. Stern, *Ernst Juenger* (New Haven: Yale University Press, 1953), p. 39.

19. Ibid., p. 38.

20. Ernst Juenger, *Storm of Steel: From the Diary of a German Storm-Troops Officer on the Western Front*, trans. Basil Creighton (New York: Howard Fertig, 1975).

21. Ernst Juenger, *Copse 125: A Chronicle from the Trench Warfare of 1918*, trans. Basil Creighton (New York: Howard Fertig, 1993), p. 254.

22. For example, von Moltke the Elder's *"wagen, denn waegen"* (weigh, then bet) and von Schlieffen's *"in der Bewegung liegt der Sieg"* (in maneuver lies victory).

23. Malte Plattenburg, *Guderian: Hintergrunde des Deutschen Schicksals 1918–1945* [Guderian: Fundation of German Destiny, 1918-1945] (Dusseldorf: ABZ Verlag, 1950), p. 20

24. Erich Weniger, in *Wehrmachtserziehung und Kriegserfahrung* [Armed Forces Education and War Experience] (Berlin: G. G. Mittler and Son, 1938), pp. 265–269, referred to *Befehlsgebung* in identifying a bipolarity between the Principle of War of "unity of command" and the tradition of granting junior leaders initiative, and argued that striking that delicate balance required sophisticated sensitivity to chronic inconsistencies and the ability to balance close control in the defense against loose reins in the attack.

25. Wilhelm Diest, *The Wehrmacht and German Disarmament* (Toronto: University of Toronto Press, 1981), p. 111.

26. N.a., *Truppenfuehrung: German Field Service Regulations* (Fort Leavenworth: Command and General Staff School Press, 1936) [Report No. 14, 507]; also see Friedrich E. A. A. von Cochenhausen, *Die Truppenfuehrung: Eine handbuch fur den Truppenfuhrer und Seine Gehilfen* [The Troop Leader: A Handbook for Troop Leaders and Their Assistants] (Berlin: E. S. Mittler, 1935).

27. For example, N.a., *Tag Und Nacht Am Feind: Afklarungs—Abteilungen in Westen* [Day and Night Against the Foe: Reconnaissance Detachments in the West] (Gutersloh: C. Bertelsmann Verlag, 1942), pp. 142–143, 176, and 213.

28. For example, see Hans V. Hube, *Der Infanterist: Handbuch fur Selbstunterricht und Ausbildung des Jungen Soldaten der Infanterie* [The Infantryman: Handbook for Self-Instruction and Education of the Young Infantry Soldier] (Berlin: Verlag "Offene Wort," 1934); and Cochenhausen, *Der Truppenfuehrung*, esp. pp. 332–335.

29. *Nuremberg Trials*, vol. xxi, p. 49.

30. Diest, *Wehrmacht and German Disarmament*, pp. 100–101.

31. For example, see Wiegand Schmidt-Rochberg, *Die Generalstab in Deutschland, 1871-1945: Aufgaben in der Armee und Stellung im Staate* [The General Staff in Germany 1871-1945; Its Tasks in the Army and Position in the State] (Stuttgart: Verlags-Anstalt, 1962), pp. 91–92.

32. For perspective on how the *Schwerpunkt* concept fit into the command process, see Helmut Volkmann and Friedrich-Joachim Fangohr, *Befehlstekhnik* [Order Technique] (Berlin: E. G. Mittler and Son, 1938), p. 30.

33. Albert Seaton, *The German Army 1933–1945* (New York: St. Martin's Press, 1982), p. 176.

34. Hans Speier, *From the Ashes of Disgrace: A Journal from Germany, 1945-1955* (Amherst: University of Massachusetts Press, 1981), p. 166.

35. Hermann Hoth, *Panzer-Operationen: Die Panzergruppe 3 und der operative Gedanken der deutschen Fuerhrung Sommer 1941* [Panzer Operations: Panzer Group 3

and the Operational Thinking of the German Leadership in the Summer of 1941] (Heidelberg: Kurt Vowinckel Verlag, 1956), pp. 140-141.

36. Gunther Blumentritt, "The Battle for Moscow," in Seymour Friedin and William Richardson, *The Fatal Decisions*, trans. Constantine Fitzgibbon (New York: William Sloane Associates, 1956), p. 78.

37. Quoted in Walter Goerlitz, *Paulus and Stalingrad*, trans. R. H. Stevens (New York: Citadel Press, 1963), p. 192.

38. Frido von Senger und Etterlin, *Neither Fear Nor Hope* (New York: E. P. Dutton, 1964), pp. 219–226.

39. Ray Merriam, ed., *Interview with Lieutenant General Heinz Gaedecke* (Bennington, Vt.: World War II Historical Society, 1995), pp. 12–13.

40. Erich Weniger, "Der Selbstaendigkeit der Unterfuehrer under ihr Grenze ["The Independence of the Junior Leader and Its Limits"], *Militarwissenschaftlichen Rundschau* [*Military Science Review*], August, 1944, p. 115.

41. At Nuremberg, von Manstein described himself as "nothing more than a soldier . . . and not a political general," *International Military Tribunal*, vol. xxi, p. 10, but also defended adhering to Hitler and rejecting the July 20, 1944, coup on the basis that "the troops believed in Hitler and consequently it was the duty of the officers to carry on," *International Military Tribunal*, vol. xlii, p. 108.

42. Guderian issued orders Nazifying the Army's command and discipline structure, including establishing "Courts of Honor" that handed officers over to the Gestapo, cf. Alan Bullock, *Hitler: A Study in Tyranny* (New York: Bantam, 1961), pp. 676-678; for von Manstein's inconsistencies on the Waffen SS, see Heinz Hoehne, *The Order of the Death's Head: The Story of Hitler's SS*, trans. Richard Barry (New York: Ballantine Books, 1969), p. 494.

43. For example, see Hildegard von Kotze, ed., *Heeresadjutant bei Hitler, 1938–1943: Aufzeichnungen des Majors Engel* [Army Adjutant with Hilter, 1938–1943: Records of Major Engel] (Stuttgart: Deutsches Verlag-Anstalt, 1974), p. 129.

44. Burkhardt Mueller-Hildebrand, *Der Blitzfeldzuge, 1939–1941: Das Heer im Kriege bis zum Beginn des Feldzuges gegen die Sowjetunion im Juni 1941* [The Lightning Campaign 1939-1941: The Army at War at the Beginning of the Campaigns Against the Soviet Union in June 1941] (E. S. Mittler and Son, 1956), pp. 113–115; and Hansgeorg Model, *Der Deutsche Generalstaboffizier: Seine Auswahl und Ausbildung in Reichswehr, Wehrmacht und Bundeswehr* [The German General Staff Officer: His Selection and Training in the Reichswehr, Wehrmacht and Bundeswehr] (Frankfurt-am-Main: Bernard and Graefe Verlag, 1968), pp. 35–36. For a survey of German command philosophy and method from the 1880s to World War II, see Hans L. Borgert, *Grundzuege der Landkrieg-fuehrung von Schlieffen bis Guderian* [Foundations of Land Warfare Leadership from von Schlieffen to Guderian] (Munich: Bernard and Graefe, 1979), esp. p. 427.

45. See Militargeschichtlichen Forschungsamt, *Verteidigung im Bundnis: Planung, Aufbau und Bewahrung der Bundeswehr 1950–1972* [Military History Research Office, Defense in Alliance: Planning, Build-up and Testing of the Bundeswehr 1950–1972] (Munich: Bernard and Graefe Verlag fur Wehrwesen, 1975), esp. pp. 55–57.

46. Eike Middeldorf, *Taktik im Russlandfeldzug: Erfahrungen unter Folterungen* [Tactics in the Russian Campaign: Learning during an Ordeal] (Frankfurt: E. S. Mittler and Son, 1950), pp. 232–235.

47. For example, Antulio J. Echeverria II, "*Auftragstaktik:* In Its Proper Perspective," *Military Review,* 6:10 (October, 1986), pp. 51–56.

48. For example, see Deborah Shapley, "The New Army's Fighting Doctrine," *New York Times Magazine,* November 28, 1982, esp. pp. 40-41.

49. *FM 100-5 Operations* (Washington, D.C.: Office of the Chief of Staff, U.S. Army, 1976); William E. De Puy, "Technology and Tactics in Defense of Europe," *Army,* 29:4 (April, 1979), pp. 14–25, and "'One Up and Two Back,'" *Army,* 30:1 (January, 1980), esp. p. 21.

50. For example, see Stephen W. Ritchey, "The Philosophical Basis of the Air Land Battle," *Military Review,* 54:5 (May, 1984), esp. p. 49.

51. See F. W. von Mellenthin, R. H. S. Stolfi, and E. Sobik, *NATO under Attack: Why the Western Alliance Can Fight Outnumbered and Win in Central Europe without Nuclear Weapons* (Durham, N.C.: Duke University Press, 1984), pp. 145–146.

52. Martin Van Creveld, *Fighting Power: German and U.S. Army Performance, 1939-1945* (Westport, Conn.: Greenwood Press, 1982).

53. I am grateful to Lieutenant Colonel Russell Hiller, USMCR, Retired for insights on the "truck-load of dog-tags" infantry versus supporting arms' mindsets.

54. Albert Kesselring et al., *Small Units Tactics Manual for Command and Combat Employment of Smaller Units* (Heidelberg: Historical Division, European Command, 1952), pp. 26–30, 34, and 99.

55. For a sharp criticism of Guderian et al., see Omer Bartov, *Hitler's Army: Soldiers, Nazis and War in the Third Reich* (New York: Oxford University Press, 1991), p. 137; a recent perspective is David P. Harding, "Heinz Guderian as the Agent of Change: His Significant Impact on the Development of German Armored Forces between the World Wars," *Army History,* 31 (Summer, 1994), pp. 26–34.

56. Quoted in L. Larionov et al., *World War II: Decisive Battles of the Soviet Army,* trans. William Biley (Moscow: Progress Publishers, 1984), pp. 522–523.

5

Chaos versus Chaos: The *Nationalsozialistische Fuehrungsoffizier* (NSFO) Program

In the opening phase of World War II, from 1939 to 1941, the fighting elements of the Wehrmacht rode the crests of the chaos of battle like surfboarders, sometimes falling, but winning victory after victory by being able to stay upright more often and longer than their foes amid the metaphorical breakers of war. Many German officers recognized at the outset that there were problems with the free-flowing blitzkrieg tactics, and they undertook reforms during the pauses between campaigns; but to those watching at a distance it did not seem to matter all that much as one after another of the Wehrmacht's opponents was caught off balance, unprepared, astonished, awkward, and unmotivated. The first shift in that tide came in the air in the Battle of Britain in the late summer of 1940 and in the first substantial reversal of the German Army at Moscow in December 1941. But despite those setbacks, the Nazis and and their allies seemed to hold the strategic initiative in World War II in mid-1942, imposing apparent strategic symmetry by closing pincers from the Caucasus and Egypt on the Suez Canal, capturing the Crimea and besieging Stalingrad, and cutting the Atlantic and Mediterranean lifelines. Then, from late October 1942 onward, it all went awry. By mid-July 1943, the Allies had won major victories on every front except the air war over Germany and were imposing their patterns of order on the chaos of war.

Amid those vortices, Hitler agreed to the creation of the National Socialist Leadership Staff (*Nationalsozialistische Fuehrungsstab*), whose

main purpose was to select and train political officers—
Nationalsozialistische Fuehrungsoffiziere (NSFOs)—to bolster faltering
morale in the Wehrmacht, especially the Army's. That program left only
a faint imprint on history, partly due to its brief organizational life span
and thin documentary evidence, and partly because many saw the
NSFOs' role in the final and most chaotic phase of World War II in
Germany as cosmetic cheerleading, little more than a faint carbon copy
of Soviet commissars. That is somewhat puzzling, since it contrasts
with the respect awarded other Nazi propaganda efforts and with the
creation of the *Innere Fuehrung* indoctrination program in the Bundeswehr a decade later. If implanting ideology didn't work, why was
that function institutionalized later in the Bundeswehr? Beyond that,
assigning the NSFOs a marginal role in history is consistent with the
minimal attention paid by professionals and historians to the influence
of National Socialism on German war-fighting in World War II in
general. There is some evidence, however, that the NSFOs were not
wholly inconsequential, nor were they forced on a reluctant military by
the Nazis. Before World War II, various high-ranking Army officers
accepted or encouraged attempts to infuse the Wehrmacht with Nazi
ideology and the spirit of the Nazi street fighters of the *Kampfzeit* (battle
time) as Hitler struggled for power.[1]

Despite their special hatred for Freud and distrust of intellectuals, the
Nazis were sensitive to the role of psychology in politics and war. They
saw Germany as having been bested in that arena in World War I by the
Allies, and attributed the literal chaos of mutiny and revolution that
erupted in late 1918 to their foes' propaganda, including the considerable talents of the Bolsheviks. Hitler presented his thoughts on such matters at length in *Mein Kampf* in 1924, and many still see him and Dr.
Goebbels as master propagandists half a century later, although mainly
in terms of their effect on their foes and German civilians, rather than on
the armed forces. There was also a great deal of concern about morale
and psychological warfare in other quarters in Germany under the Weimar Republic, especially in the Reichswehr, its 100,000-man army. From
1919 to the mid-1930s that small force, its limits set by the Versailles
Treaty, served openly as a constabulary, or what John Wheeler-Bennett
called "the nemesis of power," and covertly as a cadre for mobilization
amid the "chaos of Weimar," a term used often by many Germans and
those observing its ordeal in the wake of the 1918 collapse. The major
surviving symbol of the Kaiserine Empire and as a bastion of order and
legitimacy, the Army struck a pose of apparent political aloofness and
stability amid chaos. That stance was embodied in Field Marshal Paul
von Hindenburg, the widely revered President of the Republic. Many
Germans saw the "Wooden Titan" as a stand-in for a constitutional mon-

arch until his death in 1934. In World War I, Hindenburg served as Chief of the General Staff and Minister of War. He gained further prestige by not fleeing the country in 1918 like the Kaiser and the Chief of the General Staff Erich von Ludendorff. Both showed some sensitivity for propaganda. Ludendorff laid the groundwork for the *Ufa* film combine, which became a key element in the Nazis' propaganda apparatus, while Hindenburg managed to transfer the onus of negotiating the Armistice and peace to the liberals. He also placed the blame for the military defeat on a *dolchstoss* (stab-in-the-back) by dissident elements on the home front. That claim, based on the betrayal of Siegfried in the *Volsungsaga* and Wagner's opera *Die Gotterdammerung*, was accepted by many embittered Germans, since it meshed with the militarist-nationalist myths of a *Diktat* (dictated) peace and of the Weimar Republic, demanded by the victorious Allies, being the concoction of liberals, leftists, and Jews. German militarists and the Nazis also endorsed the fantasy that victory or at least a stalemate was militarily possible at the war's end and denied the fact that the German Army was falling back along the Western Front when the Armistice was signed. Thus Hindenburg and the Rightists wounded the Weimar Republic in its cradle by linking democracy with defeat and humiliation, and the persistent use of the epithet "chaos of Weimar" added to that alienation. The military's efforts went beyond the manipulation of symbols and political maneuvering. In 1919, the Army ordered Corporal Hitler, as a *Bildungsoffizier* (political officer) to infiltrate one of the tiny splinter parties that flourished under the Weimar Republic's electoral system—the National German Socialist Workers Party, the NDSAP or "Nazis" for short.

The Nazis and the Reichswehr did not march in step, although they shared some basic goals, especially rearmament and the rejection of the hated Versailles Treaty. Also, with the 1918 collapse fresh in their memories, Army officers and Nazi Party officials and military reformers began looking for ways to prepare the nation and the armed forces for mobilization, mechanized warfare and *Totalenkrieg* (total war). Differences outweighed similarities, however, and when the Nazis attempted a coup in Munich in 1923, Reichswehr troops opened fired on them, including Hitler. That opened a scar that never healed, and the event was written into the Nazi Party's anthem.[2] Leftists among the National Socialists, especially Ernst Roehm, head of the *SA*, called for replacing the Army and its Kaiserine traditions with Nazi Party military organizations. Until the early 1930s, armed services personnel were forbidden to engage in partisan political activities, and some junior officers were discharged for joining Nazi paramilitary organizations.[3] That policy was changed when the National Socialists gained electoral strength, and senior Army officers helped maneuver Hitler into the chancellorship.

In his dealings with the military that brought him to power, Hitler had danced around the issue of dismantling the Reichswehr; and by the time he came to power in January 1933, the Nazis had been able to influence the German armed forces indirectly but substantially through propaganda and the Party auxiliaries, including the SA, SS, NSKK, RAD (Reich Air Defense auxiliaries), and Hitlerjugend. Through those and other programs—parts of what Goebbels labeled his "orchestra" strategy for bringing the various elements of German society under Nazi control—they influenced hundreds of thousands of boys and young men during the Weimar era and later tens of millions as the Nazi Party and German state fused and those programs became virtually mandatory. Thus was the German nation imbued with the chaotic Nazi weltanschauung, a revamped model of the old Romanticist-Nationalist idea of a Volksgemeinschaft—a unified, classless society, racist, bent on grandiose social change and common purpose, imbued with a hatred of Marxism and peoples labeled as subhuman—Untermenschen—and most especially Jews. In a special irony, the Nazis were aided in building their paramilitary network by the Versailles Treaty's banning of conscription, limiting the Reichswehr to 100,000 men. That was intended to suppress militarism and prevent the forming of a shadow force army like the army raised by Prussian military reformers under the French occupation of 1807-1813, but it actually created a vacuum that led all major political parties in the Weimar era to form street-fighting armies that numbered in the hundreds of thousands, including the Communists' *Rotefront* (Red Front) and the Social Democrats' *Reichsbanner* (National Flag), as well as the Nazis' SA.

Despite defeat, despair, and the dismantling of the Kaiser's army, militarism survived the armistice of 1918 and the Versailles Treaty in many guises. In 1919, paramilitary forces sprang up across Germany, including the "Black Reichswehr" auxiliaries, and the *Freikorps* (volunteer corps) who fought leftists, some of them serving under Allied command against the Bolsheviks in the Baltic states. Although many were war veterans, most of the ad hoc forces had seen no combat. Many of their members, along with Frontier guard units, "sport" clubs, and associations of war veterans were absorbed into the Nazi Party, including insignia and style. Others became close political allies,[4] like the small but elite officer combat veterans' *Stahlhelm* (Steel Helmet). The structural chaos of Weimar stood as proof of the chaos-complexity adage that chaos begets chaos. Some have attributed the rise of Nazism to the Weimar constitution's proportional representation provision, which allowed splinter parties a foothold by assigning each of them a fraction of legislative seats, which led to the forming of bizarre coalitions. That led to a number of anomalies, while the Nazis and some elements worked to undermine democracy, but played the political game under the Weimar constitution. Throughout the era of the republic, 1919-1933, many feared that if the Army, its officers obviously right of center, but officially apolitical, leaned in any direction politically, that would bring down the Weimar Republic. Those fears were realized in the early 1930s, when the Army's pose of political neutrality, actually a conservative political stance, crumbled as senior Reichswehr officers helped the Nazis come to power during the electoral battles of 1932-1933. To further complicate matters, German Communists joined the assault on democracy by helping National Socialist members to disrupt business in the Reichstag, under Stalin's perverse logic that bringing down democracy would benefit the left more than the right. Hindenburg opposed Hitler, but his iconic status and capacity were fading as he slid into senility. Although the old *Feldmarschall* was still widely respected when the Nazis came to power, a scandal arose from the maladministration of the *Osthilfe* (East subsidy) paid to Junker aristocrats whose inefficient small estates served as breeding grounds for the officer corps, which the Nazis smoothed over at the price of Hindenburg's tacit acceptance and ultimately active support.

The convergence of the Nazis and the bulk of the officer corps became apparent as Hitler consolidated his position. Initially cautious, which angered his followers, he used the Reichstag fire as a lever to absolute power. Whether the fire had been deliberately set by Nazis or not, that incident allowed him to exploit what seemed to be the threat of a Communist insurgency and to use the sense of crisis to gain emergency powers and begin moving toward establishing himself as dictator. Hindenburg's befuddled approval of Hitler's purge of deviant Nazis in the early summer of 1934, and his death soon afterward, allowed the Nazis to begin moving down the path to dominating the Army. Although Hitler always sought more than a quid pro quo in making deals, he moved against the officer corps in increments and avoided a direct confrontation. In stages, then, the Nazi Party's paramilitary organizations were given official status; they had already encroached on the Army's turf by the time that conscription returned in 1936. The implicit deal that Hitler struck with the establishment was that the officer corps and heavy industry would curb their aversion to the seamier aspects of National Socialism in exchange for rearmament, the revival of conscription, and major public works projects to cut unemployment and stimulate the economy, although the effects of the latter were beginning to ebb when war came in 1939. Only a handful of senior Army officers, most notably Ludwig Beck, the chief of staff, tried to hold the bridge against the regime's encroachments on the Army. Many officers who differed with the Nazis were more concerned about means, style, and values than the basic shared goal of remilitarization, and those who wanted to make a stand soon found themselves gravel under Hitler's tires, isolated by the popularity of his dramatic moves to regain Germany's Great Power status. Virtually no one—including perhaps the Fuehrer himself—was sure how far he might go in wielding the new armed forces in foreign policy adventures. Deliberately or not, he projected the chaos within himself to his constituency and then out into the world around Germany. As he presented the threat of force, most of the elites in the democracies who had been scarred by World War I and their constituencies saw it as too high a bluff to call. And throughout the 1930s, from the Nazi ascendancy to World War II, the ante rose steadily and steeply, as German society and the armed forces were subjected to the myriad forms of persuasion wielded by the centralist regime. All the while, support for the Nazis in the Reichswehr's middle and lower ranks grew, and those cohorts formed by the Brown Revolution flooded the armed services when conscription was renewed in 1936. In 1934, the leash was tightened sharply when officers were forced to swear their oaths personally to Hitler as Fuehrer; Nazi party *Hoheitzeichen* (an eagle grasping a wreathed swastika) were sewn onto their uniforms, and swastikas were emblazoned on the armed forces' medals, flags, and equipment. Nor did they oppose the anti-Jewish Nuremberg Laws proclaimed in 1935, or Hitler's creation of a super-headquarters under his direct authority—the Oberkommando des Wehrmacht—in 1938. Initially seen as an administrative link between the three armed forces and the head of state, it was run mainly by Army officers. Its chief was the compliant, colorless bureaucrat Wilhelm Keitel, and its most competent functionary was the able and tireless staff officer Alfred Jodl, both of whom received death sentences at the Nuremberg tribunal for aiding Nazi aggression.

The contradictions and ambivalence within the core of Nazism were visible in the Nazis' attitude toward social rank and the aristocracy. Leftist Nazis railed against stratification, but Himmler and other high-ranking Nazis aped feudalism. The leftist Nazi threat to the Army's integrity seemed to vanish in Hitler's *putsch* (purge) on June 30, 1934. In that "night of the long knives," some 4,000 left-wing and dissident Party elements were murdered, easing the concerns of many Germans other than the officer corps about the thuggish nature of the Brown Shirts. To carry out the putsch, Hitler used the more elite and "clean-cut" members of his personal SS bodyguard, formed and commanded by Heinrich Himmler, also head of the Gestapo. The deaths of Roehm, who had called most loudly for disbanding of the Army, and his homosexual entourage placated Army conservatives. They failed to see that Hitler's use of state terror increased his power, both by showing his willingness to use force and his ability to do it without a reaction from the military. The Army's role as an aloof constabulary had been negated. Mainly contradictions remained in view, however. Even after the murder of Ernst Roehm, various Nazi leaders—including Himmler—continued to call for a *Volk im Waffen* (people-in-arms) and clung to that particular ideal of the Napoleonic era until the fall of the Third Reich. On the other hand, SS officers were trained in ersatz medieval castles, and many officers continued to come from the aristocracy—mainly the lower tiers—although most had to pass through the socialist class-leveling of the *Arbeitdienst* (work service) before entering the military. But in contrast with such leftist practices and rhetoric, the Nazis courted the nobility and the crown prince, recruited a few noble members into the Party, and made overtures to the Hohenzollern Crown Prince to kindle false hopes among conservatives that the monarchy might be restored.

Amid those turbulent countercurrents, some officers who were originally enthused about the Nazis coming to power recognized they were losing control of the Army's honor and soul. Hitler, skilled at reading moods, sensed the hauteur and hostility among the *Generalitaet* (general officer corps) and read the objections that they made to his decisions on military professional grounds as symptoms of faint-heartedness or dissidence. Before and after he assumed direct command of the Army in late 1941, Hitler's considerable arsenal of carrots and sticks included the power of his personality, the ever-expanding security services, mass promotions of generals and field marshals, grants of conquered lands—the so-called *dotationen*—and the techniques of mass persuasion that he had wielded so effectively in gaining power. Even before rearmament began, the Nazis and the officer corps found common ground in seeking ways to shore up the morale of the fighting forces and civilian population if war came again—especially a prolonged one. Not only did they remember the upheaval in the Army and Navy and on the home front in 1918, but senior Reichswehr officers had witnessed the careerist infighting in the higher echelons and the hostility between "front" and "rear" elements—the "war within the war."[5] That led them to sympathize with the Nazis' desire to close the gap in privileges between officers and enlisted men[6] and to devise tactical schemes based on shock, velocity, boldness, and maneuver that would offset the superior numbers of Germany's most probable foes. Like military innovators in other countries between the world wars, those in Germany hoped that mechanized and aerial warfare would win quick, cheap victories and prevent another protracted and bloody struggle, which might erode morale.[7] Although Nazi Germany's armed forces have been stereotyped as grossly authoritarian during World War II, and certainly were more so than most elements of the U.S. armed forces during that conflict,[8] the gap was not so wide as depicted in the propaganda and popular culture of that era. The harsh "ramrod" discipline of the Kaiser's army was eased soon after the defeat of 1918, both in the Reichswehr and the paramilitary forces. The Center for Psychological Research was created in 1920, in close collaboration with the University of Berlin. Although it served as a cover for a shadow military academy, some serious military studies were conducted; by late in the decade, both the Army and the Navy adopted sophisticated selection techniques for screening officer aspirants.[9] Some of the positive leadership methods that remained in use more than halfway through World War II[10] were traced to the populist atmosphere of SA units and Freikorps, in which idleness, close cohesion, and strongly shared ideologies engendered a more collegial form of discipline.[11] The *kameradschaft* (comradeliness) of the SA, tinctured around the edges by images of trench warfare and homosexuality, was reflected in many National Socialists' contempt toward social class distinctions and the *Arbeitdienst*. Despite the aversion of many Reichswehr officers to gays, most of them shared the Nazis' desire to reestablish German power, and their anti-Semitic views as well. Others were impressed by the effects of Nazi youth programs, sound nutrition, outdoor living, physical conditioning, and field craft. In keeping with inner chaos of Nazism, the melding of Nazi and Reichswehr reforms had very mixed results, especially during World War II.[12]

Although many effects of those changes did not become visible until World War II, by the late 1930s, the Nazis were viewed as master propagandists throughout the world, although it was very hard to draw lines between substance and image. While Reichspropagandaminister Goebbels was stereotyped as the master of the "big lie," his tactics tended to be more subtle, aimed at changing perspectives and attitudes by mingling grains of truths with emotionally charged images and themes. He certainly had his work cut out for him in presenting any kind of coherent portrayal of the Third Reich. National Socialist ideology was a smorgasbord of militarism, anti-Semitism, and anti-Communism mixed with an adulation of discipline, strength, rage, and violence. Nazism, for example, meant something far different to the populist-minded Strasser brothers and Roehm than to the psychotic Hess or the elitist Himmler—or the sadistic pornographer, Julius Streicher. Fortunately for Germany's enemies in the long run, that blur of pathologies and the Nazis' Social Darwinist emphasis on dominance both reflected and generated chronic infighting within the Party. The worship of force and brutality fed a viciousness that radiated throughout the military, bureaucracy, and industry and added to the friction of war and whatever the normative levels of nastiness in complex organizations may be.

Although those bizarre metaphysics made the NS Staat far less uniform and monolithic than it seemed at the time, there was no mistaking who was in charge. After Roehm's death removed the most visible threat to the Army in the Nazi hierarchy, Hitler used a lighter hand on the reins, but drew them in steadily nevertheless. And there were many reins. In the late 1930s, the Gestapo—*Geheim Staatspolizei* (secret state police)—intruded into the upper tiers of the military hierarchy and undermined the reputations of uncooperative senior officers. Nor did Roehm's death end the hopes of some Nazi leaders of some day being able to create a "pure" National Socialist armed force. Reichsfuehrer SS Heinrich Himmler, and those who later became SS generals, like Felix Steiner and Sepp Dietrich, clung to that vision as the Nazification of Germany allowed them to advance in that direction without directly confronting the old order. They could take heart from advances along several axes. Himmler, the bland-faced ex–chicken farmer who headed the Nazi organs of state security, slowly expanded the paramilitary units of his SS—the *Schutzstaffel* (security squads). Created as a small bodyguard unit in the mid-1920s, it grew into the *Allgemeine SS* (general SS), with ceremonial and praetorian duties, but its members also served as concentration camp guards to sharpen their bullying skills. On the eve of World War II, it was much smaller than the SA, the NSKK, or the Organisation Todt; at that point, and throughout the war, the major Nazi military force was the Luftwaffe, the air force created when Germany rejected the Versailles Treaty limits in 1935. Its head, World War I fighter ace Reichsmarschall Hermann Goering, was designated a Reichsfuehrer like Himmler and also oversaw German war production from 1939 to 1943 as head of the "Four Year Plan." Beyond its air units, the Luftwaffe included most of the Wehrmacht's parachute troops, and several field divisions.

The larger organizational crazy-quilt of which those elements were only a part allowed Hitler to play various parts of the NS Staat against each other, and to put sizable portions of the armed forces beyond the *Generalitaet*'s (General Officer Corps') authority. Despite their mutual mistrust, most senior officers went along with the preparations for war, and some of them eagerly; they later justified their compliance by pointing to Hitler's having been elected and to his hold on the loyalty of the nation, and especially the Wehrmacht rank and file. That the Nazis met relatively little resistance in stifling democracy or encroaching on the military was partly due to the series of diplomatic and domestic political coups that he carried out successfully against the best judgment of advisors—renouncing the Versailles Treaty, leaving the

League of Nations, rearming, taking back the Rhineland from France, aiding Franco, annexing Austria, humiliating the British and French at Munich, and finally, signing the Nazi-Soviet Pact. Those triumphs not only dashed the expectations of both colleagues and foes that he would falter,[13] but bolstered the populist-Romanticist view that vigor, intuition, and willpower were superior to professional and technical expertise, a tension visible throughout Western culture but especially deeply rooted in German culture and which led von Moltke the Elder to define war as a "free, practical, artistic activity."[14] Hitler and his admirers certainly thought so, while they were winning.

Some of those contradictions and the resultant inner chaos became visible as Hitler's wave of triumph was cresting. Nazi propaganda images were visible outside Germany from the mid-1920s onward, but with the German government's weight behind them after 1933, they were disseminated more widely. Reichspropagandaminister Goebbels found much grist for his mills when the Olympic games were held at Garmisch and Berlin in 1936, impressing visitors with hospitality and efficiency as German athletes won the largest share of gold medals, despite American black athletes' unexpected victories in the track and field events. Official anti-Semitism in the Berlin area was temporarily suspended by the regime during the contests, and warm feelings abounded. It was, however, an epicenter of order in a growing maelstrom. Mussolini had just conquered Abyssinia; Hitler had reoccupied the Rhineland in the spring, was openly rearming, and sending German forces to fight in the Spanish Civil War; and Japan was preparing to invade China on a major scale.

As the three major European dictatorships' propaganda organs became engaged at full volume in Spain, Nazi ideology was pervading the German armed forces, despite persisting Party-Army hostility. As the Wehrmacht went to war in 1939, the friction was serious enough that an *Ehrenabkommen* (agreement of honor) was signed by General Wilhelm Keitel, OKW Chief of Staff, and Nazi Party officials, a "pact" that created special courts of military and Party officials to deal with tensions between Nazis and non-Nazis and prevent discrimination against Party members.[15] Other accommodations preceded that formal agreement. Beyond the common views of some military and Nazi reformers on tactical methods, many military leaders allowed the Nazi Party substantial leeway in inculcating troops with their worldview. In January 1936, Minister of War Blomberg required that formal instruction at the higher war schools include National Socialist content; a year later, other steps were taken to imbue troops with the "spiritual basis" of the regime. From that point on, as Manfred Messerschmidt noted, the Nazi Weltanschauung served as "the main pillar of the German state and its armed forces," and history was rewritten to link National Socialism with the old Prussian Army.[16] After the Munich crisis in the autumn of 1938, the low motivation among mobilized troops led Army, Party, and civilian government officials to create a special OKW course for public relations officers and to form propaganda units and institute the *Wehrmachtsbericht* (periodic communiqués).[17] Despite those measures, however, the Nazi Party did not directly control the armed forces' indoctrination. Goebbels left military propaganda matters to Keitel[18] and to party leaders like Labor Minister Robert Ley, Alfred Rosenberg in the role of director of "spiritual and ideological education," and Martin Bormann, who was maneuvering toward dominance over Party affairs. There was little need for a tight rein at that point. On the eve of the war, an anti-Semitic propaganda booklet, *The Jews in German History*, was distributed to the troops through Army channels.[19]

Despite the extensive osmosis between the Party and the Army, and the latter's accommodations, the image of firm Nazi control over the Wehrmacht would become a major theme in Allied propaganda toward the end of World War II. That, however, contrasted with the Nuremberg Tribunal prosecutors' model of a high-level conspiracy of Nazis and militarists, with Allied propaganda earlier in World War II,[20] and with the image of "pure" German militarism propounded during the Cold War.[21] That picture has also been blurred by American and British scholars of the Third Reich focusing on either civilian or military aspects of the NS Staat[22] and being less inclined than some German historians and memorists to examine Nazi-military linkages.[23] Military historians, professionals, and buffs have tended to focus on the blitzkrieg campaigns during the first third of World War II, when the Nazification of the Army and even the Luftwaffe was less apparent than it was later on. As Omer Bartov and others have pointed out, since the Waffen SS (SS-in-arms) did not take the field in strength until 1942, Anglo-Americans' initial perceptions of the Wehrmacht were shaped by the relative dearth of Nazi elements visible in the campaigns in Poland, France and the Lowlands, Norway, Yugoslavia, and Greece and in North Africa and the Mediterranean. U.S. forces encountered no Waffen SS units during their first year in combat, and public portrayals of the Wehrmacht in the United States rarely reflected the extensive commingling of German Army, Luftwaffe ground combat, and Waffen SS units. Most Hollywood films and media illustrations showed Germans using World War I uniforms, equipment, and terms. In a parallel distortion, mass atrocities committed by German forces on the Eastern front and in the Balkans were usually less publicized than smaller excesses in Italy and France. In general, reports of excesses were also often discounted as updated versions of Allied propagandists' exaggerations in

World War I. By the time America went to war in 1942, "psychological warfare" had become something of a fad, and Nazi propaganda was widely featured in the media; Edmond Taylor's *Strategy of Terror* and William L. Shirer's *Berlin Diary* were best-sellers.

The playing field changed rapidly from early 1942 onward. The German military and political hierarchy's views on psychological warfare were shifting at the same time that the United States and Britain were building up substantial propaganda establishments, in response to their perceptions of the Third Reich's having softened up its victims for the Wehrmacht's coup de grace by using diplomatic and economic maneuvers and psychological warfare. That was true, but perhaps not to the degree that the Allies estimated, and they had little sense of the sea change under way in Germany. Early in the war, the Wehrmacht's triumphs led the High Command to see psychological stress and breakdown in the armed forces as marginal problems, best dealt with by effective leadership. Philosophically, that was in keeping with the trends toward relatively consensual leadership techniques and the principle of Selbstaendigkeit, and with the apparent realities. Hitler's vision in *Mein Kampf* of mechanized elite forces winning quick, decisive victories were apparently realized in the blitzkrieg era. The rapid operational tempo, quick decisions, relatively low casualties, clear outcomes, minimal exposure of the troops to heavy bombardment and enemy air attack, the exhilaration of advancing, and the widespread use of stimulants all served to buffer German ground and air forces from the kinds of pressures that had ground down their predecessors in World War I. Concerns that arose among lower-level commanders before the war and in the early campaigns did not dim optimism at the top. Despite the setback in the Battle of Britain, the German Army was beginning to demobilize when Hitler attacked Russia in June 1941; while some faint signs of public unrest in Germany appeared here and there, the initial victories in the East kept the problem of troop motivation out of focus.

The hard winter of 1941 and continued resistance of the Red Army led many to realize the war was not about to end. When morale in some units in the East took a dip, the Wehrmacht's medical services had no clear sense of the gravity of the problem and no system of treating the surge in stress casualties. Until the major Soviet victory at Kursk in July 1943, the Nazi hierarchy believed that the end of the war was at hand, reflective of the wishful thinking that prevented the German medical services from framing an index of the mounting malaise and gathering data that would have shown how the pathology was intensifying in 1941–1942.[24] The lack of statistics reinforced the sense at the top that things were under control until they reached a level where the problem became apparent to them through grosser forms of feedback, from anecdotes to the reports of the organs of state security. Although that crude adherence to ideology and denial might be attributed to the blinkered mentality of a regime that idealized willpower, a similar ethos was visible in the Royal Air Force's Bomber Command, whose leaders attributed most major psychological breakdowns to a failure of will and nerve, or "low moral fiber," as did some American officers.

Growing awareness of difficulties led Nazi leadership and senior German officers to abandon the clinical psychological apparatus for selecting leaders and military skills that had been erected between the wars. Again, those systems had been created in hopes of avoiding the kind of morale problems that infected Germany in World War I, a concern shared by both the Nazis and the Reichswehr. In mid-1943, as it became clear that things were much grimmer than they had been willing to accept up to that point, the Army and the Party did a mutual about-face and regressed to using simplistic and brutal methods, although historians would later tend to portray the Wehrmacht's psychic state of health in broad and positive terms. The destruction of many German military medical records during the war made it easy to infer that the Wehrmacht was relatively immune to the scale and kinds of psychological problems that afflicted the Western democracies' armed forces.[25] The image of psychic toughness also meshed with Nazi propaganda images of the Wehrmacht in newsreels, documentary films, and graphic periodicals. Widely reprinted in American and British media, they presented scenes of a highly efficient and ruthless meshing of men and machines. There was little sense that they were carefully edited to show none of the error and confusion in combat that alarmed many German officers, or that the Wehrmacht's early victories were won against foes who were disunited and a generation behind in their practice of the military art.

In late 1941, however, when the first major cracks in the facade appeared as the Wehrmacht endured the worst Russian winter in forty years, some Allied intelligence analysts began to sense its declining morale. A ripple of unrest in the Reich paralleled outbreaks of panic in some Wehrmacht units in Russia, as German civilians realized that the heavily battered Red Army was not vanquished. At the front, some German officers read memoirs of French officers of Napoleon's 1812 campaign and drew anxious parallels.[26] When the Army failed to take Moscow in early December, many senior officers urged a general withdrawal. The High Command had already lost face by failing to prepare for cold weather operations, and massive logistical floundering weakened the troops' confidence in their leaders. When it later became clear that Hitler's intransigence probably prevented a massive rout, the Fuehrer extended his dominance over the military professionals by assuming direct command of the Army after its exhausted commander in chief, von Brauchitsch, stepped down. Amid that turbulence, with the Wehrmacht's morale out of focus because of the lack of clinical monitoring and reporting, Hitler and the OKW drew ever more heavily on what was a much weakened storage battery as they found themselves deep in the mess they hoped to avoid: the protracted chaos of high-casualty static warfare. At that point, some Army leaders were more eager to create political officers and to structure troop indoctrination than were the Fuehrer or Himmler, both of whom had seen problems arise during World War I from trying to do that. After four years in the trenches in World War I, Hitler had been assigned as a *Bildungsoffizier* (education officer) to the fledgling Nazi Party by the German General Staff's political arm. Himmler, as an enlisted conscript, witnessed the turmoil of revolution and defeat. Both saw the alienation born of the gap between official pronouncements and actual conditions and feared that Nazi versions of Red Army commissars might be harmed by combat troops and that Party credibility would be eroded by gaps between rhetoric and reality. Hitler, as a veteran, also knew commanding officers were likely to send their least able officers to special duties[27] and, from 1941 to 1943, rejected the urging of Martin Bormann and some OKW functionaries that political officers be assigned to combat units.[28]

Although the Wehrmacht engendered respect and fear throughout World War II, in spite of increasing setbacks and defeats, signs of the growing stress became visible within the Nazi hierarchy, and even beyond. Hitler's quirks and rages became routine fare for Allied political cartoonists and filmmakers. An epidemic of suicide rippled through the Luftwaffe, from combat pilots to its upper echelons,[29] including its technical head, Ernst Udet, in 1941 and its Chief of Staff Hans Jeschonnek, in 1943. Less visible were losses of inexperienced pilots, due to their being committed to combat without adequate training and to keeping fliers on operational status when they were stressed and exhausted.[30] The Luftwaffe had also used up much of its "seed-corn" (veteran instructor pilots) in such maximum efforts as the airborne operations of 1940–1941, the Stalingrad airlift, and the "Palm Sunday Massacre." Beyond the immeasurable but substantial impact of those cumulative disasters on comrades and those in the rumor circuit was the erosive effect of being involved in, witnessing, or hearing rumors of atrocities.[31] The rising sense of doom led those in the higher echelons to consider desperate measures. Perhaps the most bizarre scheme was a proposal that human pilots ride V-1 "buzz-bombs" to their targets, which gained momentum in the Wehrmacht's upper echelons but was finally thwarted by artful bureaucratic delay and sabotage.[32]

In 1942, as noted earlier, the angstful unrest in Germany eased; and as spring approached, many now expected victory in Russia, North Africa, and the Battle of the Atlantic. The Allied bomber offensive was just getting under way and was not yet viewed as a major strategic threat. Hope did not spring in every breast, however. Many Wehrmacht officers in Russia now recognized that an Axis victory or even a negotiated peace settlement was unlikely, and the OKW's realization that morale was declining led to the creation of a small effort for politically educating Wehrmacht officers in June 1942—the *Wehrgeiste Fuehrung* (martial-spirit leadership) program, under which 278 officers underwent intense ideological training.[33] On a parallel track, Himmler authorized a structured indoctrination program in the Waffen SS, whose units were controlled by the Army in combat, but under his administrative authority. While he was not opposed to instilling fanaticism and hatred to enhance fighting-spirit performance, Himmler kept the Ideological Educational Officers of the SS subordinate to unit leaders and denied them command authority.

The tide ebbed as quickly as it rose. In early November 1942, the Anglo-American invasion of western North Africa coincided with the British victory at El Alamein, and greater reverses followed, at Stalingrad in February 1943 and in the Atlantic two months later, on the heels of the Axis collapse in Tunisia in May. In mid-summer, as the Anglo-American bomber offensive began in earnest, the western Allies' invasion of Sicily paralleled the Red Army's major victory at Kursk. Autumn saw Mussolini toppled and major landings in Italy. The only substantial success for German arms in 1943 was the bloodying of U.S. daylight bombers that forced a three-month suspension in raids. The newsreels that showed hordes of grubby, sullen German prisoners of war captured at Stalingrad, Alamein, and Tunis seemingly punctured the myth of the Wehrmacht's invincibility.

In the German High Command, that litany of defeat and Hitler's close supervision of operations aggravated tensions between the Nazi Party and the Army,[34] but they agreed on some issues, including personnel selection. When troop morale first became a concern in the winter of 1941–1942, Party officials attacked the armed forces' modernist psychological apparatus; and in February 1942, Goering ended the Luftwaffe's psychological selection program. Many military professionals shared the Reichsmarschall's hostility toward objective measurement techniques, although more on traditional than ideological or political grounds.[35] The Romanticist Nazis extolled the venting of violent impulses and dominant personalities, while German militarists idealized feudal fealty, Fuehrerprinzip (absolute obedience to superiors), and intellectual rigor. In any case, at that point, both the Party and armed forces agreed to abandon personnel screening and selection systems based on clinical psychological testing and measurement in stages, including aptitude tests for flying duties.[36] That shift toward bold primitivism included the infusion of Nazi Party terms into the armed forces' training lexicon, like *Umschuelung* (indoctrination) and *Menschenfuehrung* (leadership by individuals). [37]

That deliberate harnessing of inner chaos in the form of rage steered the Wehrmacht several points further away from the dull but crucial rationalism that was at a premium in administration, industrial process, and military operations. That adds to the burden of sorting out Nazism's influence on the German people and the Wehrmacht,[38] difficult enough in view of the inhibiting effects of a police state on keeping diaries, writing letters, and even casual conversation that would have allowed the security services to accurately map popular attitudes. Until the very end, disaffection and war-weariness were often expressed in jokes and aphorisms, like the popular saying: "The Prussianesque Army, the Kaiserist Navy, and the National Socialist Luftwaffe."[39] We can only guess, then, as to how much the regime's attempts to use ideology to enhance morale made combat forces fight more tenaciously, or workers produce more—or less. We do know that large numbers of German troops surrendered to Allied loudspeaker units or safe-conduct leaflets, and there are glimpses of sabotage, working to rule, corner cutting, delays, tardiness, or malingering.[40] That is especially murky, since many, whatever their sentiments toward the regime, would have seen an attempt to hamper the war as treasonous, especially if it put German troops at hazard.[41] Loathing their respective heads of state did not prevent millions of Russians, Chinese, Italians, Britons, and Americans from fighting for their nations' cause. The degree of order within that particular swirl of chaos is beyond discerning, and the data needed to paint a clear picture of the intricate dynamics of allegiance and allegiance are out of reach. True, Allied inspectors studying Luftwaffe production after the war found little evidence in the workplace of tampering by German or even foreign forced laborers,[42] although that assumes that workers would not have been able to disguise their efforts. Beyond that, many results of notional sabotage and tampering would have become visible only after leaving the manufacturing site, when dud bombs were dropped, defective ammunition was fired, or contaminated fuel was burnt. Nor would such effects have been apparent in the chaos of combat.

The question of allegiance is also rendered fuzzy by the fusion of the Army and the Nazi party over time, both in terms of the flow of men indoctrinated in their youth and growing overlaps within the great organizational tangle of the NS Staat. Until World War II began, for example, the SA and the NSKK, the two largest Nazi paramilitary groups, remained separate from the Wehrmacht, although many members entered the services individually or trained and supported motorized forces. Some small elements of the SS (as security squad), which was very small at that point, had been militarized since the mid-1930s at the initiative of Nazi military theorist Felix Steiner. But, as noted earlier, the bulk of it was not, and only a few *Allgemeine* (general) SS units went on active service in 1939. It was only after the fall of France that the Waffen SS was expanded, eventually to about half a million men. Its uniforms, rank titles, and administrative and training system differed from the Army's, as did the strength and quality of its twenty-nine divisions. That was also true of their "Aryan purity" as well, since many volunteers were raised from prisoners of war and in occupied areas.[43] While the Army controlled Waffen SS units in combat, they remained formally under Himmler's authority and discipline, just as Luftwaffe *Fallschirmjaeger* (paratroop) units and field divisions under *Heer* (Army) tactical control were rewarded and disciplined by Goering.[44] To add to that complexity, paramilitary security and intelligence services, like the *Sicherheitdienst* (SD) (security service) and *Einsatz-kommandos* (special units) that often operated in the same zones as military forces, were also directly under Himmler's control.

That organizational mishmash was reflected in the increasing use of the term Wehrmacht as a synonym for the German ground forces, even though those included more and more Party elements, including police divisions. An Army general who claimed to be a *"nur Soldat"* had to wear very narrow blinders or be grossly insensitive when growing numbers of Army staff officers were detailed to Waffen SS division staffs, and SS officers received Army staff training.[45] By August 1944, seven of thirteen SS corps–level chiefs of staff were Army officers who volunteered for the SS or were seconded to it[46] and, later in the war, chose to wear Waffen SS rank badges. On the other hand, a few Waffen SS units donned Army insignia and saluted in Army manner by touching the cap brim, rather than using the customary *Deutsche Gruess*, the stiff-armed "Heil Hitler" salute. A further smearing of organizational borders came from the cross-assigning of Waffen SS combat troops and concentration camp guards.[47]

Despite all the steps taken to increase Army-Party rapport and Nazi dominance, some Nazi leaders continued to fear the dilution of National Socialist purity. In mid-1943, with Hitler and Himmler still opposed to political officer concepts, Alfred Rosenberg, principal Nazi Party political theorist, in his role of State Minister for the occupied Eastern territories, was wrestling with Bormann, Party Chancellery secretary, for control of junior Army officer indoctrination. The former, whose murky and convoluted treatise *Myth of the Twentieth Century* was widely cited as the intellectual core of Nazi ideology, was a colorless personality and supremely drab speaker, and no match in political infighting for Bormann.[48] Although Hitler's mistress Eva Braun loathed Bormann for his crudity and toadyism, he had gained considerable influence in the Fuehrer's inner circle and was determined to revive the combative spirit of the National Socialist movement of the 1920s and early 1930s. Hitler thwarted Bormann's hopes of purging the Wehrmacht of its chaplains,[49] but the Party secretary did manage to gain bureaucratic control over military promotions and to increase the Nazis' growing dominance over the military, symbolized when he awarded gold Nazi Party badges to Army chief-of-staff Zeitzler and his OKW counterpart, Jodl.[50]

In August 1943, Hitler finally gave way on the political officer issue when his former adjutant, Hans Junge, visited his East Prussian head-quarters while on leave from the Russian front. In describing conditions at the front, Junge described propaganda leaflets printed in red and black, the German national colors, which called for an uprising against the Nazi regime. The troops, Junge reported, were shaken by the argument that "all thoughtful officers" and the nation as a whole knew Germany had lost the war.[51] The leaflets were ostensibly the product of General der Artillerie Walter von Seydlitz-Kurzbach's *Bund Deutscher Offiziere* (BDO) (League of German Officers), including four of the two dozen German generals captured at Stalingrad and about a hundred officers of lower ranks.[52] The BDO called for a democratic regime in Germany and purported to be apolitical, although linked with the *Nationalkomite Freies Deutschland (NKFD)*, which was composed of German Communist exiles.[53] Complexity was not confined within the limits of the Third Reich. It remains unclear whether those groups were a Soviet political warfare ploy designed to pressure the hesitant western Allies into assaulting northwest Europe,[54] Stalin's hedge against a coup in Germany, or an Allied appeal to anti-Fascist elements in the Axis camp.[55] Nor is it clear how attractive the BDO and NKFD were to Germans seeking a way out of the cul-de-sac created by the Casablanca Declaration.

In any case, Junge's account reinforced the Fuehrer's long-standing concern about disloyalty in the officer corps. In that respect, the BDO was the last straw. Hitler had been irked by the officer corps' pessimism and hesitancy since the early 1930s, especially in the winters of 1939 and 1941 and early in the campaign in Russia. That put a special edge on von Seydlitz's defection, since he embodied the Prussian tradition as a descendant of Frederick the Great's famous cavalry commander, after whom a German cruiser was named. Although there was no firm evidence regarding the effect of that dissidence on troop morale,[56] Hitler's fears now drove him to expand the dimensions of the Wehrgeiste program far beyond Rosenberg's and Bormann's designs by ordering that officers of all ranks be subjected to indoctrination. Hitler would fixate on the BDO for the rest of the war, as both his physical and mental health deteriorated, imagining that it was the result of NKVD Orwellian rat tortures and proof of a vast conspiracy throughout the Wehrmacht officer corps. The depth of those terrors became visible late on the day of the failed July 20 coup, when a *Fuehrerhauptquartier* teletype directive proclaimed that von Seydlitz and his associates were behind the coup attempt.[57] Even though the plotters had rejected links with the BDO or NKFG, did not intend to de-Nazify their regime, and avoided the *Judenfrage* (the Jewish question),[58] Hitler was alarmed by the fact that some German generals captured when the Soviets shattered Army Group "C" in the Ukraine in the summer of 1944 had made anti-Nazi proclamations.

On December 22, 1943, the Wehrmacht National Socialist Leadership Staff was formed to select, train, and assign NSFOs, who were to be recruited mainly from the ranks of outstanding combat leaders with Nazi party ties, although some were Party officials.[59] The program was headed by General of Infantry Hermann Reinecke, known as *"der kleine Keitel"* (little Keitel), since he was another military bureaucrat, otherwise undistinguished, who had proved his loyalty to National Socialism in such administrative roles as the head of the *Allgemeines Wehrmachtsamt* (general Wehrmacht office) in the late 1930s. During the war, he evolved from drone to killer bee, trumpeting the Nazi party line as he rose in influence and rank.[60] Reinecke's significant services to the regime beyond promulgating ideology and ardent dedication to duty included signing two major Army-Party agreements in 1941 with Reynard Heydrich, Himmler's principal deputy, later known as the "Hangman of Prague"—the *Kommissarbefehl* (Commissar Order) ordering the execution of key Communist functionaries[61] and an interorganizational "pact" giving Himmler's security elements access to Russian prisoners-of-war held by the Army.[62] Reinecke also supported the Reichsfuehrer SS's brutal treatment of Russian POWs , including starvation and mass execution by *SS Einsatzkommandos* (Special Commando death-squads), and fended off the complaint of Admiral Canaris, head of the *Abwehr* (Secret Service), that excluded Russian prisoners of war from Geneva Convention protection was demoralizing the Army.[63] After convening a secret OKW conference on biological warfare in July 1943,[64] Reinecke helped Bormann wrest political control of indoctrination efforts from Rosenberg by requiring that NSFO field reports be routed through Nazi Party channels.[65] At the end of March 1945, deemed "too old . . . and too inflexible" by Goebbels,[66] Reinecke was relieved during a major shakeup and "comb-out" of the Nazi bureaucracy.[67] After receiving a life sentence at Nuremberg for having issued orders for the *Sonderbehandlung* (special treatment) of Jewish prisoners of war, Soviet and otherwise, he was released from prison in 1954.[68]

When the NSFOs assumed their duties, the earlier concerns of Hitler and Himmler proved valid. Fighting troops saw them as another form of the regime's *mundpropaganda* (mouth propaganda) and coined an informal slogan: *"NS Offizier hier, Politruk dort"* (NS Officer here, commissar there).[69] Bormann extended his control over the program and struggled to infuse fighting spirit and Nazi "faith and fanaticism" into the war-weary armed forces, blending political and martial symbols by recruiting distinguished combat leaders with Nazi party links as NSFOs to further impose Party identity on the Army.[70] Increasingly isolated from reality, Bormann and other Nazi leaders denied the imminent collapse and failed to recognize how their assuming more and more authority was drawing the onus of defeat away from the military and onto the Nazi Party and themselves, an echo of 1918, when the officer corps managed to shunt blame for the defeat onto the politicians. Although Hitler's last act was to place the mantle of power on the shoulders of Admiral Karl Doenitz, that came too late. A solid foundation had been laid for making a case that Hitler and his OKW lackeys had lost the war by overriding commanders in the field.

As the war had dragged on and morale declined, many Germans, for whatever reason, remained determined to see things through. Thunderous applause met Goebbels's call for a "total war" in his carefully staged speech at the *Sportspalast* in late 1943. From that point until the end of the war, he and other top-level Nazis tried to energize faltering morale by creating a siege mentality that echoed the World War I theme of *Eine Ganze Welt Gegen Uns* (the whole world against us). Despite the mounting chaos, theoretical and virtual, they were able to exploit their foes' propaganda fumbles. At the beginning of 1943, Roosevelt and Churchill gave away a trump card by issuing the "unconditional surrender" proclamation at the Casablanca Conference. That was meant to show Stalin that the Western allies meant to fight the war to the finish, since the Soviets, openly skeptical after repeated Anglo-American postponements of a "Second Front"—a major invasion in northwest Europe—had been holding secret talks in Sweden with Nazi representatives. Beyond any dubious gains, the declaration undercut the position of Germans who hoped to form a resistance movement and depose Hitler.

Another product of the Casablanca meeting, the western Allies' strategic bombing offensive, failed to produce a general breakdown or uprising, as some of its proponents hoped, but also played into the hands of Nazi propagandists by forcing the survivors of the destruction of over forty large German cities to turn to the regime for medical and rescue services, air defense, shelter, and evacuation. The cracks in the facade grew larger and more numerous and spread. The venality and brutality of Party functionaries became increasingly visible to ordinary Germans, feeding the fatalistic sense that the end was in sight. Goebbels's imagery of siege became reality after the bomb plot in July 1944 revealed discontent in high places. Growing casualties among the civilian population, defeats on the fighting fronts, and increasing Gestapo crackdowns, along with the Allied threats of vengeance, led many Germans to fight more fiercely as the ring of foes tightened around the boundaries of the Third Reich. In September 1944, Goebbels was able to leverage reports in the British and American press of U.S. Secretary of the Treasury Henry J. Morgenthau's plan to "pastoralize" postwar Germany. Stressing the fact that Morgenthau was Jewish, the Reichspropagandaminister called on Germans to rally to the fight at the last point in the war when the Third Reich seemed to have a chance to fend off the Allies. As V-1 "buzz-bombs" and V-2 stratospheric rockets began to fall on Antwerp and London in the summer and the Luftwaffe's first jet squadron prepared to enter service, the Allies' advances in the east, west, and south had all ground to a halt. Their airborne thrust into Holland ended in disaster, and Albert Speer's realigning and expansion of German war production, begun by in late 1942, yielded an expanding flow of weapons. The Wehrmacht was secretly preparing for the major counterstroke in West in mid-December that led to the Battle of the Bulge, after which the roof began to collapse in early 1945. Anglo-American strategic bombing bit deep into the Third Reich's oil and transportation systems, the Allies regained momentum, crossed the southern and northern Rhine, encircled the Ruhr, drove into Czechoslovakia and Denmark, and took Berlin—all in the last few weeks of a war that lasted five-and-a-half years. By the late winter, more and more Germans had had enough. Millions of civilians fled from the East, while hundreds of thousands of troops began to surrender before the final collapse.

Since the NSFOs were deployed amid that turbulence, we cannot draw a neat diagram that shows that "x" number of them shored up the troops' faith that Hitler would turn things around, while "y" number hindered commanders doing their business, or "z" number stood back or helped end the madness.[71] Hitler and Himmler's earlier fears were realized when some NSFOs became targets of pent-up resentment, including brown-uniformed Party officials whom Bormann dispatched to stiffen the front in various places as things came unglued. After the war, there was some stereotyping of NSFO's behavior as inconsequential, and skimpy portrayals of the troops' reaction to them in history or literature,[72] but no firm estimates of their effect on the Wehrmacht's combat performance.[73] The NSFOs received little attention, mentioned usually in passing as frail craft launched into a vortex, as faint background detail in the death-struggle of the Nazi regime. That is not surprising, since appraising their impact on German military effectiveness is even more difficult than judging Puritan chaplains' influence in the English Civil War, or that of Bolshevik commissars.[74] We cannot be sure what documentation could effectively capture the NSFOs' day-to-day activities in the Wehrmacht's many headquarters or their effect on combat operations, since such informal dynamics and nuances usually go unrecorded. The analogy to chaplains holds there as well; anecdotes may convey some essence, but not general patterns. Nor can we easily separate NSFOs' impact from the influence of Nazi indoctrination and propaganda on Germans, civilian and military. As Stephen Fritz observed, "the consequence of incessant Nazi indoctrination in the schools, in the Hitler Youth and in the Army seemed to be body of men with a remarkable cohesion in the face of the tribulations of war"; he concluded that "National Socialist goals had seeped into the consciousness of the rank and file." That view meshed with some German generals' insisting after the war that Nazi paramilitary training had enhanced morale and fighting capacity, especially when troops were cut off, alone or in small groups,[75] and with the American sociologists Shils's and Janowitz's observation that the better-performing Wehrmacht units were built around a strong Nazi core.[76]

The evidence of that indoctrination seems very bizarre indeed, a kind of intellectual chaos reflecting the inner turbulence of the regime and many of the top Nazis, including Hitler. Himmler, like Bormann and many other Nazi leaders, firmly believed that imbuing fighting forces with the zeal of the Kampfzeit and absolute faith in Hitler might reverse the tide of battle.[77] That led him to insist on a 1:1 ratio of military topics in military training programs and service schools to provide the fullest opportunity to imbue the forces with such morale-boosting material as lectures on the Fuehrer's life, the history of the SS, the "Jew as world parasite," the Reich's role as Europe's bulwark against Bolshevism, degenerate American culture, German folk values, and National Socialist attainments.[78] Nor, as noted earlier, was such instruction limited to lower ranks or to the heroic homilies in the widely distributed *Wochensprache* (weekly inspirational quotes) propaganda leaflets. Senior Wehrmacht commanders also received heavy doses of Nazi dogma, as well as insights into the regime's most sordid inner workings and purposes. On January 26, 1944, a month after the NSFO program began in earnest, a high-level National Socialist leadership meeting was or-

ganized by Reinecke in Posen. There, in a theater, Himmler told some
300 senior Wehrmacht officers of his "horrid assignment" and the
imminent solution of the "Jewish question."[79] The next day, at
Koenigsberg, East Prussia, Hitler chided the Generalitaet's lagging
spirit in a cheerleading speech on "faith" as the key to victory. Although
von Manstein later claimed he responded sarcastically to the Fuehrer
on that occasion,[80] he and his colleagues stayed in harness, whatever
their private reservations, until a few kicked over the traces in the
attempt on Hitler's life in July 1944.[81]

From this distance, it is easy enough to judge the NSFOs a last-ditch
strategem, purposeless and without value. From the standpoint of
chaos-complexity, at first glance, they look much the same. In attempting to negate the increasing chaos of defeat and retreat by generating
an anti-chaos and by imbuing military leaders and troops with a rageful
spirit, the NSFOs stand as a case of the dictum that chaos begets chaos,
since they added an increment of confusion to the Wehrmacht's tangled
command-and-control system. They served to fragment authority in a
culture in which deference to centralized authority was a core value.
They undercut the independence—Selbstaendigkeit—of lower levels of
command at a time when simplicity, clarity, and cohesion were at a
premium. Debits all, then, but were there credits? What did that balance
sheet look like? How much did the NSFOs infuse fighting spirit into the
Wehrmacht, or undermine morale? Or did they, on the whole, have little
effect? Here, too, statistics are sparse and unhelpful. There were some
60 million Germans; 3 million were Party members, perhaps 15,000
were involved in the July 20 plot, and an estimated 10,000 aided Holocaust victims.[82] That tells us very little about what individuals or the
aggregate really thought or did. Anecdotes are no more help here than
in military history.

Since the NSFOs, like the *kamikazes* and the Soviet *politruks*, highlighted the cost-benefit ratio implicit in inculcating a nation and/or its
armed forces with specific ideologies for some apparent advantage,
relativists may swoop in here to suggest that doing that is unavoidable
to some degree, and Marxists might remind us that all acts are political
acts. That quandary was recognized during World War II, when early
Nazi and Japanese victories were ascribed to those regimes' hardening
and militarizing their youth. Subsequent British and American attempts to indoctrinate their forces produced unanticipated side effects.
In World War II, Royal Army Education Corps officers helped bring the
Labour Party to power in 1945, while in the United States, the major
ideological debate over prisoner-of-war behavior that followed the
Korean War resulted in the Code of Conduct. Those guidelines for
holding out against coercion led to hideous suffering as American

servicemen strove to uphold it while being tortured in North Vietnam. (Paradoxically, officers who attempted anti-Communist indoctrination of their troops in the 1950s were punished.)

From the standpoint of chaos theory, the course of the July 20 plot offers a grim example of the sensitivity of complex processes to slight influences, not only at the outset, but all along the way. Here, too, unfortunately, secrecy—the conspirators' and the Gestapo's—along with the slaughter of many involved and the uncertainty of the evidence, makes it difficult to know whether officers were driven to act or inhibited from doing so by being exposed to Nazi "philosophy" or having their authority usurped by NSFOs. Immediately after the failed bomb attempt, it was lower-echelon officers loyal to the regime who foiled the coup.[83] While the assassination attempt has often been portrayed as a redemption of the Army's tarnished honor, many if not most Germans saw it as treasonous, which adds some luster to those who stood their moral ground here and there, like the officer cadets who walked out of a showing of a film of the slow-hanging of some of the plotters.[84] One of the regime's responses to the coup was a sharp increase in the number of NSFOs, and the requirement that they review orders issued by senior Army leaders. Similar authority was granted to Nazi Party officials who commanded units in the newly formed *Volksturm* (People's Assault Force),[85] another by-product of the bomb plot. In an exquisite irony, Hitler directed Himmler, Minister of the Interior since early 1944, to form and command a "National Socialist People's Army," the *Volksarmee (VA)*. Thus was Ernst Roehm's dream realized by his nemesis in the lurid twilight of the Third Reich, albeit partially and shabbily.[86]

The first hesitant steps toward creating the Volksarmee (People's Army) had been taken before the attempted assassination, when Hitler ordered that deputies to *Gauleiters* (Nazi Party political district overlords) focus their attentions on regional defense matters,[87] and that Nazi militia organizations be created in areas where enemy invasion seemed likely. The stilted recasting of the populist ideal of a *Volk im Waffen* and the Prussian peoples' militias during the Napoleonic Wars gave Himmler the role he long sought, as a major field commander with authority to dominate the military professionals whom he and many top Nazis loathed.[88] The VA also served as a symbolic counterbalance to his arch-rival Goering's Luftwaffe ground units, but in fact the lightly armed *Volksdivisionen* were the scrapings of the German military manpower barrel, including schoolboys and sick and elderly men. They were minimally trained and were led by officers selected for their political reliability, most of whom lacked training and combat experience. Their marginality was reflected in the requests of many capable

VA members to transfer to the Army or Waffen SS, which were rejected.[89]

As such stratagems and blind optimism failed to turn the tide, hope gave way to despair and fury. In the final days of the war, Hitler denounced his Waffen SS bodyguard units for failing to perform tactical miracles and ordered them to remove their distinctive armbands. As the Fuehrer withdrew into drug-induced befuddlement, Bormann expanded his influence over the Nazi inner circle. Bureaucratic squabbling continued amid the virtual chaos at the center of the NS Staat until the regime's final hours, all to the greater misery of millions and to no purpose. At the end, the Fuehrer judged his old comrades Goering and Reichsfuehrer SS Himmler unworthy to succeed him and also denied the latter his prime ambition of heading the Army. After condemning the German people as unworthy of his sacrifices in his will, he bestowed authority as head of state to Admiral Doenitz; and after marrying Eva Braun, he killed himself. So did Goebbels, and soon afterward, Himmler, whose performance as a *Feldmeister* fell far short of his pretensions. The latter's authority had been undercut by Bormann, whom many saw as virtual head-of-state in the final days of the war and who in the last days oversaw the NSFO program through a staff in the Party Chancellery,[90] having gained full dominance over it in late March, when Reinecke was relieved.

Although the NSFOs did not seem trivial to the Party Secretary, how did they appear to those inside the Wehrmacht? Some German soldiers at lower echelons viewed them positively, while higher-level commanders tended to leave them out of view or were guarded their appraisals.[91] General Frido von Senger und Etterlin, a corps commander in Italy, divided the NSFOs he dealt with into two categories—a relatively small number of feared fanatics and informers and a substantial majority of "credulous . . . [but] 'decent fellows,' " more likely to have had battle experience and decorations than be a Nazi Party "wild man,"[92] despite Reinecke's successor's expressed hope of implanting "hate and the uncontrollable urge to destroy."[93] While von Senger also noted that, as Hitler had long feared, Wehrmacht unit commanders tended to nominate more marginal officers for the NSFO program,[94] the general's revulsion toward National Socialist cheerleading and false optimism led him to title his memoirs *Neither Fear Nor Hope*, and he admitted he had been cautious in dealing with them.

OKW's granting the NSFOs authority equal to Army operations officers after the July 20 coup attempt supported captured German generals' claims in early 1945—then doubted by western Allied observers—that they had been "completely subjugated" to the NSFOs.[95] The first Order of the Day issued by Guderian as Chief of the Army General

Staff ordained that each General Staff officer would be a National Socialist Leadership Officer, "not only by his knowledge of tactics and strategy, but also by his attitude to political questions and by actually cooperating in the political indoctrination of the younger commanders in accordance with the tenets of the Fuehrer."[96] Guderian also acceded to another major National Socialist incursion onto Army turf when Himmler, in his new role as head of the Home Army, established traveling military courts. Like the tribunals that attended the early French revolutionary armies, these overrode local military commanders who appeared to be too lenient toward miscreants[97] and used summary judgments and speedy executions to instill ardor. At least one general was tried for hampering an NSFO in the performance of its duties.[98]

Five years after the war, Siegfried Westphal, Rommel's chief of staff in North Africa, defined the NSFOs as "a decisive step towards the burial of the authority of the commanders . . . mainly directed against the Army, because Hitler doubted their 'Nazi Faith.'"[99] Other Wehrmacht officers' memoirs tended to follow that line,[100] but attributed more to Hitler's micromanaging than to the NSFOs. The focus on Hitler's meddling aligned more closely with the image of a clear gap between the Nazi regime and the Wehrmacht and left the fact that most NSFOs were Army officers out of focus. Nor did all the evidence bear out the image of Hitler overriding his able generals and leading Germany to defeat.[101] Sir Alan Bullock pointed out that Hitler's early triumphs, political, diplomatic, and military, far exceeded his predecessors' achievements and confounded his critics' expectations. Bullock posed the quandary that "If Hitler . . . is . . . made responsible for the later disasters . . . he is entitled to the major share of credit for the victories of 1940: the German generals cannot have it both ways."[102] But they certainly tried, and succeeded to a great extent despite the linking of the Wehrmacht's tactical effectiveness to Nazism by Field Marshal Jodl in the dock at the Nuremberg War Crimes Tribunal, when he tenaciously defended the strong bonds between the armed forces and National Socialism. Nor did the defense attorneys at Nuremberg point out that German officers' view of military victory as something transcending politics, ethics, and personal honor was also shared by their opponents, most of whom also deferred to their civilian overlords.

Field Marshal von Rundstedt, perhaps anticipating future revelations of the German Army's atrocities,[103] defended his colleagues' behavior by citing the "very ancient [Prussian] tradition that an officer does not concern himself with politics"[104]—a rule to which there were myriad exceptions.[105] Nor did claims by military defendants at Nuremberg and their apologists that they acted out of fear of Nazi coercion align with subsequent evidence that many who refused to go along had gone unpunished.[106] At Nuremberg, as in postwar memoirs and histories, the NSFOs were well out of the limelight and were seen as but one of the puppet masters' strings, like Himmler's *Bevollmachtige* (plenipotentiaries), uniformed Nazi expediters who intruded themselves into German war industries, empowered to micromanage programs in crucial areas. But there is a contradiction here, too. Those functionaries were later judged a significant in their influence, while the much larger NSFO program was portrayed as inconsequential foam in the vortex. The greatest tribute to the NSFOs came indirectly, in its imitation in the Innere Fuehrung program created by former Wehrmacht officers in the Bundeswehr in the 1950s, purged of Nazi content, by retaining the institution of indoctrinating troops and leaders.

Both the NSFO and Innere Fuehrung highlight the dilemma of using ideology to instill fighting spirit in armed forces in war or in preparing for it. Ideally, using one kind of chaos against another would compensate for or cancel out turbulence, but, again, it also risks generating further chaos. That leads to another dilemma. If stirring up deep emotions to cope with the disorder of war was brought within the reach of chaos-complexity dynamics, it might prove useful, like administering a stimulant to a tired athlete, but there might also be a deferred price. That crosses the boundary into the same realm that the Nazis and the Reichswehr entered after World War II—psychology and pharmacology. Here lies yet a further quandary. As ongoing advances in command-and-control technology and "information warfare" put an increasingly high premium on the cool judgment and accurate perception of system monitors and battle managers, at what point will the benefits transcend cultural and ethical constraints that have been crumbling throughout the twentieth century? Will that, too, be left to impressionistic, lyrical historians, leaving the mapping of crucial parameters within the turbulence of war outside our reach? If the NSFO program and Nazi indoctrination bolstered the fighting power of the Wehrmacht and the nation's morale like a stimulant, that implies a hangover. Perhaps that helps to explain why Germany shed Nazism to a degree that stunned the Allies at the time.

Taking a longer view, the NSFOs can be seen as only one case among many attempts to cope with chaos by stirring up waves of it, like building backfires in fighting forest fires. After all, the Germans lost World War II. Focusing on facets of their system is rather like becoming fascinated with the earlier successes of bankrupt speculators or the elegant style of unsuccessful surgeons. If more is transplanted than the gardener intends, that puts a very harsh light on the implications of Omer Bartov's conclusion that "the *Wehrmacht*'s troops did indeed come to accept the Nazi view of reality" and that "belief in the regime's propaganda . . . kept them fighting even when their units disintegrated and military discipline broke down" even though they were not dedicated National Socialists.[107] Did, then, the NSFOs amplify the chaos they were supposed to negate or actually keep the wobbling top of the Third Reich spinning longer? As tempting as it is to say, "probably a bit of both," chaos-complexity theory raises the possibility that leaving the NSFOs and Nazi indoctrination out of view in appraising the Wehrmacht's combat effectiveness over the last two generations was a far greater oversight than anyone realized.

NOTES

1. For example, Russel Lemmons, in *Goebbels and der Angriff* (Lexington: University of Kentucky Press, 1994), p. 6, attributes the "Chaos [that] characterized the early history of National Socialism in Berlin" to "the atmosphere of the capital after the revolution of 1918."

2. *The Horst Wessellied*—"Kamaraden die Rotefront und Reaktion erschossen" [Comrades Shot by the Red Front and Reactionaries].

3. Joochen von Lang and Claus Sibyll, *The Secretary—Martin Bormann: The Man Who Manipulated Hitler*, trans. Christa Armstrong and Peter White (New York: Random House, 1979), p. 254.

4. Some traced a direct lineage between the *Freikorps* and the Nazis, for example, Hans Ernest Fried, *The Guilt of the German Army* (New York: Macmillan, 1943), pp. 170–186.

5. Fried, *Guilt of the German Army*, pp. 162–163 and 342–343.

6. Ibid., p. 169; and B. H. Schwertfeger and E. D. Volkman, "The Rift between Front and Rear," *Deutsche Soldatenkunde* [*German Soldiers' Lore*], 1 (1937), pp. 523–535.

7. For example, see Walter Nehring, *Heere von Morgen: Ein Beitrag zur Frage des Heeres Motorisierung des Auslandes* [Army of Tomorrow: An Essay on the Question of the Mechanization of Foreign Armies] (Potsdam: L. Voggenerreiter, 1935), esp. pp. 63–65; and Heinz Guderian, *Panzer Leader*, trans. Constantine Fitzgibbon (London: Michael Joseph, 1952), p. 30.

8. For example, the characterizing of German troops as mindlessly deferential to authority in Operation OVERLORD fiftieth-anniversary media presentations.

9. See Paul M. Fitts, "German Applied Psychology During World War II," *American Psychologist*, 1:5 (1946), pp. 151–161.

10. A contemporaneous overview of that state of the art is Ladislas Farago et al., eds. *German Psychological Warfare: Survey and Bibliography* (New York: Arno Press, 1972 [1942]), esp. pp. 76–89.

11. Ibid., pp. 87–89; also see H. L. Anspacher and K. R. Nichols, "Selecting the Nazi Officers," *Infantry Journal*, 49:5 (November, 1941), pp. 44–48.

12. Emphasis on stern discipline survived the war, as in the exhortation that "Discipline must be maintained! Even the severest corrective measures should be applied," in Albert Kesselring et al., *Small Units Tactics Manual for Command and*

Combat Employment of Smaller Units (Heidelberg: Historical Command, European Command, 1952), p. 218.

13. See A. P. Young, ed., *The "X" Documents: The Secret History of Foreign Office Contacts with the German Resistance, 1937–39* (London: Andre Deutsch, 1974), esp. p. 77.

14. Quoted in Antulio J. Echeverria, "Moltke and the German Military Tradition: His Theories and Legacies," *Parameters*, 26:1 (Spring, 1996), p. 94.

15. Donald M. McKale, *The Nazi Party Courts: Hitler's Management of Conflict in His Movement, 1921–1945* (Lawrence: University Press of Kansas, 1974), pp. 171–172.

16. Manfred Messerschmidt, "The *Wehrmacht* and the *Volksgemeinschaft*," trans. Anthony Wells, *Journal of Contemporary History*, 18:4 (October, 1983), pp. 732–735.

17. Marlis G. Steinert, *Hitler's War and the Germans: Public Mood and Attitude*, ed. and trans. Thomas E. J. de Witt (Athens: Ohio University Press, 1977), pp. 11–13.

18. See Jay W. Baird, *The Mythical World of Nazi War Propaganda 1939–1945* (Minneapolis: University of Minnesota Press, 1974), p. 27.

19. Lucy S. Dawidowicz, *The War against the Jews 1933–1945* (New York: Harper and Row, 1975), pp. 114–115.

20. The Inter-Allied declaration signed at St. James' Palace in January 1942 referred to Germany's "policy of aggression" and "regime of terror" and set as war aims "the punishment, through the channel of organized justice, of those guilty or responsible ... whether they have ordered [war crimes], perpetrated them or participated in them," *Punishment for War Crimes* (New York: United Nations Information Office, 1942), pp. 5–6.

21. For example, see Charles T. Rogers, "Intuition: An Imperative of Command," *Military Review*, 54:3 (March, 1994), pp. 38–50.

22. For example, see Edward N. Peterson, *The Limits of Hitler's Power* (Princeton, N.J.: Princeton University Press, 1969), pp. 439–449.

23. A point noted by Omer Bartov in *Hitler's Army: Soldiers, Nazis and War in the Third Reich* (New York: Oxford University Press, 1991), p. 135; for an exception, see David Irving, *Hitler's War* (London: Hodder and Stoughton, 1977), pp. xi–xii.

24. See Robert J. Schneider, "Stress Breakdown in the Wehrmacht: Implications for Today's Army," in Gregory Belenky, ed., *Continuing Studies in Combat Psychiatry* (Westport, Conn.: Greenwood, 1987), pp. 87–101.

25. For example, see Omer Bartov, "The Myths of the Wehrmacht," *History Today*, 42:4 (April, 1992), pp. 32–36.

26. See B. H. Liddell Hart, *The Other Side of the Hill* (London: Cassell, 1951), pp. 284–287; Wladyslaw Anders, *Hitler's Defeat in Russia* (Chicago: Henry Regnery, 1953), pp. 78–79; for a contemporaneous view, see Curt Reiss, *The Self-Betrayed: Glory and Doom of the German Generals* (New York: G. P. Putnam's, 1942), pp. 346–367.

27. Eleanor Hancock, *National Socialist Leadership and Total War* (New York: St. Martin's, 1991), p. 123.

28. Sigrid Schulz, *Germany Will Try It Again* (New York: Reynal and Hitchcock, 1944), pp. 99–101.

29. See Paul M. Fitts, "German Applied Psychology During World War II," *American Psychologist*, 1:5 (1946), p. 155.

30. About one-third of Luftwaffe fighter losses in April–May–June 1944 were due to accidents, cf. Matthew Cooper, *The German Air Force, 1933–1945: An Anatomy of Failure* (London: Jane's Publishing Co., 1983), p. 348.

31. For example, the nervous breakdown of senior SS official Erich vom dem Bach-Zelewski and the suicide of the driver of a commander of an *Einsatzkommando;* for other examples, see Heinz Hohne, *The Order of the Death's Head: The Story of Hitler's SS,* trans. Richard Barry (New York: Ballantine, 1967).

32. Werner Baumbach, *Broken Swastika: The Defeat of the Luftwaffe,* trans. Frederick Holt (New York: Dorset, 1960 [1949]), pp. 184–186.

33. Reports of incidents appeared in the neutral and Allied press from 1942 on, for example, see Curt Riess, *The Self-Betrayed: Glory and Doom of the German Generals* (New York: G. P. Putnam's, 1942), p. 363. A succinct overview of the concerns regarding troop morale and education in the Army leading up to the creation of the NSFOs is Siegfried Grimm, . . . *der Bundesrepublik Treue zu Dienen: Die Geistige Rustung der Bundeswehr* [. . . to serve the Federal Republic Faithfully: The Spiritual Roots of the Bundeswehr] (Dusseldorf: Droste Verlag, 1970), pp. 28–33.

34. Marlis G. Steinert, *Hitlers Krieg und die Deutschen* [Hitler's War and the Germans] (Dusseldorf: Econ Verlag, 1970), p. 278.

35. Selecting officers by competitive objective criteria has been unpopular in armed forces, including those of the Western democracies. The argument that "intangible aspects of character" were "more important than aptitude or skill," in Fitts, "German Applied Psychology," pp. 153 and 160, has been echoed in defenses of subjective screening of candidates for the British Army's Brigade of Guards and U.S. service academies and in the use of superior-subordinate ratings as the exclusive promotion index.

36. See Ulfried Guenter, *The Profession of Psychology in Nazi Germany,* trans. Richard Holmes (Cambridge: Cambridge University Press, 1993), pp. 233–237.

37. An overview of that dichotomy is Dieter Rebentisch and Karl Teppe, eds., *Verwaltung Contra Menschenfuehrung im Staat Hitlers* (Gottingen: Vandenhoek and Ruprecht, 1986).

38. For example, see James J. Sheehan, "Totalitarianism and Everyday Life," *Arts and Sciences* (Northwestern University), Spring, 1978, pp. 7–10.

39. Siegfried Westphal, *Erinnerungen* (Mainz: Von Hase and Koehler Verlag, 1975), p. 53.

40. For comments on Nazism in the German Army officer corps by former senior Wehrmacht generals, see n.a., *Command and Commanders in Modern Warfare: Proceedings of the Second Military History Symposium, U.S. Air Force Academy, 2–3 May, 1968,* 2nd ed. (Washington, D.C.: U.S. Government Printing Office, 1971), pp. 170–172, 174, and 180–183.

41. See Elizabeth Noelle and Erich Peter Neumann, *The Germans: Public Opinion Polls 1947–1966* (Allersbach and Bonn: Verlag fur Demoskopie, 1967), pp. 195–206; Peterson, *Limits of Hitler's Power,* p. 449.

42. Baumbach, *Broken Swastika,* p. 56.

43. A contemporaneous, but useful, perspective is Alfred Vagts's *Hitler's Second Army* (Washington, D.C.: Infantry Journal Press, 1943).

44. Siegfried Westphal, *The German Army in the West* (London: Cassell, 1951), pp. 54–55.

45. Bernd Wegner, *The Waffen SS: Organization, Ideology and Function,* trans. Ronald Webster (Oxford: Basil Blackwell, 1990), p. 323–324 and 366.

46. Ibid., p. 366.

47. See Charles W. Sydnor, "The History of the *SS Totenkopfdivision* and the Postwar Mythology of the *Waffen SS*," *Central European History*, 6:4 (December, 1973), pp. 339–362.

48. Dietrich Orlow, *The History of the Nazi Party, 1933–1945* (Pittsburgh: University of Pittsburgh Press, 1973), pp. 460–461.

49. Lang and Sibyll, *The Secretary*, p. 255.

50. Walter Warlimont, *Inside Hitler's Headquarters*, trans. Richard Barry (New York: Praeger, 1964), p. 419.

51. Hans Martens, *General von Seydlitz, 1942–1945: Analyse eines Konfliktes* [General von Seydlitz, 1942–1945: Analysis of a Conflict] (Berlin: Von Kloeden, n.d., c. 1971), pp. 83–86.

52. For a full account, see Bodo Scheurig, *Free Germany: The National Committee and the League of German Officers*, trans. Herbert Arnold (Middletown: Wesleyan University Press, 1969); for recent overviews set in broader contexts, see Klemens Klemperer, *German Resistance against Hitler: The Search for Allies Abroad 1938–1945* (Oxford: Clarendon Press, 1992), pp. 244–249; and Franz Wilhelm Fiedler, *Fahnenflucht: der Soldat Zwischen Eid und Gewissen* [Desertion: The Soldier Between Oath and Conscience] (Munich: F. A. Herbig, 1993), pp. 82ff.

53. David Irving, *Hitler's War* (London: Hodder and Stoughton, 1977), p. 594; Lang and Sibyll, *The Secretary*, p. 258.

54. Soviet historians saw these groups as a sub-element of the anti-Hitlerite German front organized by Walter Ullbricht and other exiled German Communist leaders, for example, see M. M. Kozlov, *Velikaya Otechestvennaya Voinya 1941–1945 Entsiklopediya* [Great Patriotic War Encyclopedia 1941–1945] (Moscow: Sovyetskaya Entsiklopediya, 1985), pp. 484–485; for details, see Earl F. Ziemke, *Stalingrad to Berlin: The German Defeat in the East* (Washington, D.C.: Center for Military History, 1984), p. 149; and John Erickson, *The Road to Berlin* (Boulder, Colo.: Westview, 1983), pp. 92–93, 134, and 229.

55. Paulus did not join the group until after the failed coup against Hitler, when it had lost status in the Soviets' eyes, cf. Walter Goerlitz, *Paulus and Stalingrad*, trans. R. H. Stevens (New York: Citadel Press, 1963), pp. 289–290.

56. See Erich von Manstein, *Lost Victories* (Chicago: Henry Regnery, 1958), pp. 531–532.

57. Baird, *Mythical World*, p. 229.

58. Konrad Kwiet, "The Jewish Resistance," in David Clay Large, ed., *Contending with Hitler: Varieties of German Resistance in the Third Reich* (Washington, D.C.: German Historical Institute, 1991), p. 68.

59. For a transcript of Reinecke's briefing on the NSFO and discussion including Hitler, Keitel, and Bormann, see Gerhard L. Weinberg, "Adolf Hitler und der NS-Fuehrungsoffizier (NSFO)" [Adolf Hitler and the NS-Leadership Officer], *Viertelshefte fur Zeitschrift* [*Historical Quarterly*], 12:4 (October 1964), pp. 458; for perspective on the propagandistic tone of the NSFO program, see Kurt Zentner, *Illustrierte Geschichtes Zweiten Weltkriegs* (Munich: Sudwest Verlag, 1963), p. 481.

60. Some of his efforts were entered into evidence in the Nuremberg trials, cf. *Trial of Major War Criminals before the International Military Tribunal Nuremberg: Documents in Evidence 14 November 1945–10 October 1946* [Hereinafter referred to as *Nuremberg Trials*], vol. 34 (Nuremberg: International Military Tribunal, 1948), pp. 132–135.

61. Winfried Meyer, *Unternehmen Sieben: eine Rettungsaktion fur vom Holocaust Bedrohte aus dem Amt Ausland/ Abwehr im OKW* [Operation Seven: A Rescue Operation for Those Threatened by the Holocaust, Out of the Foreign Office / Secret Service in OKW] (Frankfurt: Meyer, Winfried, 1993), p. 109.

62. Helmut Kraminick et al., *The Anatomy of the SS State*, trans. Richard Barry, Marion Jackson, and Dorothy Long (New York: Walker and Co., 1965), pp. 72 and 523–524; and Gerald Reitlinger, *The SS: Alibi of a Nation, 1922–1945* (New York: Viking Press, 1968), pp. 177–179.

63. Excerpts from Nuremberg Tribunal proceedings, quoted in Alexander Werth, *Russia at War 1941–1945* (New York: Avon Books, 1964), pp. 644–645.

64. *Nuremberg Trial Documents*, vol. 21, p. 549.

65. Reitlinger, *SS: Alibi of a Nation*, p. 385.

66. Paul Goebbels, *Final Entries 1945: The Diaries of Joseph Goebbels*, ed. Hugh Trevor Roper, ed. trans. Martin Secker (New York: Avon Books, 1978), p. 273.

67. Ibid.

68. *Trials of War Criminals by the Nuremberg Military Tribunals Under Control Council Law No. 10*, vol. 10 (Washington, D.C.: U.S. Government Printing Office, 1950), pp. 648–661; Israel Gutman, ed., *Encyclopedia of the Holocaust*, vol. 3 (New York: Macmillan Publishing Co., 1990), pp. 1194–1195.

69. Manfred Messerschmidt, *Die Wehrmacht in N.S.–Staat Zeit der Indoktrination* [Indoctrination of the Wehrmacht in the NS-State Era] (Hamburg: R. V. Decker, 1969), p. 487; also see Rudolf Hamann, *Armee in Abseits?* (Hamburg: Hoffman & Campe, 1972), p. 42.

70. For example, Bartov, *Hitler's Army*, p. 145; and Ian Kershaw, "The Hitler Myth," *History Today*, 35:11 (November, 1985), p. 29.

71. See Robert L. Quinett, "The German Army Confronts the NSFO," *Journal of Contemporary History*, 13:1 (January, 1978), pp. 53–64.

72. One exception is the Nazi zealot in the film *The Enemy Below*.

73. For varying perspectives on the NSFOs' influence see Albert Seaton, *The German Army, 1933–1945* (New York: St. Martin's Press, 1982), pp. 219 and 230–232; Steinert, *Hitlers Krieg und die Deutschen*, pp. 37, 540–541, and 552–560; Burkhart Muller-Hillebrand, *Die Zweifrontkrieg* [The Two Front War] (Frankfurt-am-Main: E. S. Mittler, 1969), vol. 3, pp. 165–167; Hamann, *Armee in Abseits?*, p. 42; and Quinett, "The German Army Confronts the *NSFO*," pp. 53–64.

74. For example, see John Erickson, *The Road to Berlin* (Boulder: Westview, 1983), pp. 84–85.

75. For a sampling of such views, see B. H. Liddell Hart, *The Other Side of the Hill* (London: Cassell, 1951), pp. 425–427; for a perspective on the influence of Hitler Youth training, see Ian Kershaw, *The "Hitler Myth": Image and Reality in the Third Reich* (Oxford: Clarendon Press, 1987).

76. Edward Shils and Morris Janowitz, "Cohesion and Disintegration in the *Wehrmacht* in World War II," *Public Opinion Quarterly*, 12:2 (Summer, 1948), pp. 285–286.

77. Hancock, *National Socialist Leadership*, p. 89.

78. Steinert, *Hitler's War*, pp. 296, 540–541.

79. Gerald Fleming, *Hitler and the Final Solution* (Berkeley: University of California Press, 1984), p. 53; for detailed extracts see Irving, *Hitler's War*, pp. 594–632.

80. According to Manstein, in Erich von Manstein, *Lost Victories*, ed. and trans. Anthony G. Powell (Chicago: Henry Regnery, 1958), pp. 511–512; also see Alex Stahlberg, *Bounden Duty: The Memoirs of a German Officer 1933–1945*, trans. Patricia Crampton (London: Brassey's, 1990), pp. 323–325. Von Manstein praised and deprecated the Waffen SS, Hoehne, *The Order of the Death's Head*, p. 494, and later claimed he did not recall signing a field order in 1941 that began, "The Jewish-Bolshevist system must be exterminated," Alexander Werth, *Russia at War 1941–1945* (New York: Avon Books, 1964), p. 646.

81. In re von Manstein, see John Mendelson, ed., *Nuremberg War Crimes Trials: Records of Case 9* (Washington, D.C.: National Archives and Records Service, 1978), p. 272.

82. For example, see Letters *Section, The New York Times*, December 8, 1996, p. 8, sec. 4, p. 14.

83. For example, General Otto Remer; see "Nazi Who Foiled Anti-Hitler Coup Dies," *Houston Chronicle*, October 7, 1987, p. 16A [Reuters].

84. Reitlinger, *SS: Alibi of a Nation*, p. 337.

85. Burkhart Muller-Hillebrand, *Der Zweifront Krieg*, vol. 3 (Frankfurt-am-Main: E. S. Mittler, 1969), pp. 165–166.

86. For a detailed overview, see Hans Kissel, *Der Deutsche Volkssturm 1944/45: Eine Territoriale Miliz in Rahmen der Landesverteidigung* [The German Volksturm 1944/45: A Territorial Militia in the Framework of National Defense] (Frankfurt: E. S. Mittler and Sohn Verlag, 1962).

87. Walter Hubatsch, ed., *Hitlers Weisungen fur die Kriegfuehrung: Dokuments der Oberkommando des Wehrmacht* [Hitler's Instruction for Conducting the War: Documents of the Wehrmacht High Command] (Frankfurt-am-Main: Bernard and Graefe Verlag fur Wehrwesen, 1962), pp. 259–260.

88. Hohne, *The Order of the Death's Head*, pp. 612–614.

89. Steinert, *Hitler's War*, p. 302.

90. Wolfgang Schumann, et al., eds., *Deutschland im zweiten Weltkrieg* [Germany in the Second World War], vol. 5 (Cologne: Pahl-Rugenstein), p. 214.

91. See Fritz, *Frontsoldaten* [Frontline Soldiers], pp. 199–201.

92. Frido von Senger und Etterlin, *Neither Fear Nor Hope*, trans. George Malcolm (New York: E. P. Dutton, 1964), pp. 294–295.

93. Messerschmidt, "The *Wehrmacht* and the *Volkgemeinschaft*," p. 735.

94. Dietrich Orlow, *The History of the Nazi Party, 1933–1945* (Pittsburgh: University of Pittsburgh Press, 1973), p. 481.

95. See Edward Shils and Morris Janowitz, "Cohesion and Disintegration in the *Wehrmacht* in the Second World War," *Public Opinion Quarterly*, 12:2 (Summer, 1948), pp. 304ff.

96. Quoted in Charles H. Allen, Jr., *Heusinger of the Fourth Reich* (New York: Marzani and Munsell, 1963), p. 153.

97. Erich von Manstein, *Lost Victories* (Chicago: Henry Regnery, 1958), p. 519.

98. Trevor Roper, *Final Entries*, p. 156.

99. Siegfried Westphal, *The German Army in the West* (London: Cassell, 1951), p. 59.

100. Grimm, *der Bundesrepublik treu zu Dienen*, pp. 31–32.

101. For example, see Donald Abenheim, *Reforging the Iron Cross: The Search for Tradition in the West German Armed Forces* (Princeton, N.J.: Princeton University Press, 1990).

102. Alan Bullock, *Hitler: A Study in Tyranny* (New York: Bantam Books, 1961), p. 526.

103. For details of a case in World War II, see Mark Mazower, "Military Violence and National Socialist Values: The *Wehrmacht* in Greece, 1941–1944," *Part and Present*, no. 134 (February, 1992), pp. 129–158.

104. *Nuremberg Trials*, vol. 21, p. 37.

105. For example, the liberalism of Gneisenau and Scharnhorst and the defections of Clausewitz and Yorck, to the reactionaryism of Manteuffel's and Roon's reforms, the Zabern affair, and Ludendorff's complicity with Hitler.

106. See Herbert Jaeger, *Verbrechen unter totalitaerer Herrschaft: Studien zur nationalsozialistischen Gewaltkriminalitaet* [Crimes Under Totalitarian Authority: Studies of National Socialist Criminal Process] (Frankfurt am Main: Suhrkamp Verlag, 1981).

107. Omer Bartov, *Hitler's Army: Soldiers, Nazis and War in the Third Reich* (New York: Oxford University Press, 1991), p. 144.

6

Grisly Fractals: Tracing the Holocaust's Roots and Branches

The *Endloesung*, what the Nazis called the mass extermination of Jews and other "subhumans" and which became widely known as the Holocaust in the 1960s, was far less chaotic than it has been portrayed in popular culture since World War II. Indeed, it was too well organized. The sense of disarray is due to the newsreels and photos of the camps when they were overrun by the Allies. There was, of course, a great deal of chaos around the edges of it, as well as that stirred up afterward by analysts trying to trace the origins of Holocaust back into history and into the depths of the human mind. Those vortices have not only made it more difficult to determine why and how all that happened,[1] but have also blurred the boundaries between the *Endloesungapparat* (the Holocaust infrastructure and process) and the inner chaos of the Nazi Party and administrative structure of the NS Staat, as well as the role of Allied and neutral nations, in helping the Endloesung along its course.

As the bubbles of evidence keep rising to the surface, looking at all those convolutions and contradictions makes it easy to understand why some have argued that the Holocaust is not tractable to effective historical analysis and explanation. For example, the Nuremberg Laws of 1935 put German Jews beyond the pale of citizenship, but the complicated rules they set forth enfolded vast numbers of *mischlinge* (Germans of "mixed blood") into the *Volksgemeinschaft*.[2] In the early 1940s, as the trains rolled and furnaces flared, Nazi leaders argued about whether to exterminate or exploit Jews. The hard-liners raged at attempts, including some by Nazi Party members, to rescue Jewish "pets" from the scythe of the Endloesung, as many Germans found themselves trying to sort out how they felt about Jews in general versus those they knew. Some ambivalence and confusion is also due to chaos at the inner boundaries in German society. Despite centuries-long isolation in ghettos, Jews and Germans were not so sociologically or historically distinct as Nazi propagandists insisted when they tried to erase the traces of cordiality and creative fusion between German and Jewish culture in the arts, science, and society.[3] In Germany, as in other European nations, such links were closer and tolerance was greater in the upper classes, but so was the virulence that led Bernard Lazare, after the Dreyfus affair in the late 1800s, to describe French anti-Semitism as universal, and as old as the Jewish faith.[4] Plagues and other natural misfortunes had often been blamed on Jews in earlier times, and Passion Plays kept alive the image of Jews as "Christ killers." When large numbers began to leave the ghettos of Europe from the French Revolution onward, scapegoating continued. In 1807, for example, Prussian aristocrats, after being defeated by Napoleon at the Battle of Jena, vented their fury on Jews; and anti-Semitism flavored the work of Marx, the historian Treitschke,[5] and even so dedicated a rationalist as the Prussian military theorist Karl von Clausewitz. In a letter to his wife from Poland in 1814, he described "Dirty German Jews, swarming like vermin in the dirt and misery" and wrote, "A thousand times, I thought if only fire would destroy this whole anthill so that this unending filth were changed by the clean flame into clean ashes."[6]

In Central Europe, from the 1840s on, much was made of the fact that Jews were overrepresented in a few professions,[7] and little allowance was made for the fact that for many generations, Jews did work that was forbidden or anathema to Christians. The moneylender stereotype in Shakespeare's Shylock and Dickens's Fagin ran back to medieval times, when Jews were denied both noble and peasant status. As de-ghettoization progressed, they were allowed some marginal opportunities in the military, civil service, the judiciary,[8] and manufacturing, but they became more visible in finance and the arts. They emerged as intellectuals and artists, drawing on the strong literary and intellectual traditions of Judaism.[9] The long-standing anti-Semitism of peasants, a blend of religious prejudice[10] and resentment toward Jews who served as middlemen in the economy,[11] was blended with modern nationalism in Austrian and German anti-Semitic political movements in the late nineteenth century. Some Jews, in the tradition of the Middle Ages, continued to enter unpopular businesses or activities or to pioneer new ones, most notably department stores. Encounters with persistent social snobbery and open hostility led others to join political movements that promised major social change, tolerance, and opportunity, although there, too, they were sometimes rejected.

As a result, from the late eighteenth century onward, Jews were widely seen as a major destabilizing force throughout Europe, partly because they were out of phase with rising nationalism and racism and partly because their increasing visibility in society threatened those threatened by social change, especially the trend toward secularization. Visions of Jewish intrigue and conspiracy, including myths of international networks and ritual murders, offered simple explanations for the intricate interplay of powerful but less tangible forces such as population growth, mass migrations, industrialization, mass-marketing, and public education. Anti-Semitism was bolstered by bizarre theories churned up in the wake of the scientific revolution that seemed to validate old prejudices. The rise of literacy and the revolution in communication disseminated those images, allowing many otherwise powerless to feel superior to those who were visibly different. Racial and ethnic stratification also gained legitimacy from European-centered imperialism, which reached its final flowering in the late nineteenth and early twentieth centuries. Hitler's concept of the *Herrenvolk* (master race) was based on his stilted perception of the British Empire, including the khaki uniforms, Sam Browne belts, and jackboots. Since the Nazis defined Slavs, Jews, and other ethnic groups of eastern and Central Europe as potential underlings, their anti-Semitism seemed to be one thread in a tapestry of group hatred, not unique to National Socialism. As a result, the scale and virulence of their particular version of prejudice blended into a larger tapestry of prejudice, one not confined to Europe. From the middle of the 1800s, eugenics and pseudo-scientific racism became primary themes as politicians increasingly harnessed hatred in electioneering and propaganda and fueled various forms of racial segregation throughout the world, including the United States. Aside from the brief interlude of Japanese conquests, 1942–1945, the broad pattern of whites ruling yellow, brown, and black peoples finally began to crumble in the mid-1950s, although fragments of that deeply entrenched hostility survived in many countries to the end of the twentieth century. On a parallel and often convergent track, as Jews became a visible if very small minority in the urban middle classes in the major cities of eastern and Central Europe,[12] popular anxieties about Jewish influence in the media grew far out of proportion to the actual state of affairs—as they did in the United States in the 1930s and 1940s and in the 1990s.[13] The fear of their eagerness and intelligence was reflected in the term *intelligentsia*, a Russian term used by the Nazis and others as an anti-Semitic code word.

Intellectual chaos also resulted from the Nazis' ransacking history for bits of data, which they wove into political fantasies. For example, they held Oliver Cromwell in high regard as a prototypical modern dictator, looking past the fact that the Lord Protector brought Jews back into England, centuries after they had been expelled by Edward III. And they drew anti-Semitic stereotypes from such diverse images as the fictional *Jud Suess*, pseudo-scientific, anthropologically based racist typologies, pornography, conspiracy theories, and Jewish involvement in political radical movements. In that era of tabloid politics, themes presented in newspapers, posters, pamphlets, books, and films by the Nazis and other Fascistoid factions across Europe between the world wars were drawn from the broad range of history.[14]

There were other inconsistencies. For example, although Hitler was from Austria—the most anti-Semitic region of *Grossdeutschland* (Greater Germany)—and was raised as a Catholic and although the Papacy was ambivalent toward the Axis and protective of some Nazis after World War II, Catholic regions of Germany gave National Socialism less electoral support during the Weimar era than did other regions. As the Nazis layered fresh rationales for anti-Semitism onto old ones, they stressed the differences between ghettoized Jews' language, religion, and customs and the surrounding Christian society, even though such distinctions had been fading for over a century. Beyond that nostalgic fury, as noted earlier, many blamed the Jews for the 1918 defeat and the revolutions and mutinies that swept across Germany at that time. The "stab-in-the-back" myth[15] was bolstered by a Bolshevik diplomat's claim that he had paid a major Jewish politician to support the November Revolution in Berlin.[16] Many Germans accepted the rightists' depiction of the Weimar Republic as a product of the "Diktat" peace forced on a nation undermined by left-wing elements and Jews, an animus reinforced by the Republic's constitution giving Jews full citizenship for the first time in German history.[17] A prominent postwar Jewish radical activist, Rosa Luxemburg,[18] was murdered by nationalist officers during the suppression of the 1919 Spartakist uprising, which she led with Karl Liebknecht. Throughout the world at that time, many saw Russian Bolshevism, several of whose leaders were Jewish, as an international revolutionary conspiracy; some, untroubled by the contradiction, linked their fears to the older model of a cabal of Jewish financial elites bent on world dominion depicted in the forged *Protocols of the Elders of Zion*.[19]

A similar increase in anxiety was visible in exaggerated perceptions of Jewish power and influence, despite the fact that relatively few Jews held key positions in German society. The pattern was uneven. Although many were lawyers, for example, very few were judges or held high rank in the civil service.[20] The best known of the latter, Walter Rathenau, was killed after World War I in one of a series of rightist political murders. After World War II, a Nazi-era diplomat reflected the perspective of those earlier times by claiming that "Intelligent Jews had admitted before 1933 that with the great opportunities they had in the Weimar Republic they had overdrawn their account."[21] That sense of very little being far too much was also expressed by Alfred Rosenberg in his memoirs, in which he claimed that "The war [sic] against Jewry came about because an alien people on German soil arrogated the political and spiritual leadership of the country, and believing itself triumphant, flaunted it brazenly."[22] Beyond arguments that Jews failed to "stay in their place"—at the margins of German society—were many louder rumbles of the coming storm. For all its rambling coarseness, Hitler's autobiographical political testament *Mein Kampf* (my battle) was far less crude than Nazi tracts like Julius Streicher's pornographic newspaper *Der Sturmer*.

Such vitriol was not exclusive to the National Socialists. Propagandists of other political factions used grotesque caricatures of Jews to attack Bolshevism, Socialism, and pacifism,[23] and the Weimar flag was often depicted as a Jewish banner.[24] The slogan *"Deutschland erwache!"* (Germany, Wake Up!) emblazoned on the Nazi Brown Shirts' standards had been a popular code phrase for anti-Semitism since the early nineteenth century. General Erich von Ludendorff, head of the German General Staff at the end of World War I, was a major proponent of Jewish conspiracy theories. After suffering a nervous breakdown and fleeing to Sweden at the end of 1918, he returned and marched with Hitler in the abortive coup in Munich in 1923. While Ludendorff would be singled out for his eldritch view of a "world republic" being formed by "supernational wire-pullers"—Jews, Freemasons, and the Vatican— such fantasies and rabid sloganeering abounded in German political life for generations before the Weimar era.[25] Images of cabals and conspiracies gave form to the vortex of massive impersonal forces that threatened and sometimes shattered the economic security of millions throughout the 1920s and early 1930s.[26] During the last half of the 1920s, desecrations of their cemeteries led Jewish war veterans to refute charges of slacking in World War I,[27] but such arguments failed to brake the nationalist extremism sweeping through the universities, students and faculty alike, as well as the courts. Some rightist radicals, like Ernst von Salomon, who were jailed briefly for political murder found it easy to justify their crimes on the basis of patriotism, as did some judges.

Throughout the 1920s, as the fluctuating turmoil wore on the nerves of a generation of Germans already severely jangled by defeat and humiliation, the Allies' hope of implanting liberalism in Germany

faded. Amid what many observers labeled chaos, as Saul Friedlander
pointed out, the "involvement of Jews in the revolutionary movements
of the war and the postwar period" became an "antagonizing element
of the greatest significance."[28] The shift in stereotype from capitalist to
Bolshevik villain was entwined with other social anxieties, including
fears of genetic "pollution" as Jews "passed" as Gentiles[29] and a long-
standing association of Jews with disease and filth in German semantics
since the time of the ghettos.[30] The concerns about cleanliness and
epidemiology, especially venereal infection, that increased throughout
the world following the discovery of microbial infection in the 1880s
were central themes in Nazi propagandists' depictions of Jews as lustful
predators. Sexual exploitation of Gentile women by Jews, one of
Hitler's preoccupations,[31] was mirrored in the torture of some concentration camp inmates.[32] The Nazis' raising of legal barriers and sharp
distinctions in the mid-1930s was in reaction to the steady increase in
Jews marrying non-Jews,[33] which they saw as "polluting" their "racial
purity,"[34] even though that was also a matter of concern to many Jews
who saw such assimilation eroding their cultural identity.[35] In the late
1920s and 1930s, German attitudes toward Jews ranged from cordiality
to apathy to complicity or involvement in street bullying, roundups,
and re-ghettoization, on through to attempts to save individual Jews.
As noted earlier, that ambiguity was evident in the decision of those
who conspired against Hitler in 1944 to steer clear of the *Judenfrage* (the
Jewish question).[36]

How, then, did that bubbling cauldron, which many saw as another
version of chronic anti-Semitism in Europe, boil over into the Endloesung? It means little to assert that chaos begat chaos, if the actual
generative process remains invisible. Was it the result of a myriad of
causal lines crossing at one point, one most or all had crossed before,
but with nowhere so terrible a result? We now sense, half a century later,
that the Nazis tried to keep it secret, but which Nazis did so? Were they
so successful that some aspects were erased and will never be revealed?
Why did they try to do that, given their open statements of intent from
the early 1920s on? From 1935 on, with the publication of the
Nuremberg Laws, anti-Semitism was German state policy and a mainstay of Nazi propaganda, popular culture, and indoctrination. Were
attempts to keep the Endloesung secret mainly intended to keep their
victims off guard and much easier to round up and transport or to
prevent the Allies from realizing what was happening, under the assumption that they would try to stop it? The Allies knew a good deal
about it as it unfolded, and so did many Germans, but how many knew
and looked away, as opposed to taking part? How much were these
reactions due to fear, obedience, or enthusiasm? Some historians have

agreed with the claims of Speer and other Nazi principals and military leaders at the Nuremberg war crimes trials that most Germans saw the Nazi restructuring of life in the Third Reich as a source of surety, order, and pride and Hitler as a benevolent and paternal figure.[37] While some critics conceded that, on the eve of World War II, Konrad Heiden envisioned the roots of that social contract rising from "the emptiness of an existence which lacked a larger significance" and labeled it an alliance with the Devil.[38] An appropriate metaphor, to the extent that the Holocaust was the product of Hitler's and some of his colleagues' deliberately arousing and channeling the human reflex to demonize and kill and torture, in an amalgam with high technology and state authority.

Some of the more lurid aspects of the Hitlerzeit, like the top Nazis' fascination with the occult and sadists' fascination with the Third Reich's symbols and trappings since World War II, have been pushed off to the margins of serious analysis into the realm of tabloid history, or wholly discounted. That is understandable enough, considering the dangers of sliding into devil and conspiracy theories of causation, but chaos-complexity theory raises the question of whether anything can be labeled as trivial in a domain where things are sensitive to initial conditions. As noted earlier, anti-Semitism was one among many ferocious anxieties that emerged as racial and ethnic identities began to crumble throughout the modern world. At the same time that rabblerousing and baiting minorities became common in Europe—and in Britain and the United States—science was twisted to support stereotyping and stratification, from Freud and Pavlov on the left to Darwin and Mendel on the right. Bizarre polemics and crank theories were so common by the time that World War II began that extremists' calls for exterminating Jews or other "subhumans" were often dismissed outside the Axis orbit as inconsequential ravings. In 1937, for example, when a leader of the Iron Guard movement in Rumania urged that the "Jewish problem" be "solved by wholesale murder,"[39] very few serious-minded people among the western democracies took it seriously. Nor would they have believed a historian, journalist, policy maker, or an often successful seer like H. G. Wells, who had set forth a detailed accurate prediction of the unfolding of the Holocaust. It was like so many other sudden lurches—or phase-changes—in the flow of history that were not predicted by experts or those in power.[40] Scholars' tendency to focus on more mechanistic aspects that left a documentary trail, while also understandable, leaves a great deal out of consideration.

The major difference of opinion among historians of the Hitler era is over just how it began.[41] The "intentionalist" school contends that Hitler and/or other top Nazis deliberately made a key decision that began the Holocaust, while "functionalists," as Christopher Browning has suggested, see its origins in a "gradual, almost imperceptible" increase in momentum produced by the aggregate of attitudes, impulses, and incremental decisions and acts within the Third Reich's bureaucracy.[42] Some scholars have suggested that the wheels only began to roll toward mass extermination when emigration from Germany was blocked by the coming of World War II, thwarting Nazi plans to ship Jews to Palestine and Madagascar. On the other hand, some moves were made in that direction before the war, including the euthanasia program in Germany and, very soon after fighting began, mass executions of "Jewish-Bolshevist"[43] elements in the wake of the Wehrmacht's conquests in the East. Of course, for individual victims, it did not matter whether they were killed by a crucial high-level decision or by whatever process flowed "by degrees" to mass executions and the building of the death camps, most notably the one at Auschwitz-Birkenau.[44]

So far, "Intentionalists" have not found a "smoking gun." While that leaves them in a cleft stick, that is also true of the "revisionists" who have denied that the Holocaust happened. Even if the Nazis had prepared documents spelling out such actions, it seems obvious that those records would have been the first to be destroyed in the face of imminent defeat. Himmler, after all, in his 1943 speech to the Nazi hierarchy at Posen, taped and related by various witnesses, described the Endloesung as "a never-recorded and never-to-be-recorded page of glory in our history."[45] Nevertheless, thanks to the many pockets of traditional German administrative thoroughness within the bureaucratic chaos of the NS Staat, enough evidence of lower-level processes survived to provide clear traces of the vast undertaking. Claiming the Holocaust was a hoax requires denying at one sweep such tangible circumstantial evidence, from all the statements of murderous intent made by various Nazis from the early 1920s onward to the testimony of defendants and witnesses at the Nuremberg war crimes trials, during which defense attorneys did not challenge the validity of prosecution evidence. Beyond that lies the question of who had the gigantic resources, will, and perfect foresight required in preparing an effective hoax. Forged evidence would have to stand up under the scrutiny of historians for centuries and mesh perfectly with administrative practices and materials of the NS Staat. Not only would hoaxers have needed virtually perfect knowledge of Nazi bureaucratic processes, including materials, but would have had to begin that effort just before the war or immediately after the war began so that it would mesh perfectly with public announcements and journalists' reports, as well as bureaucratic flow. But why bother? The decision to commit the extensive and scarce talent resources to do all of that would have required certainty of an Allied victory at a time when that was not at all a sure thing. An Axis victory would very likely have wiped out traces of such fabrication—and put its architects at special risk. If notional hoaxers foresaw the future so clearly, that would have been in sharp contrast with their inability to do so in so many other cases. Since any hitch, break, or discrepancy would have brought down the intricate house of cards of a hoax, a virtual army of forgers, printers, ink, and paper makers would have been required, along with exact, continuous, and complete intelligence about the minute workings of the Nazi bureaucracy and security apparatus.

Who, then, would have done that, and why? Since the Soviet Union was a virtual ally of Nazi Germany from 1939 to 1941 and such an elaborate effort was well beyond the capacity of faction-ridden Jewish groups, who had enough resources and motivation to structure such a deception that would risk monumental embarrassment? The U.S. government was just putting its toe in the pond of the strategic intelligence business. Many among the American elites were isolationist, and some were anti-Semitic. No major constituency favored taking concerted action to help the Nazis' victims or refugees. Until Pearl Harbor, most Americans opposed going to war or lowering immigration restrictions, and many were anti-Semitic.

Who else, then? France had the resources for such an effort, and anti-Semitism was stronger there, especially in the officer corps; but most of it was occupied by the Nazis from 1940 to 1944, and the Vichy government actively persecuted Jews. Basically, then, only the British had the resources to undertake such an effort, but did they have a reason to do it? They had been badly burned for their World War I propaganda campaign. A Holocaust hoax would have consumed substantial resources in a nation approaching bankruptcy in 1940 when Britain faced Hitler and Mussolini for a year all alone. If detected during the war, it would have been a propaganda disaster. But why would they have done it? As World War II began, they were squabbling with Zionist groups over Palestine and were concerned about the large Muslim populations within the British Empire, some of them close to oil supplies, and Turkish neutrality. If the Axis had won the war, such a hoax would have been irrelevant, and if the Germans had occupied Britain, it would have been a massive liability. Why, then, would the British have tried to conjure up a vast array of bureaucratic minutiae that required virtually perfect orchestration and meshing of thousands of details to avoid detection, but which offered no clear advantage or purpose, and which was pregnant with major embarrassment? Even a single discontinuity or admission or detection of involvement of a single participant would have brought down such a house of cards.

There are many other puzzles in that hall of mirrors. Why, in expending all that effort, would notional hoaxers not forge evidence of a "smoking gun" that would have assigned specific guilt? Why generate literal mountains of tedious documents requiring exhaustive sifting for circumstantial evidence? At first glance, Holocaust denial arguments seem to be aimed at the credulous and unsophisticated at a time when the World War II generation is passing away, and historical education is pretty thin. Beyond many cases of deliberate historical distortion and myth-making, popular perceptions of the past have been shaped more and more by journalism, fiction, and the arts than "serious" academic history. Relatively few have a sophisticated sense of the complexity of power processes. Ironically, Holocaust scholars' tendency to frame elaborate arguments in a scholarly format and to devote their energies to debates among themselves has abandoned much ground to "revisionists" by underscoring the uncertainties of historical interpretation. Some have argued that the Endloesung stands outside the flow of history and was a unique aberration, or "ultimate mystery," since treating it as one historical event of a particular type diminishes its iconic significance and power.[46] To understand such concern about "progressively more sterile debates . . . [that] drain the subject of either emotion or a wider philosophical dimension,"[47] we need only scan the many definitions of the Holocaust and the range of dates between 1939 and 1942 that various historians have set as its point of inception.[48]

The Functionalist–Intentionalist polarity and all the grappling with incomplete evidence and contradictions highlight problems that historians routinely deal with in their craft. Here, too, like biologists who kill to dissect, their abstracting, categorizing, selection, and analysis tend to blur the gritty texture of events. Yet much horror still shines through, and some of it because of ill winds. In the 1970s, just when the Holocaust seemed to be fading toward academic abstraction with the thinning of the ranks of survivors and witnesses, the appearance of Holocaust deniers brought it back into the spotlight. There is no way to be sure if it will eventually become a dim historical benchmark, like the leveling of Carthage, the sack of Rome and Byzantium, the St. Bartholomew's Day Massacre, or the slaughter of Armenians in World War I. At the end of the twentieth century, looking back across the intervening landscape of fifty years, the Holocaust, a looming peak in the foreground in 1945, now appears as one of a range of horrors that includes Cambodia, Indonesia, Rwanda, the Balkans, and Stalin's and Mao's enormities.[49] While placing it in that array of mega-atrocities may appear to diminish the gravitas of the Endloesung, it does undercut attempts to suggest that reports of Nazi crimes were trumped-up exaggerations because such horrors were beyond the range of likely human behavior.

That leads us to the farthest and most minute branches of the causal fan of the Holocaust—all the individual human beings, including those who designed it, set it in motion, and carried it out, its victims, and spectators in Germany and all over the world who turned a blind eye or worked against it, each to a varying degree. Since there is no way to distill all that and as arrays of suggested causes, anecdotes, and statistics overlap, but not exactly or completely, it is not surprising that analysts have framed broad explanations, like assertions made from the time the Nazi Party first appeared that its leaders were neurotic and psychotic. Beyond providing a virtual insanity defense, that clashes with the claims of the Nuremberg Tribunal prosecutors that the Third Reich's top military and industrial leaders and bureaucrats were criminal conspirators, that is, essentially sane men who were guilty of making the wrong choice. Trying to sort out "normal" and "sane" Germans in the Hitler era leads to another double-bind, a "Catch-22," since it is not easy to accept the possibility that sane persons could have been dedicated Nazis, or have "merely" done their duty under those ghastly circumstances. Again, individuals made all kinds of choices, and shadings and contradictions abounded. While some Nazi leaders tried to slow the momentum toward extermination,[50] Jews in the ghettos' *Judenrat* (community councils) screened Jews for transportation, and others in the death camps participated in the extermination process to survive. That revival of the "old calumny of the Jews somehow having murdered themselves"[51] served to blur the fact that a great many Germans were involved in rounding up, moving, detaining, killing, and disposing of millions of people. In the parlance of management science, that massive effort required planning, managing, coordinating, and controlling. It depended not merely on compliance but the effort and initiative of many beyond the Nazi inner circle, from large numbers of transport and industrial workers to the engineer who designed crematoria at Auschwitz. Not a Nazi party member, that engineer later claimed that he had "only respected and acted according to the laws of my country,"[52] much in the spirit of a *Waffen SS* veteran who expressed regret over the concentration camps but deemed a former superior who later headed the Dachau camp as a "true commander for his homeland" whose "life overall was a positive one."[53]

From the very detached perspective of what might be deemed antisocial science, just how did that work? What were the crucial variables and causes? Or was there a chaos within those who acted that was created by that of the Nazi regime and reverberated and amplified? What should be made of German historians' attempts to relativize the

Holocaust by comparing it favorably with the Stalinist terror,[54] when there are no scientific gauges or indices by which we can measure those assertions—or challenge them with absolute certainty? Where, indeed, do logic, meaning, and truth lie in all that—or do they lie somewhere beyond the limits of reason and meaning, incomprehensible and formless? Did Nazism bubble out of the cauldron of history? Were, as a senior SS officer, Erich von dem Bach-Zelewski, suggested at Nuremberg, the seeds of Nazism born of Germany's somber heritage war, militarism, defeat, occupation, atrocity, and humiliation? When he argued that "If for years, for decades, a doctrine is preached to the effect that the slave race is an inferior race, that the Jews are not even human beings, then an explosion of this sort is inevitable,"[55] that assertion was only one hypothesis of many. Helen Fein, for example, pointed out the bewildering contradiction of the Nazis trying to remove Jews from German life even though anti-Semitism was the unifying "mortar" that made "the blocks of National Socialism cohere."[56] That weakens the case for the Holocaust arising from military defeat and frustration in 1941–1942, since when the Final Solution began in earnest, somewhere in late 1941 or early 1942, the Nazis seemed to hold the upper hand in all theaters of war. When anti-Semitic propaganda rose to a polemical apex in 1942 with the release of the films *Der Ewige Jude* and *Jud Suess*, it seemed to be an effort by the regime to divert "the population from the economic and social measures that the regime had promised but had failed to deliver."[57] But Nazi attempts to link Jews with Germany's enemies had little impact, and there was substantial resistance to the *Endloesung* within the government and Nazi Party beyond the exploitation of Jewish skilled laborers in the war machine,[58] and opposition among the public at large as well.[59] Despite the Nazis' shrill polemics and bullying of Jews on the street, there was no precedent for the relentless, methodical industrialized slaughter. Himmler's anguish in telling senior *Wehrmacht* commanders about the Holocaust may look like crocodile tears, but why did the Nazis, who never shied away from promising to annihilate them try to keep those deeds secret? The Warsaw uprising of 1943 offers a suggestion that if it was due to fear of concerted resistance, that was a valid concern.[60]

However shocked and guilty any individual German felt when the grisly images of the Holocaust became public, many in the Allied nations also realized that things were done and not done on their side of the battle lines that compounded the Nazis' crimes—Stalin's complicity with Hitler from 1939 to 1941, American isolationism, Anglo-American restrictions on immigration, and the western Allies' faltering and cautious strategy. Claims made toward the end of the twentieth century that the Allies strove to end the Holocaust by bending every effort to win the war quickly notwithstanding, there is very little evidence of attempting to align strategy and military efforts with that goal in the high councils of power. It is extremely puzzling that Churchill did not mention the Holocaust in his war memoirs, and neither Roosevelt not Stalin left any kind of testament. Even a half-century later, ongoing revelations of sordid dealings of various nations and interests during the Holocaust added an edge to the question of Allied apathy and complicity—and to David Schoenbaum's provocative hypothesis that "there might be a Third Reich in every industrialized society." The full evidence is apparently not yet in hand, nor has the shock of the revelations of the Holocaust and the Maoist and Stalinist terrors impeded outbreaks of mass murder. Whatever the causes of those, individually or generically, even when such slaughters happened in plain view of the world throughout the twentieth century, little or no attempt was made by observers, great or small, to interfere. Despite the literally hundreds of visions and proposals proposed since the Middle Ages for ways to block and suppress war and aggression, there is no counterpart on the international scene to a fire department to douse outbreaks of chaos and horror. On the contrary, throughout the twentieth century, despite occasional firm resolves forged in the immediate aftermath of defeat, the world's nations have been like reluctant members of a ramshackle volunteer fire department whose sense of privacy and property inhibit their willingness to act until a catastrophic conflagration threatens them directly. That tolerance for chaos, traditional as well as theoretical, will be starkly visible when we consider the Allies' disinclination to use military force against the *Endloesungapparat* from the perspective of chaos-complexity.

NOTES

1. A concise recent discussion of attempts to trace Holocaust causality is Christopher Hitchens, "Hitler's Ghost," *Vanity Fair*, 430 (June, 1996), pp. 72 and 74.

2. A recent broad-gauged perspective is Klaus L. Berghahn, ed., *The German-Jewish Dialogue Reconsidered* (New York: Peter Lang, 1996).

3. See the lists of German-Jewish rapport in Marion Graefin Doenhoff and Gordon Craig's letters to the editor on Goldhagen's *Hitler's Willing Executioners*, in *New York Review of Books*, 43:9 (May 23, 1996), p. 52.

4. Bernard Lazare, *Anti-Semitism: Its History and Causes* (Lincoln: University of Nebraska Press, 1995), pp. 8–9.

5. For example, Treitschke's saying "the Jews are our misfortune," quoted in Richard Grunberger, *Germany 1918–1945* (London: Batsford, 1964), p. 67.

6. Quoted in Peter Paret, *Clausewitz and the State* (Oxford: Clarendon Press, 1976), p. 213.

7. Ibid., pp. 5 and 12–15.

8. In the Weimar era, 1919–1933, Jews held four of the 250 government ministries, and fifteen of the top 500 high civil service posts, and 0.16 percent of government posts overall; see Charles A. Madison, "Perish the Jew!" *American Scholar*, 8:3 (July, 1939), p. 282.

9. Paul W. Massing, *Rehearsal for Destruction: A Study of Political Anti-Semitism in Imperial Germany* (New York: Harper and Brothers, 1949), pp. 162–163.

10. For example, Rohan D. O. Butler, *The Roots of National Socialism* (New York: E. P. Dutton, 1942), p. 221.

11. See Helen Fein, *Accounting for Genocide: National Responses and Jewish Victimization During the Holocaust* (New York: Free Press, 1979), pp. 88–91; and Michael H. Kater, *The Nazi Party: A Social Profile of Members and Leaders 1919–1945* (Cambridge: Harvard University Press, 1983), pp. 26–27.

12. See G. J. Peter Pulzer, *The Rise of Political Anti-Semitism in Germany and Austria* (New York: John Wiley, 1964), pp. 3–17.

13. For example. see *Hitler's Secret Conversations, 1941–1944* (New York: Signet Books, 1953), p. 437.

14. See the citing of Deuteronomy 20:16–17 as a "subterranean and grimly ironic contribution to that indisputably historical instance of genocidal intentionality known as the Holocaust," by David A. Lupher, in a letter to the editors, *Chronicle of Higher Education*, August 10, 1994, p. B5.

15. Fein, *Accounting for Genocide*, p. 18.

16. Erich Eyck, *A History of the Weimar Republic*, trans. Harlan P. Hanson and Robert G. L. Waite (Cambridge: Harvard University Press, 1962), p. 135.

17. Lucy S. Dawidowicz, *The War against the Jews 1933–1945* (New York: Holt, Rinehart and Winston, 1975), p. 46.

18. Nigel H. Jones, *Hitler's Heralds: The Story of the Freikorps 1918–1923* (London: John Murray, 1987), p. 76.

19. Reuben Ainsztein, "Soviet Jewry in the Second World War," in Lionel Kochan, ed., *The Jews in Soviet Russia Since 1917* (Oxford: Oxford University Press, 1978), pp. 281–299.

20. 16% of lawyers; 10% of doctors; 5% of professional writers; 45% of accountants; 3% of academics, artists, entertainers; 2% of bankers; see George Victor, *Hitler: Pathology of Evil* (Washington, D.C.: Brassey's, 1998), p. 142.

21. Ernst von Weizsaecker, *Memoirs*, trans. John Andrews (London: Victor Gollancz, 1951), p. 86.

22. Alfred Rosenberg, *Memoirs*, trans. Eric Posselt (Chicago: Ziff-Davis Publishing Co., 1949), pp. 112–113.

23. See Abraham Cronbach, *The Quest for Peace* (Cincinnati: Sinai Press, 1937), pp. 145–147.

24. Hermann Schwab, *A World in Ruins: History, Life and Work of German Jewry*, trans. Charles Fullman (London: Edward Goldston, 1946), pp. 80–81.

25. Erich von Ludendorff, *The Coming War* (London: Faber and Faber, 1931), p. 9.

26. For a contemporaneous view, see Marvin Lowenthal, *The Jews of Germany: A Story of Sixteen Centuries* (Philadelphia: Jewish Publication Society of America, 1936), p. 369; for details of professionals' attitudes and actions toward Jews, see Michael

H. Kater, *The Nazi Party: A Social Profile of Members and Leaders, 1919–1945* (Cambridge: Harvard University Press, 1983), pp. 26–27, 30, and 110–111.

27. For statistics of Jewish military participation in World War I, see Charles A. Madison, "Perish the Jew!" p. 282.

28. Saul Friedlander, "Some Aspects of the Historical Significance of the Holocaust," in Michael R. Marrus, ed., *The Nazi Holocaust: Historical Articles on the Destruction of European Jews* (Westport, Conn.: Meckler, 1989), pp. 158–159.

29. John M. Steiner, *Power Politics and Social Change in National Socialist Germany: A Process of Escalation into Mass Destruction* (The Hague: Mouton Publishers, 1976), p. 288.

30. See Harold Kaplan, *Conscience and Memory: Meditations in a Museum of the Holocaust* (Chicago: University of Chicago Press, 1993), p. 127.

31. Lowenthal, *Jews of Germany*, p. 370.

32. For a philatelic perspective, see Ken Lawrence, "Sexual Slavery in the Concentration Camps," *American Philatelist*, 108:8 (August, 1994), p. 727.

33. See Ruth Gay, *The Jews of Germany: A Historical Portrait* (New Haven: Yale University Press, 1992), esp. Chapter 6.

34. Detlev J. Peukert, *The Weimar Republic: The Crisis of Classical Modernity*, trans. Richard Deveson (New York: Hill and Wang, 1987), p. 159.

35. See Abba Hillel Silver, *Where Judaism Differed: An Inquiry into the Distinctiveness of Judaism* (New York: Macmillan, 1956), pp. 80–82.

36. Konrad Kwiet, "The Jewish Resistance," in David Clay Large, ed., *Contending with Hitler: Varieties of German Resistance in the Third Reich* (Washington, D.C.: German Historical Institute, 1991), p. 68.

37. For example, Eberhard Jaeckel, *Hitler in History* (Boston: University Press of New England, 1984), p. 94.

38. Konrad Heiden, *Der Fuehrer: Hitler's Rise to Power*, trans. Ralph Mannheim (Boston: Beacon Press, 1969 [1944]), p. 774.

39. Henry C. Wolfe, "Terror in Bucharest," *Coronet* 2:4 (August, 1937), p. 4.

40. Other major examples include the outbreak of the world and Korean wars, the 1929 stock market crash, the fall of the Shah of Iran in 1979, and the collapse of the USSR.

41. For recent succinct statements of the opposing positions, see Henry Friedlander, "Step by Step: The Expansion of Murder, 1939–1941"; and Richard Breitman, "Plans for the Final Solution in Early 1941," both in *German Studies Review*, 17:3 (October, 1994).

42. Christopher Browning, *The Final Solution and the German Foreign Office* (New York: Holmes and Meier, 1978), p. 10.

43. See Christopher R. Browning, "A Reassessment of Nazi Jewish Policy," in Thomas Childers and Jane Caplan, *Reevaluating the Third Reich* (New York: Holmes and Meier, 1992), p. 219.

44. Nora Levin, *The Holocaust: The Destruction of European Jewry* (New York: Thomas Y. Crowell, 1968), esp. pp. 268 and 290–298; and Raul Hilberg, "The Anatomy of the Holocaust," pp. 85–102, in Henry Friedlander and Sybil Milton, eds., *The Holocaust: Ideology, Bureaucracy and Genocide* (Millwood, N.Y: Kraus International Publications, 1980).

45. Quoted in Heinz Hoehne, *The Order of the Death's Head: The Story of Hitler's SS*, trans. Richard Barry (New York: Ballantine Books, 1969), p. 413.

46. Kaplan, *Conscience and Memory*, p. 11.

47. Michael Burleigh and Wolfgang Wippermann, *The Racial State: Germany 1933–1945* (Cambridge: Cambridge University Press, 1993), p. 96.

48. For example, Richard Breitman suggests March 1941 in his *The Architect of Genocide: Himmler and the Final Solution* (New York: Alfred A. Knopf, 1991).

49. A survey of conceptual issues is George J. Andreopoulos, ed., *Genocide: Conceptual and Historical Dimensions* (Philadelphia: University of Pennsylvania, 1994).

50. For example, the skirmishes between some Wehrmacht elements and security forces in the Ukraine in late 1942, cf. Gerald Fleming, *Hitler and the Final Solution* (Berkeley: University of California Press, 1984), pp. 131–133.

51. Yehuda Bauer, *The Holocaust in Historical Perspective* (Seattle: University of Washington Press, 1978), pp. 4–5.

52. For example, see Gerald Fleming, "Engineers of Death," *New York Times*, July 18, 1993, p. 19.

53. James M. Markham, "4,000 Germans Protest an SS Reunion," *New York Times*, April 1, 1984, p. 9A.

54. Martin Suskind, "A Voice from Bonn: 'History Cannot Be Shrugged Off,'" *New York Times*, November 2, 1986, p. 2E.

55. Quoted in Telford Taylor, *The Anatomy of the Nuremberg Trials: A Personal Memoir* (New York: Alfred A. Knopf, 1992), p. 260.

56. Fein, *Accounting for Genocide*, p. 25.

57. David Welch, *The Third Reich: Politics and Propaganda* (London: Routledge, 1993), p. 73.

58. Fleming, *Hitler and the Final Solution*, pp. 117–125 and 132.

59. For example, see Bernard P. Bellon, *Mercedes in Peace and War: German Automobile Workers, 1903–1945* (New York: Columbia University Press, 1990), pp. 256–257.

60. See Ian Kershaw, *Popular Opinion and Political Dissent in the Third Reich: Bavaria* (Oxford: Clarendon Press, 1983), p. 371.

7

Chaos versus Chaos II: Using Military Power against the Holocaust

From the perspective of chaos-complexity, the Allies' reluctance to use military power against the Holocaust during World War II offers a special paradox, since such an attack would have systems designed to create chaos against an extremely well-organized system—the End-loesungapparat, or Holocaust infrastructure—which was designed to impose order in its ultimate form, death. Such an attack or attacks would also been extremely complex, since a literal host of people and organizations would have been involved in planning and operations, such as the Anglo-American air forces, the Allies' intelligence, diplomatic and military bureaucracies, refugee groups, special operations "assets," the Soviets, and / or the Polish governments-in-exile. Although proposals and requests for a military effort were being made throughout the Allied camp from early 1941 onward,[1] the subject faded out of view after World War II to reemerge in a debate among historians in the early 1960s, following the trial of senior SS functionary Adolf Eichmann in Jerusalem. The main questions examined subsequently include the feasibility and utility of a military attack on the Endloesungapparat and whether it might have done more harm than good by bringing forth some further horror from the dark pit of Nazism. Much discussion has revolved around the scenario of a daylight strategic air attack, and on the rejection by Assistant Secretary of War John J. McCloy in the summer and autumn of 1944 of four requests by John Pehle, head of the War Refugee Board, that the extermination facilities at the Auschwitz-

Birkenau concentration camp be bombed. Beyond the closely linked aspects of intelligence and camp inmates' safety,[2] the most recent debate has revolved around the validity of McCloy's claim in his final reply in mid-October that such military operations would detract from the larger war effort, which he and many of his colleagues saw as holding the greatest promise for ending the mass exterminations, which had nearly run their course. The Red Army overran the camp in mid-January 1945.

The Allied policy process was fairly chaotic unto itself. McCloy, of course, was deeply involved in shaping policy in the War Department, but he did not make such crucial decisions on his own.[3] His letters echoed earlier official views on using military force against the Endloesungapparat, including a War Department statement in June that rejected attacks on death-camps that were not part of "operations conducted with the objective of defeating the armed forces of the enemy."[4] In a parallel vein, the State Department opposed retaliation for Nazi atrocities by "indiscriminate bombing of civilian populations in enemy countries."[5] Nor did Jewish leaders agree about what to do. Some rejected the reports of mass horrors, and those who wanted to act disagreed about methods.[6] It is not surprising, then, that there were inconsistencies in McCloy's letters. He overlooked the fact that inmates who might be killed or injured by bombing were doomed if the Endloesungapparat continued to function. Nor did his comments about "uncertain" and "dangerous" effects of bombing Auschwitz align with actual practice. True, the safety of civilians in France and other occupied countries was of concern to the western Allies from time to time, and even in Germany during the Anglo-American air offensive.[7] Broadcasts and leaflets often warned German city dwellers to flee, and many did, but the knowledge that many of them and civilians of other nationalities as well were being killed did not always put a brake on air operations.[8] At the same time, while German women and children and the elderly might be sent to the countryside, concentration camp inmates and ghetto dwellers had no such option. In some cases, the Allies were aware of what was happening. In 1943, for example, the Allied planners of a raid on a key *Vergeltungswaffen* (vengeance/ V-weapons) site knew that some 600 forced laborers were at risk, including informants at the site who were not heard from afterward.[9] Beyond "round the clock" attacks on many German cities, "collateral damage" and civilian casualties were also inflicted in heavy bombing raids, including those on V-weapons complexes, submarine pens, the Norsk hydroelectric facility (a suspected source of crucial materials for a Nazi atomic bomb), and the battleship *Tirpitz*. Nor were such concerns weighed in the balance by Allied airmen and planners when they argued in early 1944 over whether strategic bombers should assail Nazi transportation system or oil production facilities after the Normandy invasion.[10] From time to time, objections to area raids were raised. Some senior American airmen objected to "throwing strategic bombing at the man in the street,"[11] and British pacifist Vera Brittain spoke out against the Royal Air Force Bomber Command's terror bombing. But such caution and dissent had little effect. As McCloy implied in his letter to Pehle, the low accuracy of medium- and high-altitude bombing had made area raids more the rule than the exception by the time that stiffening German defenses forced a three-month halt in American daylight raids in late 1943.

What other military options were open the Allied armed forces, earlier or when Pehle asked for action? In his last letter to the War Refugee Board, McCloy mentioned the low-altitude attack on the Gestapo jail in Amiens by Royal Air Force Mosquito bombers, but not those on government buildings in Budapest in early July 1944, which forced Hungary's dictator, Admiral Horthy, to stop handing Jews over to the Nazis. The Free French Lorraine Squadron and certain RAF units had carried out low-altitude "surgical strikes" on key Nazi facilities in Denmark, Holland, Belgium, and France. Nor, as McCloy implied, was dive-bombing absolutely out of the question. Both the RAF and the USAAF had abandoned it earlier in the war, but the U.S. Navy and Marine Corps and the Royal Navy had not. Nor, as Table 7.1 shows,[12] were Auschwitz-Birkenau and its supporting rail net "beyond the maximum range of medium, low flying or dive bombing aircraft located in the United Kingdom, France, or Italy." The camp had been bombed accidentally.[13] In mid-September 1944, USAAF B-17s escorted by fighters were able to drop supplies to the Polish Home Army in Warsaw, 150 miles further from Allied air bases in Italy and western Europe than Auschwitz-Birkenau. Two of 250 planes on the mission were lost, and most went on to land in the USSR.[14] Beyond those numbers, of course, other factors would have affected the operational radius, including variations in wind, evasive maneuvers, damage, varying bomb and fuel loads, wind speed and direction, and navigational aids.

Generating scenarios is more art than science, and elaborate and rigorous analyses have led to diversive conclusions.[15] Perhaps future historians will have access to more data and be able to use computers to simulate different kinds of missions, plans, or force mixes that allow them to draw firmer conclusions. Calculating the effect of a notional mission by projecting data from previous raids would have been problematical then, and still is. Some missions went very well, while others were disastrous or far off the mark. By October 1944, the Allies had overrun many airfields in Belgium and northeastern France and built more. Forward staging might have been difficult, but it was not im-

Table 7.1
Maximum Range of Allied Aircraft in 1944

Type	Range (mi) at a maximum load
A-20 Havoc/Boston light bomber	1,050
A-26 Invader light bomber	1,400
B-25 North American Mitchell medium bomber	1,500
B-26 Martin Marauder medium bomber	1,150
De Havilland Mosquito bomber	1,370
P-38 Lockheed Lightning heavy fighter	2,260
SB2C-IC Curtiss Helldiver dive bomber	1,895
Distance of Auschwitz-Birkenau from East Anglia	750
Distance of Auschwitz-Birkenau from Eastern France and Italy	600

Note: Most USAAF B-29 Superfortress very-long-range bomber forces were re-deploying to the Marianas from bases in southwest China overrun by a Japanese offensive. Roosevelt opposed using them elsewhere, except for the secret atomic bomb–delivery SILVERPLATE unit.

possible. What, however, if attacks had been made earlier, say in 1942, when the details of the Endloesung first came to the attention of Allied leaders? Would that have been merely symbolic or wholly futile? We cannot be sure how the Nazis would have reacted to that or to the attendant publicity, whatever the physical effects. Did that really matter, since it was clear to many in Britain and America, and perhaps the Soviet Union, that they were doing their worst? The Nazis did sometimes shown acute sensitivity to public opinion in Germany and abroad. They accepted Roosevelt's call for restraint in bombing cities during the first year of World War II and, in 1943, invited neutral journalists to examine the evidence of the Soviet massacre of Polish elites in Katyn Forest. They treated Allied prisoners of war—except the Russians—much better than their Japanese colleagues did; and Hitler rescinded his order that commandos be manacled and dealt with outside the laws of war when the British threatened to retaliate against German prisoners of war. The Germans' anger at the Soviets' Kharkov war crimes trials in 1944 also revealed some sensitivity on such issues.

At the heart of the matter, the use of military power against the Holocaust hinged on the will of the highest Allied political authorities, that is, the Big Three—Churchill, Roosevelt, and Stalin. Beyond periodic rhetorical threats, however, there was very little substance to their professions of vengeful resolve. Churchill offered joint citizenship to the French during the 1940 collapse, but no one proposed extending the magical umbrella of sovereignty to refugees or victims. Pehle's request was dealt with well down the U.S. military chain of command, and options other than air attacks were not considered. Each of the Big Three was an epicenter of chaos unto himself, and each was awash in the turbulence of managing a massive conflict. None played their cards face up. FDR's tendency toward deviousness was widely known, and his health was failing. So was that of Churchill—who also exulted in crypticity. As leaders of democracies, all constantly grappled with the attendant chaos. Roosevelt yawed and waffled on many matters, including occupation policy and war crimes. The assertion that FDR steered as close against the wind of anti-Semitism as political constraints allowed[16] do not quite align with the argument that decisions not to bomb Auschwitz had "little to do with War Department policies, indifference, military ineptitude, or negative ethnic attitudes."[17] That hot-potato model leads to a dead end, although Roosevelt's hesitancy and ambivalence were paralleled by differences between Rabbi Stephen Wise and Chaim Weiszmann and in the American Jewish community over Zionist aspirations and policies—and on whether military action should be taken against the Holocaust, and if so, how.[18]

In weighing such questions, we should not forget what the general military situation was when McCloy wrote to Pehle, especially the Allies' fear of the Third Reich, which lasted to the very end. Even now, it is hard to pinpoint when the Allies really concluded that Germany was beaten or that the goal of unconditional surrender was really attainable. Not long after McCloy wrote his letter, the persistent anxiety in the Allied high command about Nazi military potential was reflected when Eisenhower responded to a request from refugee groups, forwarded by President Roosevelt, asking Ike as Supreme Commander to issue a warning proclamation to the Germans regarding the safety of forced laborers and concentration camp inmates. After SHAEF's Psychological Warfare Division advised him that "that original wording would give Germans powerful propaganda line," Eisenhower asked for a formal request from the Combined Chiefs of Staff and approved a modified draft with a recommendation that the original phrase mentioning Jewish prisoners be changed to refer to "religious faith" in general.[19] That also reflects less than a feverish urgency at high levels regarding the plight of Holocaust victims.

It is easy enough to invoke wartime exigencies and priorities, which was often done. But when there was a will at the top to carry out "special operations," ways were found to get the job done. In early 1942, for example, when resources were much scarcer, the U.S. armed forces collaborated and improvised quickly and effectively under such pressures. One spectacular case was the Navy and Army air forces' surprise air attack on Japan in April 1942. Under heavy criticism for lack of coordination and inertia, the services mounted the "Doolittle raid," in which Army medium bombers were launched from the aircraft carrier *Hornet*. A year later, in a few hours, Navy commanders in the South Pacific gained almost instant approval from the highest levels to dispatch a quickly improvised mission by Army Air Force long-range fighters, which intercepted and shot down Admiral Isoroku Yamamoto.

What about "will" at the very top? Contrary to the currently popular myth of World War II as a golden age of detached management from on high, Roosevelt, Churchill, and especially Stalin intruded themselves into military and naval matters regularly. Before America entered World War II, for instance, FDR urged the Navy to build small escort vessels, ignored seniority in choosing top leaders in the Army and Navy, sanctioned such covert projects as the creation of the O.S.S. and the "Flying Tigers," set military aircraft production goals, and launched the Manhattan Project. During the war, he insisted that American commando-type units be formed, ordained the times and places of some invasions, and with Churchill, approved the Combined Bomber Offensive. Nor did FDR mind linking military operations to politics. In 1942, he wanted to schedule the North African landings a week before the Congressional elections (Marshall fended that off), and in 1944 he rejected Churchill's Balkans invasion scheme, pleading the potential loss of Polish-American votes in the impending presidential race. Churchill's reaching down the chain of command in both world wars were legion. Perhaps most spectacular was his shunting of British Empire forces to Greece from North Africa just as Rommel and the Afrika Korps appeared in Libya. And Generalissimo Stalin, who wore the hat as head of every major Soviet wartime organization, ran his part of the war on a very close leash, with detailed up-to-date situation maps maintained by a special section of the Soviet general staff.

If any or all of the Big Three had ordained the use of military force against the Endloesungapparat, there is no way to know who would have planned, commanded, and carried out such an attack, if it would have succeeded or failed—or how that would have been measured. Nor can we be sure of its effects, from physical damage and casualties to the political and psychological effects in many directions. In some carefully designed bombing attacks, like the Peenemunde and final *Tirpitz* raid, things went very well, but others, like the Schweinfurt-Regensburg and Ploesti mission, were disasters. In the latter, in keeping with chaos-complexity theory, small things—persistent fog in the first case, early sighting of the force and a navigational glitch in the second—had major consequences. If an Allied air raid or raids killed several thousand inmates at Auschwitz-Birkenau but failed to halt the gas chambers and/or crematoria, that would have been grist for journalistic, diplomatic, and historical mills long afterward. When McCloy wrote his final letter to Pehle, the ashes of the Arnhem airborne disaster were still cooling, the Allied drive across France was stalling, and presidential elections were two weeks away. Major hearings had been conducted on the Pearl Harbor attack, and it was not yet clear whether the Manhattan project would not prove to be the biggest New Deal boondoggle of all.

Looking beyond the strategic and political context, the success of a military attack on the Endloesungapparat would have depended on the quality of intelligence. How good was it? A defender of McCloy's position suggested that "before the end of 1944, the Allies lacked enough solid intelligence about the 'Final Solution'" to "adequately comprehend its hideous import."[20] What would they have needed? Beyond the reports of Nazi mass murders that appeared in Britain and the United States throughout the war, the Nazis did keep many details of the Endloesung secret, but never masked their general intentions. Hitler often repeated the promise he made in the 1920s in *Mein Kampf* to expunge Jews from European life, and so did his minions. Hermann Goering, as justice minister in Prussia in 1933, proclaimed that "We will treat the Jews like a flower, only depriving them of water."[21] We have seen how, as Nazi brutality became visible in mass media throughout the world from the mid-1930s onward,[22] reactions were fitful and feeble, due to appeasement, widespread anti-Semitism, and the fluctuations in Nazi persecutions. In early 1934, for example, during a lull, many Jews who had fled in 1933 came back to Germany, and the British government rejected pleas that it raise objections to the persecutions under Article II of the League of Nations Covenant. A year later, the Nuremberg Laws formally defined German Jews as outcasts in the Third Reich, but the picture was blurred by the Nazis' own convoluted definitions of Jewishness and the frequent bending of rules by the Nazi hierarchy.[23]

The 1935 international convention of Jewish organizations, intended to focus attention on persecutions in Germany and other eastern and central European countries, proved to be the first in a long series of such well-publicized but inconsequential meetings and empty gestures.[24] In 1937, while shiploads of refugees were being turned back by various countries, the League of Nations named a High Commissioner for Refugees, and President Roosevelt formed an Advisory Committee on Political Refugees. The next year, another major conclave at Evian led cynics to point to the reverse spelling of that city's name. A few months later, after *Kristallnacht*, Britain dropped its restrictions, but American limits were not relaxed significantly until well into the war. Both the

United States and Britain remained sensitive to mounting Arab pressure, which the Nazis and Italians also exploited effectively. In the late 1930s, as the British, who held the League of Nations mandate in Palestine, attempted to tighten immigration there, growing desperation generated a series of proposals for new homes for refugees, Jewish and others, in various parts of the world. Suggested sites included British Guiana, Switzerland, France, and Holland, but the most ambitious plan centered on the Central African highlands. It was strongly supported by such American luminaries as Bernard Baruch and Herbert Hoover, but rejected by the British Cabinet. The only tangible result of all those efforts was an arrangement by the Intergovernment Committee on Refugees for a small number of Jewish refugees to be admitted by the Dominican Republic just before the war. In January 1939, Adolf Hitler spelled things out in unambiguous terms in his promise before the Reichstag that if "another world war" came in Europe, "the consequence will not be the Bolshevization of the earth and thereby the victory of Jewry, but the annihilation of the Jewish race in Europe."[25] When war came in September, some of Himmler's lieutenants were exploring ways to send refugees to Palestine and Madagascar, while other Nazi functionaries were engaged in a massive shakedown scheme, demanding that wealthy Jews throughout the world underwrite bonds for a huge "trust fund" to subsidize German exports and guarantee the deportation expenses of German Jews. The war ended those grotesque machinations, and as the Wehrmacht overran Poland in September 1939, Himmler's security services took the first steps toward to a *Loesung* (solution) to the *Judenfrage* (Jewish question), which evolved into the Endloesung. Those mass slaughters in Poland were reported in British and American mass media, as others were throughout the war. As the blitzkrieg swept across Europe in 1940–1941, many Jews from Germany and Central Europe who had fled to other European countries before the war were now caught, or forced to flee again, along with others trying to escape the Nazis. Over the next three years, Germany openly pressed its allies and clients, reluctant to varying degrees, to round up and hand over those whom the Herrenvolk deemed Untermenschen.

Although many details of the Holocaust were not visible and although the super-secret British ULTRA intercepts of high-level Nazi encrypted radio messages contained little evidence of the death-camps throughout the war, the British Ministry of Economic Warfare's Railway Research Service monitored the German transportation system radio net.[26] In mid-1941, British signals intelligence analysts described mass murders of "'Jews,' 'Jewish,' and 'Jewish Bolshevists'" and Russian soldiers as "calculated acts of policy."[27] At the same time, as reports of the slaughters appeared in the American and British popular press, the Jewish World Congress' 1940 *Black Book* estimated a quarter of a million Jews had been killed in Poland in the first three months of the war. In March 1941, Martha Gellhorn anticipated the schism in Holocaust scholarship in her account of the mass murders of two and-a-half million Jews, when she pointed out how naive it was to expect Nazi officials to provide the world with official documents describing their activities.[28]

A special glimpse of the horror shone through in June 1942, when Nazi security forces destroyed the Czech village of Lidice to provide a grim example to those who might be inclined to give aid and comfort to the Third Reich's foes. Some villagers had sheltered the assassins of Reynard Heydrich, Himmler's deputy and Reichsprotector of Bohemia and Moravia—the "Hangman of Prague." Two of 394 survived the war. In the United States, the film *Address Unknown* dramatized the effects of the "Night-and-Fog" decree, a policy of state terrorism based on sudden arrests, deportation of suspects to Germany, and the use of summary executions to suppress active dissidence in occupied areas. Even after the United States entered World War II, many Americans who had been rendered cynical by the revelations of Allied propaganda fabrications after World War I continued to view reports and portrayals of atrocities as propaganda and discounted both the predictions of mass slaughter by emigres and observers and the Nazis' threats. Nevertheless, from early 1942 on, the Polish underground and government-in-exile in London knew what was happening, and the Allies repeatedly issued highly publicized official statements about Nazi atrocities, including the Big Three proclamations on Nazi mass killings of hostages in late 1941 and 1943 and the St. James' declaration, a White Paper supporting the Inter-Allied Declaration, which was formally signed in London and provided details of the Endloesung outside refugee circles. It described the "terrorization and ruthless destruction . . . in full force" in Poland, as "particularly tragic for the Jewish population . . . on a scale unsurpassed," including mass starvation and massacres, with estimates "of many hundreds of thousands" killed. It also identified "three 'extermination camps'" of which Oswiecim (Auschwitz) was deemed "the most notorious."[29] In December 1942, further official Allied censures followed a "day of mourning" in Jewish communities outside Europe. At that point, Varian Fry in *the New Republic* estimated that "nearly 2,000,000 European Jews . . . already been slain since the war began, and the remaining 5,000,000 . . . under Nazi control are scheduled to be destroyed."[30] A month later, Philip Bernstein wrote in *The Nation* that "innumerable Jews have perished without record" and were "being slaughtered in cold blood where the Nazis can lay hands on them."[31] Late in the year, a major shift in American public opinion led the U.S. House and Senate to pass joint resolutions in favor of taking action against the Nazi program of "extinction." But those, too, had no significant effect on the unfolding of the Endloesung.

If, then, Allied intelligence organs did not notice any of that when they were able to identify a number of less evident and subtle patterns and targets, what does that suggest about levels of concern and competence, especially at those echelons where practical decisions were made and policy was implemented? If there was a rainbow of shadings among Germans, and even within the Nazi hierarchy, what of the spectrum of attitudes in the Allied camp? How many of those who were prepared or in some cases eager to indulge Fascism or Nazism before the war remained sympathetic to various degrees during the war?[32] How many were anti-Semitic, not pro-Nazi or Fascist, but to the point that it affected their judgment and actions? As with measuring German motives and attitudes, there is no way to weight that, since official records offer no clear view of it. But there is substantial evidence of anti-Semitism in many countries during the Hitler era, including the United States.[33] Its measures were far less virulent than those in Europe—real estate contract restrictions, professional school quotas, and formal exclusions from fraternities and sororities, country clubs, and hotels, as well as subtler unwritten rules and social pressures in business, society, and the armed services.[34] In the Army, the Finance Corps was labeled the "Jewish infantry," while prominent Jews in public service were frequently attacked in the popular press, as well as in political extremists' polemics, and sometimes by government officials and legislators. Derisive humor and slang included terms like the "Jew deal" and "Jew S. of A.," coins were altered to show anti-Semitic images, and copies of the "Protocols of the Elders of Zion" forgery were circulated, feeding fears of sinister conspiracy. Roosevelt responded with gentle sarcasmto charges that he had Jewish ancestors, expressing the hope that if it were true, they had been good folk.

Some attributed the surge in prejudice in the United States in the 1930s, visible in public opinion polls and social science research, to Jewish immigrants' arriving during the Great Depression amid rising unemployment. Images of Jewish influence in high finance and the media abounded in popular culture, including Henry Luce's *Fortune*, the most prestigious business monthly, and his high-circulation weeklies *Time* and *Life*, and in the *New Yorker*.[35] The image of Jewish commercial cabals was reinforced by journalists and historians' attributing America's entry into World War I to Allied propaganda and financial-industrial conspiracies, even though, contrary to popular impression, a Jewish financial house arranged only one loan of $13.8 million out of 28 American major loans totaling $2.5 billion to Allied nations during

1914–1917.[36] American Jewish groups' calls for boycotting German products and highlighting of Nazi brutality[37] provided grist for the polemical mills of radio demagogues like Father Charles Coughlin and Gerald L. K. Smith. After war broke out in Europe in September 1939, supporters of U.S. neutrality, most notably Charles Lindbergh, chief spokesman of "America First," looked past mounting Zionist-British friction over Palestine immigration when he linked Jewish complaints to British machinations.[38] Even though congressional hearings in 1941 on undue Jewish influence in public affairs and especially Hollywood backfired on their sponsors, they made Jewish film industry leaders hesitant to make films about Nazism, even after the United States entered the war.[39]

That furor came just as the Holocaust was gaining momentum. A key milestone was the meeting of Nazi officials at Wannsee, a Berlin suburb, in January 1942, just after Pearl Harbor, where detailed planning of the Endloesungapparat began. While at the same time, a Conference of Occupied Nations highlighted Nazi atrocities, a more visible and dramatic assemblage convened at the Biltmore Hotel in New York in May,[40] where six hundred delegates approved a platform submitted by David Ben-Gurion, head of the Jewish Agency in Palestine and later Israel's first president. Demands for a Jewish commonwealth, unlimited immigration into Palestine, and the forming of a Jewish Army produced mixed reactions. The highlighting of Nazi horrors generated considerable concern and sympathy in Britain and the United States; but in the Middle East, Nazi and Fascist propagandists used the Biltmore platform to inflame Arab fears of Zionists seeking temporal power in Palestine at their expense. To further complicate that picture, from late 1940 to mid-1943, as the Holocaust unfolded, the Middle East was the main stage of Anglo-American military operations against the Nazis and the Fascists. Some Islamic leaders and factions drifted into the Axis sphere in spite of Nazi racism and Mussolini's heavy-handed treatment of Islamic colonial subjects in Libya and East Africa. Throughout the war, American elites' views on refugees and the Middle East roughly mirrored those of their British counterparts, who were juggling three roles—champion of freedom-fighting totalitarianism, master of the largest empire in history, and a major mechanized military power at war heavily dependent on Middle Eastern oil. Turkey was a major concern to all of the Allies, at once a neutral nation bridging Europe and Asia Minor and controlling the Straits and a major Islamic military power whose entry into the war on either side would have been significant, especially if it had joined the Axis before 1943.

Amid that tangle of power politics, British and American diplomats and military leaders reacted to the Holocaust cautiously. The views of "Arabists" in the U.S. State Department and British Foreign Office toward Jews varied. Some were concerned about oil and Realpolitik, and others admired Islamic culture, but none supported Zionism, nor were they responsive to the changing tide of American public opinion as major efforts mounted on the "Home Front" during World War II to encourage tolerance in business, education, and government.[41] Even though reports of Nazi atrocities changed public attitudes toward immigration limits, State Department officials repeatedly blocked refugee rescue attempts and curtailed immigration until very late in World War II, not only after the Holocaust was visible in official circles but after the shift in public sentiment as well.[42] In view of that, it is hardly surprising that relatively faint traces of the Endloesung appear in the historiography of World War II, especially in accounts of the conduct of affairs in high places.[43] While Churchill's leaving the death-camps out of his World War II memoirs may have been due to state security concerns or to the self-serving normal to that genre, the actions of the agencies of his government make it plain enough why he would have wanted to leave the matter out of focus.

Despite widespread silence on the matter, there are some fragments of evidence regarding anti-Semitism in American and British elite circles. In 1940, for example, a State Department code and cipher clerk in the American embassy in London, who accepted Hitler's claim that Jews precipitated World War II to gain profits, was caught passing high-level message traffic to the Axis.[44] At a higher level, after the United States entered World War II, Assistant Secretary of State Breckinridge Long delayed and blocked several attempts to save Jews, including a plan to ransom 70,000 Rumanian Jews and transport them to North Africa or Palestine.[45] At the Bermuda Conference in 1943, he maneuvered approval of the "rescue through victory" policy, which a British participant deemed a "facade to inaction." When Long argued that lowering immigration limits would flood the United States with "fifth columnists"—saboteurs, spies, and agitators—like McCloy, he was not steering very far from policy or from his superiors' desires. His actions required the compliance of many colleagues and subordinates and reflected the views of many members of Congress and of the public, including those of liberal bent.[46] In 1942, for example, Secretary of the Treasury Henry Morgenthau, Jr., and Rabbi Wise, on behalf of Jewish groups, asked the Council on Foreign Relations (CFR) in 1942 to support calls for vigorous government action against the death camps. Although CFR members and staff expressed concern among themselves about Nazi atrocities, they decided to maintain public silence, based on the logic that since Allies lacked military power and opportunity to express their outrage in concrete terms, that option should not be openly discussed until "later on in the war when allied power grew."[47]

Although Long's contention that the only hope for Holocaust victims lay in an Allied victory has been echoed recently by those defending Roosevelt's sluggishness on the matter and asserting that halting the Holocaust was a primary Allied strategic goal, the record does not bear that out. Before World War II, the public backlash to his 1937 "quarantine the aggressor" speech led FDR to keep his hand well hidden as he maneuvered behind the scenes to aid the Allies. Despite his covert maneuvers, Roosevelt followed public opinion polls most of the time during that era of isolationism. He signed the Neutrality Acts, approved the Munich agreement, and ran on a peace plank in the election of 1940. Steering wide of collective security, for two years before Pearl Harbor, he allowed disruptive bickering between the Secretary of War Harry Woodring and Assistant Secretary of War Louis Johnson to paralyze the War Department. As a result, America went to war without a centralized, coherent defense and intelligence structure.

After Pearl Harbor, there was little evidence of the all-out effort suggested later. The U.S. Army General Staff's original plans for mobilizing 300 divisions were scaled back to 105 in late 1941, and finally to just under ninety. Despite unprecedented rationing, the United States fought the war on a guns-and-butter basis compared with the other combatants. The bulk of production was aimed at the civilian sector, and demobilization of the armed forces began in mid-1943. Although in January 1941, in the secret ABC-1 talks, senior American officers had assured British and Canadian military leaders that no matter how and where the United States was drawn into the war, it would strive to beat Germany first, that did not happen. Most of the American ground forces that were sent overseas during the first ten months of the war went to the Pacific. Wherever the responsibility for any of that is laid, FDR seriously crimped the air offensive against Nazi Germany in early 1943 by ordering that B-29 Superfortress heavy bombers be diverted from Europe to China. In other indices of proportional effort, the bulk of Axis ground forces were engaged in Russia, the Balkans, and China; the Anglo-American invasion of northwest Europe was postponed two years running; and more British Empire than American troops were in action against the Axis in Europe until September 1944. Later that year, during the Battle of the Bulge, troop and ammunition shortages reached crisis proportions, and the close margin in American military manpower left SHAEF—Supreme Headquarters Allied Expeditionary Force—with a single division in theater reserve. Nor does the image of the western Allies hell-bent on a quick victory hold up when we consider such dead-end sideshows during World War II as the Makin raid;

Operation TIDAL WAVE, the low-level attack by B-24s on the Ploesti oil fields in 1943; Operation FRANTIC, the ill-fated basing of a U.S. B-17 Group in the Ukraine in 1945; and the Hammelburg raid, the loss of an armored task force when Patton tried liberate his son-in-law from a prisoner-of-war camp. On a larger scale, Churchill and Roosevelt's "Unconditional Surrender" proclamation at Casablanca in early 1943, by undercutting the German resistance, virtually guaranteed that the war would last longer and reduced chances of negotiating on behalf of Nazism's captives.

Small wonder that historians have puzzled at length over what Roosevelt and America's war aims really were. Churchill preferred a peripheral strategy and wanted to approach Germany through the Balkans, while many Americans, especially Admiral King, the Chief of Naval Operations, itched to avenge Pearl Harbor, strategy be damned. Although the United States went to war with some well-honed war plans, the Atlantic Charter prepared by Roosevelt and Churchill in August 1941 created a general framework for destroying Fascism and creating a new version of what looked at the time like a revitalized League of Nations. But in the long run, Allied strategy was concocted in bits and pieces along the way. Throughout his eleven years as president, Roosevelt held his cards very close to his vest, allowed no stenographers or recording devices in the room when discussing major policy questions, and left no memoirs nor political testament beyond his often vague and contradictory official statements and actions. Yet his ambivalence on the Nazis' victims plight stands favorable comparison with that of Congress, which refused to pass the Wagner-Rogers Children's Bill just as the British dropped their immigration limits.[48] Nevertheless, what the executive branch did in those times was on Roosevelt's "watch" as president and commander-in-chief.

The contrast between key State and War Department officials' efforts and Roosevelt's rhetoric, and their British counterparts' attitudes toward Churchill's calls for action and the unfolding of sharp and sordid financial practices in various Allied and neutral nations half a century later makes suggestions that the Allies knew little of the Holocaust all the more perplexing.[49] The British government, as holders of Palestine under the League of Nations Mandate, had been monitoring Jewish affairs very closely since 1919; their policy on immigration, especially the 1939 White Paper, deemed "infamous" by Zionists, had generated some tension with the U.S. State Department as well as among American Jews.[50] While that document was intended to sooth Arab sensitivities, not all among the British elites were so inclined. Churchill was an enthusiastic Zionist, and while First Lord of the Admiralty in Chamberlain's cabinet, he had critiqued a harshly worded Foreign

Office cable draft of guidelines for the British ambassador in Washington in responding to American Jews' demands that immigration into Palestine be eased. Urging a "softer and smoother" tone, Churchill suggested dropping references to the White Paper and proposed arming Jewish settlers, whom he saw as Britain's "only trustworthy friends" in the region.[51] Another enthusiastic Zionist was Orde Wingate, who later headed the "Chindits" in Burma. As a captain in Palestine in the late 1930s, he helped train the *Palmach*, the leadership cadre of the Haganah, the Jewish Agency's clandestine army.

Beyond the divided views among British officials toward Arabs, Jews, and/or Zionists, anti-Jewish attitudes and pejorative slang were as pervasive in Britain's armed forces in the Middle East as in many other nations' at that time, as was racial and ethnic prejudice against many different peoples. That tension took on a special intensity in Palestine in the early 1940s, however, as the Jewish terrorist groups *Irgun Zvai Leumi* and the Stem Gang began their campaign of assassination, bombing and kidnaping that lasted until Britain terminated its Palestine mandate in mid-May, 1948.[52] That led to the special irony of British military and security forces frequently raiding the Jewish underground, many of whose members were serving with Allied forces in North Africa and the Mediterranean.

The argument that "demands to help the Jews . . . [were] detrimental to the war effort"[53] can also be considered in light of Anglo-American relations. While the "special relationship" between Britain and America often broke down in practice, many military professionals and diplomats in both nations were involved in the closest wartime alliance of modem times, officially and personally. Much of that complex process went unrecorded, making it uncertain how much the close similarity in British and American diplomats and military professionals' rejecting calls for attacks on the Holocaust infrastructure was due to coincidence or to perceptions of common interest. McCloy's reference to "the best military opinion" in his letter to the War Refugee Board sounded much like the British Air Ministry's response to Foreign Minister Anthony Eden when he responded to Churchill's request to "Get anything you can out of the air force and invoke me if necessary." He got nothing, since the British airmen saw "no purpose" in undertaking aerial operations against the death-camps.[54] (They had been rejecting such requests since early 1941.) In a similar vein, after the British high commissioner for Palestine blocked the training of Jewish volunteers for a "special" commando force to block the movement of Jews from Hungary to Germany, an attempt to revise the project was vetoed at the highest echelons of the British military.[55] In Washington, Field Marshal Sir John Dill, chief of the British Military Mission in Washington, expressed his antipathy to Zionism in sharp terms very similar in tone with a senior British civil servant's complaint in September 1944 that "a disproportionate amount of the time of the [Foreign] Office is wasted on dealing with these wailing Jews." More private were the views of Harold Nicolson, a twenty-year Foreign Office veteran and a principal in the Ministry of Information during World War II. who had labored to rescue Jews from Germany, but who confided in his diary in June 1945 that: "Although I loathe anti-Semitism, I do dislike Jews."[56]

That foot-dragging and obstruction ultimately led to an explosion among U.S. Secretary of the Treasury Henry Morgenthau's aides, who, from mid-1942 on, watched through Treasury Department channels as several rescue deals were derailed by British and American diplomats, including a plan to move refugees from southeastern Europe into the Middle East and North Africa. From the late 1930s onward, many American Jews had urged Morgenthau to act, since they saw him as their main point of access to the Roosevelt administration, but nothing of substance came from his repeated entreaties. The final straw came after a joint House-Senate resolution that called for the creation of a commission to plan "to save the surviving Jewish people of Europe from extinction at the ends of Nazi Germany" led to further inaction. Morgenthau's deputy, Randolph Paul, prepared *A Report to the Secretary [of the Treasury] on the Acquiescence of This Government in the Murder of the Jews*, a litany of State Department and British Foreign Office hampering of refugee rescue efforts and suppression of reports on the Endloesung. By the time that the War Refugee Board was formed in late January 1944—and supported mainly by private funds—many chances to ransom victims or take military action were lost, as more would be over the next few months.[57]

Another bureaucratic roadblock was U.S. immigration barriers, which remained high until late in World War II, when they were lowered under mounting public and congressional pressure. (Special exceptions were made for British children during the Blitz.) Secretary of State Cordell Hull later claimed that he tried earnestly to help victims of Nazism and that the United States accepted more than all other nations at that time.[58] The latter was hardly surprising, since the United States was the largest nation untouched by the war, the world's greatest economic power, and short of skilled manpower from late 1938 on. However, the refugee flow into the United States from 1933 to 1945 was far less than a torrent—an average of roughly three persons per state per day. Although State Department documents of the period reflect sluggishness and caution,[59] to be fair, Hull, like Roosevelt, was buffeted by the unparalleled turbulence of wartime bureaucratic process. His hesitancy, nevertheless, contrasted sharply with the action of others who spoke out boldly on the issue, including diplomats from occupied nations, who risked much more by taking a strong stand. For example, in 1944, the Foreign Minister of the Polish government-in-exile in London "expressed the conviction that it is a matter of the utmost urgency that the United Nations reconsider means of saving the Jewish population and that responsibility for such crimes be determined with great precision."[60]

That was the milieu in which officials like McCloy and Breckinridge Long shaped refugee policy and practice, offering a glimpse of the special sensitivity of complex systems to slight influences.[61] McCloy was not a "faceless civil servant" but the member of an informal but powerful foreign policy elite, later labeled "the wise men."[62] After leaving his New York law practice to serve in the War Department in 1942, he played a key role in setting up the Japanese-American detention camps, articulating the position that constitutional rights went out the window when national security was at risk. After playing "a moderating role" in problems with black troops,[63] in early 1944, McCloy testified in front of Congress against a resolution offered by American Zionist groups urging the United States to bring pressure to bear on Britain to allow increased immigration limits into Palestine with an eye to creating a "free and democratic Jewish commonwealth there." Here, too, he was not speaking on his own, but as a War Department official.[64] Here, too, there is no way to determine just how much he was actor—or playwright. When McCloy signed the last letter rejecting the use of military force against the death camps in October 1944, he was being considered for High Commissioner in the U.S. occupation zone of Germany after the war. At the same time, with his boss, Secretary of War Henry L. Stimson, he served on a committee formed by FDR to review U.S. postwar policy toward Germany; both stood opposed to the other members, Morgenthau, and Roosevelt's principal aide, Harry Hopkins, who supported the Treasury Secretary's highly publicized plan for dismantling German industry and dividing the Reich into pastoral states to prevent its militaristic resurgence.[65] While Roosevelt and Churchill supported that scheme initially,[66] FDR backed off as a schism developed in the War Department between "soft" and "hard" schools of thought.[67] Members of the former were concerned that a harsh occupation policy might recreate the economic difficulties and resentments that followed the Versailles Treaty, and which both Nazis and Communists had used to undermine the Weimar Republic. Others, like James V. Forrestal, then Secretary of the Navy and later Secretary of Defense, hoped to use Germany as a barrier to Soviet expansion.

In the end, the "soft" school prevailed, and McCloy remained a major force in high policy circles for the next generation, gaining special prominence as chairman of the Board of Advisors of the Council on Foreign Relations. Toward the end of the war, he and several other New York attorneys steered American policy toward support of an international trial of war criminals and away from the British preference for summary executions. In a layered irony, in what a historian later deemed "1940's ethnic prejudice," McCloy justified aligning American and Soviet views by citing Anglo-Saxon standards of justice and slighting those of Latins and Slavs.[68] McCloy also argued that the prosecution's case in the Nuremberg war crimes tribunal be based on allegations of a criminal conspiracy of senior Nazi officials and military leaders at the highest levels, which left the complicity of those in the middle and lower tiers in the shadows.[69] While he also opposed creating a Jewish state[70] and lenient treatment of ex-Nazis when he was High Commissioner in Germany in the early 1950s,[71] it is not clear how much McCloy's views or acts reflected his own attitudes as opposed to policy. That was, after all, a time when the pseudo-science of geopolitics was fashionable, anti-Semitism was pervasive, and the Cold War was heating up.

There is no way to tell if ways other than bombing to bring military force to bear against the Holocaust were discussed in the corridors of power, but such speculation is not wholly fanciful. Some Jewish leaders preferred a commando raid, appropriate enough since World War II generated a host of "special operations" units, or "mobs for jobs," like the British Commandos, the Long Range Desert Group, the U.S. Army Rangers, and the U.S. Marine Raiders.[72] While many "special ops" failed and others succeeded,[73] the western Allies had a sizable array of forces that might have been considered for such a mission in mid-1944, including the paramilitary elements of the American Office of Strategic Services, British Special Operations Executive elements, Special Air Service, and various foreign contingents, including the Polish underground, who had pulled off a spectacular "special ops" coup in spiriting a German "V" weapon out of a Nazi factory. Although enthusiasts claimed SOE sabotage yielded more precise results than bombing, and at much lower cost, such methods were unpopular in some quarters, partly because they intruded upon the turf of other agencies. Special forces also symbolized military unorthodoxy and contempt for traditional militaristic methods and attitudes, and many Jews—European, Palestinian, British Commonwealth, and American—were involved in Allied intelligence and covert operations. In 1941, for instance, the SOE's efforts to impede the flow of Rumanian oil supplies to Germany were "seriously handicapped by the general attitude of the Foreign Office and His Majesty's diplomatic representatives."[74]

The outcome of any particular undertaking would have been determined by a vast and bewildering array of factors that are impossible to chart. Designing an air campaign against the Endloesungapparat would have been extremely complex,[75] considering such problems as the phasing of bombing, rocket, and/or strafing attacks over time and the uncertainties of German responses, but "laying on" a special operation would have been far more intricate. It would have involved "insertion" and "extraction," orchestrating air transport and supply with air support, and liaison with local underground elements and perhaps the Soviets. Much would have depended on who did the planning. Agencies that might have been in the inner loop in designing such an undertaking include the Combined Operations and SHAEF planning nexus in Britain, the Joint Planning Committee of the Joint Chiefs of Staff, the Combined Chiefs of Staff, the U.S. Army Air Force's network of think-tanks, the U.S. and British Air Staffs, and the Office of Strategic Services and the Special Operations Executive. The technological matrix was constantly changing, and tactics were evolving. By that point in the war, ground-sensing radar and the first generation of "smart" ordnance (the AZON "azimuth only" bombs) and various types of "earthquake" bombs were in service, and Operation STRANGLE, the major interdiction effort in Italy, was a fresh experience. Those who had a reputation for creativity in their planning, like Sir Solly Zuckerman, Basil Embry, Leonard Cheshire, Don Bennett, George Kenney, and Phil Cochran, would each have devised far different blueprints than, say, Hoyt Vandenberg or Curtis LeMay. During World War II, having those responsible for carrying out plans prepare them was a widely followed principle.

Looking at that vast range of contingencies from the vantage point of chaos theory suggests that tone of confidence in debates over using military force against the Endloesungapparat is excessive. An increased awareness of the sheer complexity of the conditions, and of the range of possible inputs and outcomes also points up the dangers of drawing deep or straight lines through the intricate webs of history and seeking simple answers to complex problems. But we do not need chaos-complexity theory to remind us that even the most rigorous and careful speculation opens up multitudes of bewildering possibilities and risks violating two basic caveats in the training of academic historians—the rules against imposing current perspectives on past situations and "what-iffing." As fascinating as that can be, it cannot lead us to an absolutely firm conclusion that if some particular thing were done or not done at any point in history, it would have produced a specific result.

Perhaps the most firm conclusion we can draw from all this at the moment, a half-century beyond the events, is that in not attacking the Endloesungapparat, the Allied elites misestimated how brightly the lights of hindsight would shine on those decisions in the future and how "history" might see that they had weighed their honor too lightly against practical considerations in the press of war—if military utility was in fact all that shaped that decision. It would, of course, be unfair to condemn the Allied elites for failing to take options that only came into focus with the passing of time, to those who had the luxury of pondering the contingencies at length and at leisure. But the increasing flow of evidence has, in an analogy to quantum physics, clouded our view on the decision not to act. If substantial numbers among the commercial, financial, and diplomatic elites in the neutral and Allied nations were more compliant in helping the Nazis carry out the Holocaust than seemed to be the case immediately after World War II, that raises the question of how much the attitudes that shaped those actions and decisions were shared by key political and military actors in that darkling scene. Why, if the Allies and Nazis carried out exchanges of wounded prisoners and diplomats, was no attempt made to negotiate some sort of quid pro quo, perhaps a broader version of the abortive scheme for exchanging trucks for Hungarian Jews, if not the easing of Allied air attacks on German cities in exchange for a halt to the mass murders?[76]

Pending the notional appearance of clarifying evidence, what light can chaos-complexity theory shed on all of this? Obviously, heightening our sensitivity to the potential of seemingly minor factors to have major effects suggests the need to delve more deeply for subtle factors and in the long run might lead to methods that would allow us to distinguish patterns amid turbulence, analogous to the developing of film. At this point, however, the greatest utility of a non-linear perspective will be in its highlighting the need to identify and map as many actual conditions as possible and to avoid clinging to any single factor or model of causality as an absolute truth or drawing firm conclusions from spongy evidence.

NOTES

1. For example, Martin Gilbert, *Auschwitz and the Allies* (New York: Henry Holt and Co., 1981), pp. 209–245; Morton Mintz, "Why Didn't We Bomb Auschwitz?" *Washington Post*, April 17, 1983, pp. D-1 and D-2; Bernard Wasserstein, *Britain and the Jews of Europe, 1939–1945* (Oxford: Clarendon Press, 1979), pp. 308–320; Richard L. Rubenstein and John K. Roth, *Approaches to Auschwitz: The Holocaust and Its Legacy* (Atlanta: John Knox Press, 1987), pp. 183–184; Roger M. Williams, "Why Wasn't Auschwitz Bombed? An American Moral Tragedy," *Commonweal*, 105 (November 24, 1978), pp. 746–751; David S. Wyman, "Why Auschwitz Was Never Bombed," *Commentary* 65 (May, 1978), pp. 37–48, and his *The Abandonment of the Jews* (New York: Pantheon Books, 1984), p. 292; and Raul Hilberg, *Perpetrators, Victims, Bystand-*

ers: *The Jewish Catastrophe 1933–1945* (New York: HarperCollins, 1993), esp. pp. 225–255. A recent argument against feasibility is David Horovitz, "Why the Allies Didn't Bomb Auschwitz," excerpted from *Jerusalem Report*, in *World Press*, 42:3 (March, 1995), pp. 44–45, and an argument for is Robert H. Hodges, "Auschwitz Revisited: Could the Soviets Have Bombed the Camp?" *Air Power History*, 44:4 (Winter, 1997), p. 74.

2. James H. Kitchens III, "The Bombing of Auschwitz Re-examined," *Journal of Military History*, 58:2 (April, 1994), p. 246.

3. A recent perspective on such questions is Richard H. Levy, "The Bombing of Auschwitz Revisited: A Critical Analysis," *Holocaust and Genocide Studies*, 10:3 (Winter, 1996), pp. 267–298.

4. U.S. National Archives, ASW 384.3 Bombardments—German Concentration Camps, Letter from John J. McCloy to John W. Pehle, November 18, 1944.

5. Cordell Hull, *The Memoirs of Cordell Hull* (New York: Macmillan, 1948), p. 184.

6. Levy, "The Bombing of Auschwitz Revisited," pp. 271–272.

7. A far-ranging major critique is Michael S. Sherry, *The Rise of American Air Power: The Creation of Armageddon* (New Haven: Yale University Press, 1987).

8. See British Public Record Office, AIR 20 4069 00388 for background on Anglo-Free French diplomatic exchanges on collateral damage caused by U.S. bombing missions in France in the spring of 1943.

9. Leni Yahal, *The Holocaust: The Fate of European Jewry, 1932–1945*, trans. Ina Friedman and Haya Galai (New York: Oxford University Press, 1990), p. 639.

10. W. W. Rostow, *Pre-Invasion Bombing Strategy: General Eisenhower's Decision of March 25, 1944* (Austin: University of Texas Press, 1981).

11. For a discussion of the dialogue within the U.S. Army Air Forces hierarchy, see Conrad C. Crane, *Bombs, Cities and Civilians: American Airpower Strategy in World War II* (Lawrence: University Press of Kansas, 1993).

12. David Brazleton, "SBD Dauntless," in Charles W. Cain, ed., *Aircraft in Profile*, vol. 9 (Garden City: Doubleday, 1971), pp. 182–185; Frank Wesley Craven and James Lea Cate, *U.S. Army Air Forces in World War II*, vol. 2 (Chicago: University of Chicago Press, 1950), p. 478; and Ray Wagner, *American Combat Planes* (Garden City: Doubleday, 1968), p. 19.

13. Richard G. Davis, *Carl F. Spaatz and the Air War in Europe* (Washington, D.C.: Center for Air Force History, 1992), p. 379.

14. See September 18, 1944, entry, *The Army Air Forces in World War II: A Combat Chronology 1941–1945* (Maxwell Air Force Base: Air University, 1973), p. 454.

15. Hodges, "Auschwitz Revisited," pp. 74–75.

16. William D. Rubenstein, *The Myth of Rescue: Why the Democracies Could Not Have Saved More Jews from the Nazis* (New York: Routledge, 1997); and William J. vanden Heuvel, *America, Franklin D. Roosevelt and the Holocaust* (Chicago: Center for New Deal Studies, 1996) [Occasional Papers, No. 2], esp. pp. 8–14.

17. Kitchens, "Bombing of Auschwitz," pp. 244–245.

18. Levy, "Bombing of Auschwitz," pp. 268–272.

19. Alfred D. Chandler, Jr., et al., eds., *The Papers of Dwight David Eisenhower*, vol. 4 (Baltimore: Johns Hopkins University Press, 1970), pp. 2220–2221.

20. Kitchens, "Bombing of Auschwitz," p. 246.

21. Chaim Weiszmann, *Memorandum Submitted to the Royal Commission on Behalf of the Jewish Agency for Palestine* (London: Jewish Agency for Palestine, 1936), p. 283.

22. N.a., "Death Trap for Jews," *Nation* 147:2 (July 16, 1938), p. 61; Georges Duhamel, *The White War of 1938*, trans. N. Hoppe (London: J. M. Dent, 1939), p. 24; and Howard Daniel, "Mass Murder in Poland," *The Nation*, 150:4 (January 27, 1940), pp. 92–94.

23. For a recent perspective, see Warren Hoge, *New York Times*, April 6, 1997, pt. 4, p. 8.

24. For background, see Paul L. Hanna, *British Policy in Palestine* (Washington, D.C.: American Council on Public Affairs, 1942), esp. p. 141; David Ben-Gurion, *Letters to Paula*, trans. Aubrey Hodes (London: Valentine, Mitchell, 1971), pp. 216–240.

25. Raul Hilberg, *The Destruction of the European Jews* (New York: Holmes and Meier, 1985), p. 393.

26. Walter Laqueur, *The Terrible Secret: An Investigation into the Suppression of Information about Hitler's "Final Solution"* (London: Weidenfeld and Nicolson, 1980), pp. 283–285.

27. F. H. Hinsley et al., *British Intelligence in the Second World War: Its Influence on Strategy and Operations*, vol. 2 (London: Her Majesty's Stationery Office, 1981), pp. 670–671.

28. Martha Gellhorn, *The Face of War* (New York: Atlantic Monthly, 1988), p. 102.

29. *Punishment for War Crimes* (New York: United Nations Information Office, n.d. [c. 1942]), pp. 53–55.

30. Varian Fry, "The Massacre of the Jews," *The New Republic*, 107:25 (December 21, 1942), p. 816.

31. Philip Bernstein, "The Jews of Europe," *The Nation*, 156:1 (January 2, 1943), p. 9.

32. For a recent debate over that issue, see David Turner's letters to the editor in the February 5 and March 5 issues of *The London Review of Books*, 1998, p. 4.

33. For an example, see Roland Marchand, *Advertising and the American Dream: Making Way for Modernity, 1920–1940* (Berkeley: University of California Press, 1985), pp. 35–36.

34. For example, Robert K. Andrist, ed., *The American Heritage History of the 1920s and 1930s* (New York: American Heritage-Bonanza, 1970), p. 382.

35. For glimpses of the tenor of of the times, see "Ownership and Control of Moving Picture Companies," Appendix A, "Jews in America," *Fortune*, 13:2 (February, 1936), pp. 142–144; Robert E. Herzstein, *Henry R. Luce: A Political Portrait of the Man Who Created the American Century* (New York: Scribner's, 1994); and the *New Yorker* cartoon annuals of the era.

36. For example, Bruce Winton Knight, *How to Run a War* (New York: Knopf, 1936), pp. 39–76, and Walter Millis, *Road to War: America, 1914–1917* (Boston: Houghton Mifflin, 1935), esp. pp. 62–121; for loan statistics, see Charles Callan Tansill, *America Goes to War* (Gloucester, Mass.: Peter Smith, 1963 [1937]), Appendix A, pp. 660– 661.

37. A study of boycott efforts is Moshe R. Gottlieb, *American Nazi Resistance, 1933–1941* (New York: KTAV Publishing House, 1982).

38. Israel Cohen, *The Zionist Movement* (New York: Zionist Organization of America, 1976), pp. 295–304.

39. The flavor of journalism during the period is reflected in Robert E. Sherwood, *Roosevelt and Hopkins: An Intimate History* (New York: Harper and Brothers, 1950), pp. 760–761; for perspectives on the 1941 congressional hearings, see Clayton R. Koppes and Gregory D. Black, *Hollywood Goes to War: How Politics, Profits and Propaganda Shaped World War II Movies* (New York: Free Press, 1987), pp. 8 and 40–47; and Joe Morella, Edward Z. Epstein, and John Griggs, *The Films of World War II* (Secaucus, N.J.: Citadel Press), pp. 5–6 and 11–15.

40. For a brief survey of the Biltmore Declaration, see Robert St. John, *Ben Gurion: A Biography* (Garden City: Doubleday and Co., 1971), pp. 87–92.

41. Robert D. Kaplan, *The Arabists: The Romance of an American Elite* (New York: Free Press, 1993).

42. For example, *Documents Related to the Foreign Relations of the United States: 1944*, vol. 1 (Washington, D.C.: U.S. Department of State, 1963), p. 1003. [Hereinafter referred to as FRUS]

43. For example, the Eisenhower papers, the Roosevelt-Churchill messages, Stephen Ambrose's *Rise to Globalism*; Chester Wilmot's *The Struggle for Europe*; James Leutze, ed., *The London Journal of Raymond E. Lee 1940–1941* (Boston: Little, Brown, 1971); and David Dilks, ed., *The Diaries of Sir Alexander Cadogan 1938–1945* (New York: P. Putnam's, 1972).

44. Anthony Cave Brown, *Bodyguard of Lies*, vol. 1 (New York: Harper and Row, 1975), pp. 74–76.

45. For an extensive analysis of Long's role, see Chapter 6, "Breckinridge Long and the Jewish Refugees," pp. 126–145, in Richard Breitman and Alan M. Kraut, *American Refugee Policy and European Jewry, 1933–1945* (Bloomington: Indiana University Press, 1987).

46. vanden Heuvel, *America, Franklin D. Roosevelt and the Holocaust*, pp. 14–15.

47. John Morton Blum, *V Was for Victory: Politics and American Culture During World War II* (New York: Harcourt Brace Jovanovich, 1976), p. 176.

48. See David Wyman, ed., *The World Reacts to the Holocaust* (Baltimore: Johns Hopkins University Press, 1996), pp. 702–704.

49. For example, vanden Heuvel, *America, Franklin D. Roosevelt and the Holocaust*, pp. 13–14.

50. For example, see FRUS, *The Lansing Papers*, vol. 2 (Washington, D.C.: U.S. Department of State, 1940), pp. 107–109.

51. Martin Gilbert, ed., *The Churchill War Papers*, vol. 1 (New York: W. W. Norton, 1993), pp. 564–567 and 748.

52. Cohen, *The Zionist Movement*, p. 301.

53. Richard C. Rubenstein and John K. Roth, *Approaches to Auschwitz: The Holocaust and Its Legacy* (Atlanta: John Knox Press, 1987), p. 183.

54. Martin Gilbert, *The Second World War: A Complete History* (New York: Henry Holt, 1989), p. 546.

55. David Stafford, *British and European Resistance, 1940–45: A Survey of the Special Operations Executive, with Documents* (Toronto: University of Toronto Press, 1983), pp. 180–181.

56. Nigel Nicolson, ed., *Diaries and Letters of Harold Nicolson: The War Years 1939–1945*, vol. 2 (New York: Atheneum, 1967), p. 344.

57. Rubenstein and Roth, *Approaches to Auschwitz*, pp. 183–184; John Morton Blum, *From the Morgenthau Diaries: Years of War*, vol. 3 (Boston: Houghton Mifflin, 1967), pp. 220–221; and Blum, *V Was for Victory*, p. 178.

58. Cordell Hull, *Memoirs*, vol. 2 (New York: Macmillan, 1948), pp. 1184, 1278, and 1291.

59. For example, see *FRUS:1942*, vol. 4, pp. 538–558; and *FRUS:1944*, vol. 1, p. 1164.

60. U.S. Department of State, *Foreign Relations of the United States: Diplomatic Papers, 1944*, vol. 1, *General* (Washington, D.C.: U.S. Government Printing Office, 1966), p. 1234.

61. For a detailed account of McCloy's exchanges with the WRB, see Kai Bird, *The Chairman: John J. McCloy: The Making of the American Establishment* (New York: Simon and Schuster, 1997), pp. 201–227.

62. See Robert D. Schulzinger, *The Wise Men of Foreign Affairs: The History of the Council on Foreign Relations* (New York: Columbia University Press, 1984), p. 102.

63. Morris J. MacGregor, Jr., *Integration of the Armed Forces 1940–1965* (Washington, D.C.: Center for Military History, 1981) [Defense Studies series], pp. 23–41.

64. Bird, *The Chairman*, pp. 208–209.

65. For a survey, see Warren F. Kimball, *Swords or Plowshares? The Morgenthau Plan for Defeated Nazi Germany 1943–1946* (Philadelphia: J. B. Lippincott, 1976).

66. A "hard line" appeared before Pearl Harbor in American academic circles, for example, see "History Lesson," *Time*, 38:22 (December 1, 1941), pp. 57–58.

67. For details, see Frank M. Buscher, *The U.S. War Crimes Trial Program in Germany, 1946–1955* (Westport, Conn.: Greenwood Publishing Co., 1989), pp. 14–15; and Elting Morison, *Turmoil and Tradition; A Study in the Life and Times of Henry L. Stimson* (Boston: Houghton-Mifflin, 1960), pp. 604–610; for a glimpse of McCloy's involvement, see Alfred D. Chandler, *Eisenhower: The War Years*, vol. 4 (Baltimore: Johns Hopkins University Press, 1970), pp. 2270–2271.

68. Bradley F. Smith, *The Road to Nuremberg* (New York: Basic Books, 1981), p. 191.

69. Telford Taylor, *The Anatomy of the Nuremberg Trials: A Personal Memoir* (New York: Alfred A. Knopf, 1992), p. 4; also see Ann and John Tusa, *The Nuremberg Trial* (New York: Atheneum, 1984), pp. 56–66.

70. Kaplan, *The Arabists*, p. 89.

71. See Christopher Simpson, *Blowback: America's Recruitment of Nazis and Its Effects on the Cold War* (New York: Collier Books, 1988), pp. 49, 93, 144, 191–192, and 251.

72. For an overview, see Roger Beaumont, *Special Operations and Elite Units: A Research Guide* (New York: Greenwood Press, 1988), esp. pp. 63–102.

73. Some disasters were the British Combined Operations–Free French attack on Dakar, 1941; the British Commandos' "Raid on Rommel," 1941; and Dieppe, 1942; successes included the British Commandos' raid that seized crucial German radar technology at Bruneval in 1942; British Special Air Service forays against Axis airfields in North Africa, 1941–1942; American prisoner-of-war camp liberations in the Philippines in 1944; and Otto Skorzeny's rescue of Mussolini.

74. David Stafford, *Britain and European Resistance, 1940–45: A Survey of the Special Operations Executive, with Documents* (Toronto: University of Toronto Press, 1980), pp. 180–181.

75. For example, see Bertram Schwartz, letter to the editor, *Journal of Military History*, 60:1 (January, 1996), pp. 205–211.

76. For example, Richard Breitman, *Official Secrets: What the Nazis Planned* (New York: Hill and Wang, 1999).

8

Searching for Patterns in the Murk

While the chaos theory pioneer Edward Lorenz has insisted that "we should believe what is true even if it hurts, rather than what is false, even if it makes us happy,"[1] that assumes certainty about what is true. That sense of fuzziness led Ron Rosenbaum, after years of studying Hitler, to express his "feeling of something still missing, something still inexplicable."[2] In a similar vein, the swirls of contradictions that made up the Hitlerzeit have led some to argue that it cannot be dealt with as a part of history without muting its unique horror or leading to some extenuation, insanity defense or not. Despite that, many have tried to nail the bug of Nazism to a specimen board and assay it through different lenses, from analyzing election statistics to mapping the bewildering bureaucracy. From the perspective of chaos-complexity, anti-Semitism looks like the fixed point in an attractor dynamic around which the Nazis orbited, the focus of their obsession even when caught in the strong gravity fields of waging a multi-front war. Other non-linear metaphors that come to mind in looking at the Third Reich are the tumbling of a woodpile when a single log is pulled out and the blind collective impulse of schools of fish and flocks of birds—and lemmings. But could something as complex as the NS Staat and the Holocaust have resulted from such simple mechanisms? Did the Nazis' mass murder of millions whom they judged to be subhumans spring from some crude collective impulse to wreak havoc, like that which drives army ants and plagues of grasshoppers? Was that upheaval wholly peculiar to Germans and Central Europeans at that particular time, or was it only one variant of a genus of shared tantrums that have sprung forth from humans' lizard brains en masse from time to time in such wholesale slaughters of varying scale as the Reign of Terror, the Indian Mutiny, the Armenian massacres, strategic bombing, and most recently, in Cambodia, Rwanda, and Bosnia (see Figure 5)? A historian's attribution of the relentless slaughter by warring tribes in Rwanda to their trying to sustain "a vision they have of themselves and the others" rather than pursuing "material interests"[3] certainly sounds a lot like a rationale for the actions of National Socialism.

Does drawing such analogies minimize the uniqueness of the Nazis' crimes—or do patterns within the Holocaust and other instances of mass slaughter reflect the often discounted power of human reflexes and impulses to make distinctions, dehumanize, and affix blame? Just as physicists examining "a simulation . . . . must wonder what bit of reality was left out, what potential surprise was left out,"[4] the Duke of Wellington sensed the limits of military history when he asserted, "no individual can recollect the order in which they [events in battle] occurred, which makes all the difference to their value and importance."[5] Squinting at the tangled landscape of the Hitlerzeit through the lense of chaos-complexity throws a different light on that and raises the question of whether the Iron Duke missed the point that "the complexity we see in the world is the result of underlying simplicity"?[6] Is the working of history, then, less like a broad flowing river and more like winking fireflies, shimmering sunspots, or irregular eruptions of energy—phase-changes that take place within a certain range from time to time, and are not predictable in scale or frequency? As contrary to common sense as that may seem, simple children's tunes and Beethoven's symphonies are made up of the same few notes of the musical scale, and all the materials that make up the universe are combinations of several dozen elements on the periodic table. The intricate patterns flowing from such simplicity offer a different perspective to historians, who have long anguished over the uncertainties of causality, what led Mark Twain to suggest that history rhymed rather than repeated itself.[7] But if Keith Windschuttle was right in proposing, "What happens in history . . . is never random, but neither does it conform to any deep-seated design,"[8] that seems to leave no option in searching for causes beyond artful guessing[9] and puts us in the same box, again, as physicists for whom "Turbulence remains an unsolved problem" with no "adequate theoretical account of the whorls and eddies that appear in waterfalls, whirlpools, and wakes."[10]

Analysts have drawn other comparisons between chaos-complexity and physics, like the warping effect of the "law of location" on an

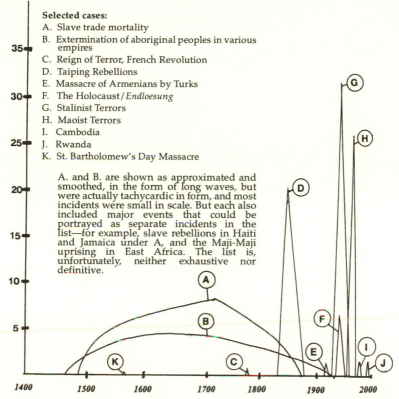

Millions of deaths

Selected cases:
A. Slave trade mortality
B. Extermination of aboriginal peoples in various empires
C. Reign of Terror, French Revolution
D. Taiping Rebellions
E. Massacre of Armenians by Turks
F. The Holocaust/*Endloesung*
G. Stalinist Terrors
H. Maoist Terrors
I. Cambodia
J. Rwanda
K. St. Bartholomew's Day Massacre

A. and B. are shown as approximated and smoothed, in the form of long waves, but were actually tachycardic in form, and most incidents were small in scale. But each also included major events that could be portrayed as separate incidents in the list—for example, slave rebellions in Haiti and Jamaica under A, and the Maji-Maji uprising in East Africa. The list is, unfortunately, neither exhaustive nor definitive.

Figure 5 Tachycardia of horror: Mass slaughter in modern history

experimenter's subjectivity. Individual perception and the choice of subject and method obviously affect all sciences, but metaphysical factors like evil, cruelty, and the "seven deadly sins" push the study of human behavior, history, and philosophy into another dimension, and too often to denial and minimization. Nevertheless, there are many theories about the sources of human viciousness; social scientists have wrangled at length over the implications of the Millgram and Berkeley studies and the research of Harry Harlow, Teodoro Adorno, and Milton Rokeach—but have come to few firm conclusions. It is not quite clear, for instance, why we turn to faux terror for diversion and amusement.

Does that provide a way to anticipate real horrors, to diminish them by building extreme models, or to serve as a hardening or numbing device? Is it the working of an ordering reflex trying to deal with a form of chaos? How much does observing faux violence reduce or amplify actual impulses? Or is such diversion akin to the tendency noted by American social scientists among combat troops in World War II to judge enemy weapons least likely to kill or wound them as the most deadly threat—and vice versa?

While the Hitlerzeit presents us with a great swirl of such imponderables, that is also true of many other historical eras and events. Fluctuations in the ratio of order and disorder abound throughout history, like the march of sunspots, differing in size and shape and displaying jumbled patterns that nevertheless allow some level of prediction. But our view of the NS Staat is dimmed and blurred by several special filters, including a very high but uneven degree of secrecy, whirlpools of turbulence generated by corrupt and inept Nazi Party administrators, and uneven documentation. Maps of the bureaucratic intricacy do not convey the organic metabolism of what many saw as an incomprehensible crazy-quilt. The latter was partly due to the Nazi elites' diverging from the orthodox procedures of well-ordered palaces and chanceries, but it also resulted from deliberate destruction and falsification of records and very high levels of war damage. Nevertheless, some of the Third Reich's administrative sub-elements—including the death-camps—recorded their business in a traditional, thorough, bureaucratic way; extensive evidence survived, including sanitized summaries of Hitler's *Tischgesprach* (table talk) and high-level command conference transcripts, as well as some local government records. Beyond that, National Socialism was a populist revolutionary movement that crumbled and blurred boundaries between the layers and compartments of society. That churning produced a mix of such contradictory ingredients as street bullies, superstitions, pornography, anti-intellectualism, paganism, and a host of academics, professionals, and intellectuals who joined the Party before 1933. The latter included "world-class" scientists who were willing to swallow or look past the Nazis' idealizing of the German peasantry under the rubric *Blut und Boden* (blood and soil, with "blood" a code-word for eugenic "purity") and euthanasia as state policy.

How much were the Nazis, their victims and foes, or individual Germans exercising free will as opposed to being caught like foam on the tide of history? In chaos-complexity terms, could we ever hope to identify the "initial conditions" in Germany that led to the Hitlerzeit? Along the metaphorical line of march, we saw how apparent causal threads ran far back in history, long before the Nazis' appearance, and the entwining of many Germans' resentment toward the "diktat" peace and the humiliation of Versailles, the blaming of democracy for the 1918 collapse, and the much longer and deeper roots of anti-Semitism.[11] Identifying such major factors is one thing, but pinning all conditions and causes on the specimen board is another.[12] Even if that were possible, it would not replicate qualitative aspects like the wispy subtleties of diplomacy, the interplay of personalities, and "back-channel" processes. During the 1920s, as the Nazis' political fortunes rose and fell, even very sophisticated observers saw them as one of many splinter parties created by the Weimar Constitution's broad-gauge rules; their appeals to bad taste and lower instincts in the attempt to attract voters of varied interests did not seem wildly different from those of many other political factions in Germany or other democracies. Like con artists at a flea market, the Nazis spread their miscellanies on the table, convincing many, with a wink and a nudge, that the particular things they liked amid that tawdry midden of ideologies and policies were *the* solid goods. As a result, some Nazi Party sub-organizations recruited mainly thugs and bullies, while others forged links with people of good taste and judgment and provided opportunities for many, talented and otherwise, to rise far higher in status than they could have under the old social and economic order. Whatever else Albert Speer concealed, he admitted that he had been drawn in, as other talented people like Goebbels, Heydrich, and Riefenstahl were, by the unique opportunity to exercise his talents.[13]

The swirls of individual motive also make it impossible to draw sharp boundaries between the dynamics of Nazism and the flow of German history or to determine how much the National Socialists' juggernaut cart was built and rolling long before they hitched a ride on it.[14] (In a special irony, Nazism inverted Hegel's "law" of the transmutation of quantity into quality, as a bizarre and tiny splinter party on the edge of German politics expanded into a massive force in less than five years.) Despite the distinct cachet of their propaganda, the Nazis' dynamic and ruthless modernism was not unique at the time, nor were rough-and-tumble electoral politics peculiar to Weimar Germany. Apparent similarities to the growing turbulence within the major European democracies and throughout their empires also warped perspective. Militant factions of varying stripes between the world wars from Bolshevism and a host of Fascistic movements to the Popular Front and New Deal spiced the bland pudding of day-to-day politics with grandiose posturing, uniforms, slogans, and symbols and attracted many intellectuals to one or another among the many polarities. But that does not explain exactly how the Nazis, in January 1933, despite the sleaziness of their goods and promises to kill democracy, ultimately attracted more votes than any other party in a single Weimar Republic election. Since the fall of the Third Reich, many historians have pored over election records, in a postmortem of the innards of German society that led to that pathology, and the search goes on. Might chaos-complexity theory help shine more light on that, beyond providing a sharper sense that one form of chaos replaced another when the Brown Revolution toppled the Weimar Republic? Could it help identify just which crucial forces, subtle or major, brought that about? Sensing that there were more levels of intricacy than we thought is not the same as determining exactly what they were.

In any case, chaos-complexity does reinforce historians and philosophers' concerns about the elusiveness of certainty in their tracing of causality. Fractals, especially, highlight how intricate the diversity of systems based on very elemental logic can be. Consider, for example, the many sources of friction in the Nazi war machine identified by historians, including German scientists' parochialism and turf-guarding, wasteful archaic and skilled labor–intensive methods, the use of forced and slave labor in industry, Hitler's idiosyncracies, Nazi functionaries' ineptitude and corruption, and individual Germans' attitudes and actions, from avid enthusiasm to compliance, foot-dragging, and sabotage. Most studies of the Hitlerzeit have focused on one or a few such elements, rather than a sprawling map. That is understandable, given the sheer complexity of constructing such arrays and tracing their linkage. Consider, for example, the following list of putative reasons for the Nazis' coming to power in January 1933 cited by various observers and historians:

resentment toward the Versailles Treaty

German authoritarian traditions in the family and culture

American isolationism

bourgeois fear of Communism

industrialists' and militarists' desire to rearm

Nazi propaganda skills

the rise of pacifism in the democracies

America's recall of war loans

the 1923 mega-inflation in Germany

secret German-Soviet military collaboration

eugenics and pseudo-scientific racism

ingrained anti-Semitism in Germany, including folklore regarding sexual abuse, ritual murder, venereal disease, Jew-baiting, and Passion Plays, and concern about competition and Jewish involvement in radical leftist movements

appeasement

the Great Depression and Smoot-Hawley tariff

the League of Nations' decline

Japan's invasion of Manchuria and exit from the League

dissonance between Britain and France at the Geneva arms talks

the Weimar constitution's proportional representation clause

disruption of the Reichstag by German extremist parties

Hitler's charisma and political canniness

As we saw earlier, roots can be drawn much further into the past, while, as with the flow of fractals, causal branches can also be extended into the future from the point the Nazis came to power to include the origins of World War II, the Endloesung, and the dramatic phase changes in Germany after World War II.[15] Where, in drawing such webs or framing equations, should we insert terms that represent the effect of unidentified subtle elements and catalysts or such ephemeral idiosyncratic quantities as Hitler's rat phobia and many top Nazis' fear of Freemasonry? Listing and weighting all such factors, stark and subtle, down to the level of individual attitudes and actions would be an impossible task. That illustrates what chaos-complexity theorists deem the "coastline of England" problem—that is, as the measuring of complex boundaries approaches reality at the micro level, dimensions increase. Hence the substantial difference between the length of a coastline when measured on a one-meter scale and when measured on the level of grains of sand. But what if chaos-complexity helped us increase our resolving power as we measured such dimensions and gave us greater insight into the dynamics of history by looking at it from a different perspective? There seems to be little hope of that if we substitute "history" for "physics" in Ilya Prigogine's assertion that "The basic vision of classical physics was the conviction that the future is determined by the present, and therefore a careful study of the present permits the unveiling of the future. At no time, however, was this more than a theoretical possibility."[16] If that is true, even the most rigorous studies of the past would yield no valid explanation of the present, let alone accurate predictions. But what if Mark Twain was right about history rhyming, and history works something like the tracing of a double attractor? If we could see that more clearly, then we might map and trace the roots of things like Nazism, Fascism, Bolshevism, and genocide and test the validity of such challenging but currently untestable assertions as "the antecedents of the Holocaust lay in European, particularly British, imperialism"[17] and "it is arguable, at least, that

Fascism (understood functionally) was born in the late 1860s in the American South."[18]

That millennium is not at hand. Lyrical impressionism remains the mainstay of historical writing, and although the electronic revolution has increased our immediate knowledge of what happens throughout much of the world, most of the "now" remains unknown. Some fragments come to us in minutes or hours, initially in the form of news or gossip, and more much later, in days, weeks, or months, as more "serious" journalism or as formal reports, and finally, in years, decades, and centuries, as history or archaeology. But most of "what's happening" remains out of reach, and we deal with that by generalizing and making broad assumptions on the basis of broad patterns and data. The gap between the assumption of knowledge and reality, often filled in by arrogance and heedlessness, is reflected in the frequency with which governments and armed forces have been caught by surprise over the last century. (Technology has made that easier, too.) But are there any stars to steer by on this turbulent and murky sea? Chaos-complexity theory may affirm that "the disdain for assigning large events small causes is not rational in a world partly nonlinear,"[19] but there is a great difference between recognizing the workings of a broad truth and identifying a specific minor factor that had a disproportionate influence or, to put it more tersely—general factors, yes; specific causes, no. Where does that leave us? Over roughly six millennia, concepts have appeared that at the time seemed to offer ways to discern new patterns and meanings. Many did, but the mixed record raises the question of how chaos-complexity theory compares with such faulty concepts as auguries, oracles, and humors and angle-of-attack theories that proved marginal, irrelevant, or dangerous.

It seems obvious enough that the more arrows we fire over a wall at a target we cannot see, the more likely one will hit it, but it is less clear whether firing randomly at a jinking target would make a hit more or less likely. Chaos-complexity theory reminds us that such ambiguities and uncertainties are all about us, part of the natural order of things, and may only be discerned and measured within certain limited ranges. Lorenz's butterfly metaphor, for example, raises the question of how much human activities are even as predictable as the weather—like wars, revolutions, financial markets, migrations, epidemics, and mass panics, all of them potentially more destructive, unpredictable, and complex than tempests and typhoons. Indeed, revolutions have often been compared to the cleansing effect of a great storm; many—usually at a distance, like Marx and Jefferson—saw them as mechanisms of beneficial change, that is, of changes they favored. But analysts from Edmund Burke to Crane Brinton have puzzled over the tendency of revolts to rebound, go off course, and generate further reactionism and repressions, hence the cliché, "revolutions devour their own children." By underscoring the tendency of apparently well-ordered complex systems to go wildly off course when nudged even slightly, chaos-complexity theory offers a different perspective on the bewilderment of those who have launched and studied revolutions. They may have grossly underestimated the scale of forces involved, especially the power produced by releasing forces from social control, especially primal urges to survive, punish, dominate, and destroy—and impulses to self-destruction. It seems most appropriate, then, that the vortex, a popular image of chaos, was a fashionable symbol of modernism and protofascism in the early twentieth century and that its sense of swirling turbulence carried over into both Fascism's fuzzy ideology and the lack of a generally accepted definition of it. Most Fascistic systems have displayed some similar traits, like stirring up and manipulating ethnic and class hatred; anti-Marxism; admiration of brutality, war, torture, and atrocity; sadistic costumery; aggressive nationalism; and mass ceremonies. Most have been xenophobic, but not all were rabidly anti-Semitic or racist. Although Fascism is widely seen as a right-wing movement, those boundaries have been blurred as well. Some variants like Peronism and Nazism enfolded populist and socialist values and rhetoric and modernist and antimodernist themes.

That ambiguity blurs our view of which elements of neo-Fascism might be merely pallid traces and which might be powerful pathologies and precursors of a significant resurgence. While it seemed unlikely from the end of World War II to the mid-1980s, Fascism was not dead but dormant. If, as David Schoenbaum and others have suggested, all complex societies harbor germs of Fascism, then, in chaos-complexity terms, it might be some sort of self-organizing system generated by the convergence of a set of not necessarily identical conditions and, like the tracings of a double attractor, orbiting within a range that produces roughly approximate pathologies. If so, or if it is an approximate whole produced by the sum of different parts,[20] that lies a long way from the Marxist view of Fascism as a stage in the evolution of capitalism. It might help explain, however, why aggregates of what seem to be roughly similar attitudes have produced such a wide range of effects. Might we be able to identify variables in a physics of mass violence, for example, that account for differences in the scale, duration, and type of violence produced by racial, religious, and ethnic prejudice in the United States, Tsarist Russia, India-Pakistan, Britain, Ireland, Turkey, Rwanda, South Africa, and the Balkans and those based on such differences as politics, ideology and class, like those in Revolutionary France, Soviet Russia, Communist China, and Cambodia during the twentieth

century? What if the twentieth century's Fascistic movements were
anomalous transient wave fronts that coalesced into a kind of coherence
amid turbulent conditions peculiar to the times? If they were as seemingly unique as Ikhnaton, Sparta, the Assassins, the Vikings, the Albi-
gensian heresy, and the St. Bartholomew's Day massacre, they
shouldn't recur. But if history is a process in which forces orbit around
sets of attractors, while absolute duplication is not likely, rough approximations are—rather like Mark Twain's view of history rhyming.

In that case, most if not all such mass slaughters were variations
on a theme, which brings us back to the workings of history. A
generation ago, Arnold Toynbee tried to discern meaningful patterns
over time by looking at civilizations as complex organisms struggling
to adapt, survive, and grow.[21] Like Marx and other advocates of
"covering laws," he treated the working of slight forces as twigs
swept along in the flood. Chaos-complexity raises the question of
whether that view of causal dynamics is right, and clusters of similar
but not identical elements converge in the turbulent flow of time, like
clumps of boulders formed in the bed of a raging river that form
rough approximations, like the English and American civil wars, the
Romanticism of the early 1800s and 1900s, or ancient and modern
imperialism. If historical events are analogous to chemical reactions
produced by roughly similar convergences of elements, temperatures,
and pressures and if some patterns do reappear, in the manner of
echoes, then chaos-complexity might help us identify attractors
around which horrors and wars take up their orbiting and plot the
roughly common conditions—the "fuzzy sets"—that lead to that.
Isaiah Berlin's claim that there is "no sharp break between history
and mythology or . . . . metaphysics"[22] brings us back to the question
of whether it might be possible to frame a view of history encom-
passing all the causes of a particular event—or the most critical ones.
Might we, then, be able to chart enough details of German, European,
and world history to find out why things really went the way they
did in the Hitlerzeit? That is certainly not a trivial question, considering that after-images of those events seem to be looming ever larger
as we move farther away from them in time.

Framing such hypotheses and theoretical models of mega-atrocities
may seem to risk putting a bland mask of rationality on them, in the
spirit of biologists killing to dissect. The plight of historians trying to
explain the Holocaust as narrative history is not too different in essence
from that of social scientists engaged "in traditional policy research and
model building [who] focus on the 'normal' or average behavior of
relevant systems," which "expedites policy-making since examining
the total gamut of possible behaviors and variables strains even the

most thorough analysis."[23] Generalizing and relying on impressionism would be all to the good if the simplicity and time gained by that produced benefits outweighing any loss of linkage with reality, but leaving the Endloesung outside the scope of rational inquiry ignores nature's attitude toward vacuums. Beyond literal mountains of historical studies of the Hitlerzeit and the many dozens of biographies of Hitler lie all the portrayals of that era in art, drama, film, and fiction, which arguably have shaped far more attitudes than academic history, or the musings, however elegant, of intellectuals like Elias Canetti, Hannah Arendt, and Sigmund Freud. It also abandons ground to the Holocaust deniers.

We should, of course, not brush past Freud in re-tracing Nazism's route of march, since he was hounded by it from home and country at the end of his life. As those shadows darkened, he envisioned, in *Civilization and Its Discontents*, a collective ferocity mounting in the first half of the twentieth century in mass cultures throughout the world, especially in Europe and East Asia. Freud saw those tempestuous forces arising from civilization's placing social constraints on violence and building up pressures bound to burst forth violently in some form or other. That model of a heating boiler is a linear one, in that x amount of heating yields y amount of energy, but it is congruent in essence with chaos-complexity theory in the sense that the ultimate result is chaos. The Freudian concerns for the potential power of perversions, pathologies, and superstitions and the Nazis' fixation on pain and cruelty both suggest, albeit loosely, a kind of attractor dynamic. So does the polarity between lofty romantic ideals and the Nazis' obsessive hatred for Jews and the heavy overtones of sadism that suffused the Third Reich's ceremonies, paraphernalia, and ultimately the Holocaust. We can only speculate whether the Nazis hated Freud not only because he was Jewish but also because he hit too close to home in searching for the roots of motive and action, even before he ultimately turned his analytical gaze on human viciousness.

When Freud made his pessimistic assessment in the late 1930s, the orchestration and stimulation of frustration, resentment, and hatred by monarchs and politicians had long been visible, feeding the illusion that they were cyclical and fell within a certain range, like undulating long-waves, not spikes of tachycardic chaos that appeared suddenly and reached far beyond expectations in scale. There were visible patterns, like the link between economic anxiety and scapegoating. In the 1870s, for example, Stoecker's Christian Socialist Worker's Party in Austria rose out of a financial depression, then fell back when it eased.[24] Religious and ethnic tensions had also ebbed and flowed in British, French, and American politics throughout the nineteenth and twentieth centu-

ries in rough conformity with economic downturns. The National
Socialists' electoral fortunes also fluctuated. They gained Reichstag
seats following the runaway inflation of 1923, lost momentum in the
late 1920s, then surged sharply as the Great Depression buffeted Central
Europe. But if we envision anti-Semitism as a kind of oscillating curve
in the flow of European history or as a variable influenced by other
variables, what made the Nazis' anti-Jewish violence soar so steeply
above earlier waveforms? What element in the shrill but apparently
traditional anti-Semitism in Europe between the world wars trans-
muted it into something far greater, all the more deadly for seeming to
be just another cycle in a longstanding phenomenon?[25] And why did
the world whistle past that graveyard—and so many others as well?

Other patterns lie embedded in the turbulence of the Hitlerzeit. For
example, what happened to the millions of Germans who warmed to
democracy during the Weimar era—more than half the voters in the
final elections—and those who voted Socialist and Communist? The
hazard of openly expressing independent action and thought in the NS
Staat blocks our view of how many Germans—including Nazis—became disillusioned as Himmler's apparatus grew and tightened its grip
and the steel gauntlet beneath the black leather gloves came into view.
That landscape is also clouded by the linking of patriotism to state,
party, and the military in the NS Staat, in a war-siege mentality from
1933 on, which kept the plotters against Hitler in 1943–1944 from
planning to depose the Nazi superstructure when they took power.
From the standpoint of chaos-complexity, were there subtle but crucial
variables in that turbulence, factors analogous to the mosquito, overlooked for centuries as a cause of malaria, but whose influence proved
to be far out of proportion to its scale? Are some causal factors not yet
recognized—and which perhaps never will be?

That brings us to another crossroads in the fog, one that looks at first
glance like a deconstructionist cul-de-sac. What if even the most sophisticated methods of research and analysis failed to provide a clear view
of the snarls of causality and if mapping the turbulence of historical
webs proved to be wholly out of reach, because the sheer complexity of
history made that impossible? That would render the search for causality futile and leave the crafting of history pretty much where it is, most
of it closer to artful musing than to science, social or otherwise. Although chaos-complexity theory seems to support that possibility, especially its principle that very slight forces may yield disproportionate
results, historians have been wrestling with the dilemmas of tracing
complex causation for a long time.

The Nazis themselves drew a cause-and-effect relationship in attributing their "triumph of the will" to the brutality, rage, and terror they

brandished in every direction, first to gain power, then to intimidate their victims and foes—and other Germans. That ferocity served to diminish the body of evidence of that era, from everyday life to the Holocaust. The hazards of committing thoughts and impressions to paper, including diaries and letters, as well as the danger that intimate conversation and offhand remarks might be overheard by the security services, made it increasingly difficult for Germans to sense each others' inner thoughts, if not their moods. It produced deference to cheerleading and led to "inner migration" or "inner emigration," as people turned to such distractions as hobbies, gardening, or reading as an apolitical refuge. Another source of social dislocation was the destruction of over forty German cities by Anglo-American bombing raids, which sent many survivors and refugees into the countryside. In nonlinear terms, chaos begat chaos.

Can chaos-complexity, then, give us a significantly clearer view of Nazism and the Holocaust, or is it just another conceptual spin around the block? If history is an uneven processional of chaotic systems "poised at the critical state" that yields "a range of responses" to certain conditions, ranging from a few, rare big ones to many small ones, with a few in between,[26] can we gather adequate evidence of those processes? If so, would that have a significant effect on power processes? The prospects are slim, given the turbulence of politics, the enduring infernos of nationalism and parochialism, and the impunity of sovereignty to bridling. Leaders routinely claim special powers of intuition and insight. Even Wilson and Gandhi did. The pose of serious-mindedness by leaders is a deeply rooted myth in many cultures, despite all the visible cases of psychopathology in high places and examples of human viciousness.[27] While making sense of such contradictions, as with Nazism, requires penetrating the swirls of chaos within individual minds and social systems, we cannot be sure of mapping that intricacy. Beyond the fact that such charting abstracts reality lies the pitfall of ignoring or minimizing subtle but significant dimensions, like the momentary blending of forces that yields transient disproportionate effects like a sudden surge that leaves only a fragmentary trace.[28] Here, chaos-complexity theory suggests the need to be cautious in accepting history as an exact reflection of actuality or as a basis for making conclusions and taking action. The frustrations of archaeologists puzzling over the meaning of artifacts from Bronze Age barrows, Pompeii, and Stonehenge shows how solid the barriers of the past can be. Despite that, historians tend to assume they are presenting reasonable approximations of reality, as do their readers, and even scientists well trained in forecasting methods ignore their solid grounding and relay on intuition, impulse, or common sense.[29]

If chaos-complexity enhances our ability to identify patterns and steer the crafting of history only a point or two closer toward absolute truth, that might put it ahead of other models of the past embraced in some cases by many millions over the last two centuries. And it may offer us a way to get around such historiographical roadblocks as searching for the Holocaust's moment of inception, treating denials of it too seriously, and obsessing on certain notional scenarios. By underscoring the danger of overlooking any particle of evidence along the way, chaos-complexity theory also raises the question of whether historical analysis requires rigor and patience beyond previous levels. The format of single-author narratives keeps history at the level of analysis of Michael Faraday's notebooks. Brilliant and thorough as they were, they fell far short of the elegant abstract analyses and equations of James Clerk Maxwell, who transformed the study of electromagnetic phenomena from philosophical investigation to scientific—and far more useful—research. Perhaps the time has come—or is perhaps long past—for historians to make the kind of transition from art to science that most other professions have and to work in teams with colleagues in other disciplines to weave and spread wider nets of finer mesh and grapple with such hypotheses as, "If you just jostle . . . a homogenous system governed by simple rules or forces . . . [a] heterogenous structure will emerge."[30] Numbing, discarding evidence, and discounting are common enough but are often overlooked or dismissed as marginal in significance. The shapers of the Versailles Treaty's vengefulness and greed led them to overlook or brush past what seemed to be ephemeral aspects, which came back to stalk them and their heirs. Even Wilson, in his struggle to gain visionary detachment, only got a step or two further away than the others. The layering of burdens on Germany—the extended blockade, war guilt, reparations, occupation, and dismantling of its Empire—that was meant to buckle and break it turned out to be more like the compressing of a spring.

The disproportionate effect of seemingly vague and trivial forces like resentment, which Schopenhauer deemed the most powerful of human emotions, adds a special edge to the revelations half a century later of the links between the Holocaust and various neutral and Allied nations during World War II, which reminds us that the seeds from which the Hitlerzeit grew are still on the wind. Just as arrogance and contempt blinded many to the Nazis' potential, so has the passing of time. Apathy and ignorance have distorted and erased details and feelings, leaving appreciation for the seductiveness of National Socialism on the margins, along with that of other cases of collective frenzy that led to mass slaughter like the Crusades, the Reign of Terror, imperialism of many hues, Fascism, Stalinism, and Maoism. Dismissing those attractions, however, loses sight of the shiniest facet on the whirling sphere of the Hitlerzeit. The wife of one of Hitler's military assistants, in recalling pleasant times at the Berghof, asked how disparaging the gifts Hitler so clearly did have made it any easier for people to live with having become bewitched by him.[31]

Pinning such wispy specimens to the specimen board is very difficult, but that does not justify ignoring them, either from the standpoint of sensitivity to initial conditions or in seeking a sharper view of chaotic forms within the turbulence of the NS Staat. But, again, is that possible? It may be, as Ian Percival suggested, that "the state of European politics may look chaotic, but you cannot study a subject of this type using chaos theory. There are many other situations that are chaotic in the ordinary sense, but not in the scientific sense of chaos."[32] Despite that possibility, the enormous toll in pain, death, and destruction of Nazism warrants looking at those grotesque and filmy specimens through the lenses of chaos-complexity. At the very least, it might provide a basis for comparison with other specimens of pathology. But optimally, it would lead to new insights and implications that would help us bridle the forces that produced the equivalent of a ferocious beast running amok before the Hitlerzeit, elsewhere at the same time, and since. It is sure to again, as long as that is left to the workings of chance in a world in which sovereignty is enshrined as the overarching design principle in the architecture of human society. That seed-crystal of potential chaos is deeply embedded in the basic structure of civilization, and it will take a great deal of poking about the ruins it has left to root it out and to discern any patterns that might lead us away from the path along which the Nazis marched to their precipice. If we are unable or unwilling to do that, our meandering may well lead us to follow them.

NOTES

1. Edward N. Lorenz, *The Essence of Chaos* (Seattle: University of Washington Press, 1993), p. 159.

2. Ron Rosenbaum, "Explaining Hitler," *New Yorker*, p. 51.

3. Gerard Prunier, quoted in Andrew Purvis, "The Roots of Genocide," *Time*, August 5, 1996, p. 57.

4. James Gleick, *Chaos: Making a New Science* (New York: Penguin Books, 1987), p. 210.

5. Quoted in David Chandler, *Waterloo: The Hundred Days* (New York: Macmillan, 1980), pp. 10–11.

6. Roger Lewin, *Complexity: Life at the Edge of Chaos* (London: J. M. Dent, 1993), p. 190.

7. For example, William Dray, "Some Causal Accounts of the American Civil War," *Daedalus* (Summer, 1962), pp. 582–598.

8. Keith Windshuttle, *The Killing of History: How Literary Critics and Social Theorists Are Murdering Our Past* (New York: Free Press, 1996), p. 7.

9. For example, see David Campbell and Gottfried Mayer-Kress, quoted in Glenn E. James, *Chaos Theory* (Newport: Naval War College, 1997), p. 46.

10. Stephen H. Kellert, *In the Wake of Chaos* (Chicago: University of Chicago Press, 1993), p. 7.

11. For a succinct overview of non-Nazi anti-Semitism in Weimar Germany, see John Weiss, "Germany's Holocaust," letter to the editor, *New York Times Book Review*, February 28, 1999, p. 4.

12. For a succinct attack on "covering law" history, see George A. Reisch, "Chaos, History and Narrative," *History and Theory*, 21:1 (1991), pp. 1–20.

13. Albert Speer, *Infiltration*, trans. Joachim Neugroschel (New York: Macmillan, 1981), p. 4.

14. An example of that line of analysis is Bill Kinser and Neil Kleinman, *The Dream That Was No More a Dream: A Search for Aesthetic Reality* (New York: Harper Colophon, 1969); more recent perspectives, amid the torrent of Hitler biographies and Third Reich histories of the 1990s, is Jane Kramer, "The Accidental Fuehrer," *New Yorker*, 75:2 (March 9, 1999), p. 91; and Gordon A. Craig, " 'Working Toward the Fuehrer,' " *New York Review of Books*, pp. 32–35.

15. For a list of twenty-seven major NS Staat organizations involved in the functioning of the Endloesung, see Raul Hilberg, *Perpetrators, Victims, Bystanders: The Jewish Catastrophe 1933–1945* (New York: HarperCollins, 1992), pp. 22–24.

16. Ilya Prigogine, *From Being to Becoming: Time and Complexity in the Physical Sciences* (New York: W. H. Freeman, 1980), p. 214.

17. Reginald Trevelyan, "A Murderous Burden," *New York Times Book Review*, August 18, 1996, p. 26.

18. Robert O. Paxton, "The Five Stages of Fascism," *Journal of Modern History*, 70:1 (March, 1998), p. 12.

19. Donald McCloskey, "History, Differential Equations, and the Problem of Narration," *History and Theory*, 21:1 (1991), p. 26.

20. Stuart A. Kauffman, "Antichaos and Adaptation," *Scientific American*, 265:2 (August 1991), pp. 78–84.

21. For an essay on the question of progress and complexity theory, see Roger Lewin, *Complexity* (London: J. M. Dent, 1993), pp. 130–149.

22. Isaiah Berlin, *Historical Inevitability* (London: Oxford University Press, 1955), p. 70.

23. L. Douglas Kiel, "The Nonlinear Paradigm: Advancing Paradigmatic Progress in the Policy Sciences," *Systems Research*, 9:2 (1992), p. 34.

24. For a review of precedents of Nazi-era anti-Semitism on the eve of the Holocaust, see Charles A. Madison, "Perish the Jew!" *American Scholar* 8:3 (July, 1939), pp. 271–284.

25. A recent analysis of German Jews' underestimations of the virulence of Nazism is John H. V. Dippel, *Bound upon a Wheel of Fire* (New York: Basic Books, 1996).

26. Lewin, *Complexity: Life at the Edge of Chaos*, p. 61.

27. For a recent speculation on this question, see Michael Moorcock's comment on Goldhagen's *Hitler's Willing Executioners* in *London Review of Books*, 19:4 (February 20, 1997), p. 4.

28. For example, the mass exodus from eastern U.S. cities in the spring of 1898, Mafeking Night, *Kristallnacht*, the Orson Welles "War of the Worlds" broadcast reaction, the V-E and V-J celebrations, and the Cuban missile crisis panic.

29. For a succinct discussion, see William Bechtel and Robert C. Richardson, *Discovering Complexity: Decomposition and Localization as Strategies in Scientific Research* (Princeton, N.J.: Princeton University Press, 1993), p. 5.

30. Lewin , *Complexity: Life at the Edge of Chaos*, p. 147.

31. Maria von Below, quoted in Gitta Sereny, *Albert Speer: His Battle with Truth* (New York: Alfred A. Knopf, 1993), p. 113.

32. For example, see Ian Percival, "Chaos: A Science of the Real World," in Nina Hall, ed., *Exploring Chaos: A Guide to the New Science of Disorder* (New York: W. W. Norton, 1991), p. 16.

Index

ABOUT THE AUTHOR

Roger Beaumont has taught history at Texas A&M University since 1974. Co-founder and former North American editor of the journal *Defense Analysis*, he has written eleven books and monographs including *Special Operations and Elite Units, 1939–1988: A Research Guide* (Greenwood Press, 1988); *Joint Military Operations: A Short History* (Greenwood, 1993); and *War, Chaos, and History* (Praeger, 1994); and over seventy book chapters and articles. Beaumont served two active duty tours in the Army as a military police officer, 1957–59 and 1961–62, has lectured at higher military schools in Europe and the United States, and was the first historian named a Secretary of the Navy Fellow at the U.S. Naval Academy (1989–90).

ISBN 0-275-96708-5

90000>

EAN

9 780275 967086

HARDCOVER BAR CODE

3 5282 00510 8207